Karen,

I hope you enjoy these stories

Phil

SURVIVING VODKA TOASTS AND RAMPAGING ELEPHANTS
A JOURNEY TO LIFE'S PURPOSE

BY PHIL LATESSA

Printed by Bookbaby
Pennsauken, NJ

First Edition, American Printing, October 2015
Copyright ©2015 by Philp F. Latessa
All rights reserved

www.philipflatessa.com

Printed in the United States of America
Typeface in Times New Roman
Cover and page design by Mary Talbert, Crafted QC

Ordering Information: Quantity sales. Special discounts are available on quantity purchases by corporations, associations, trade bookstores, wholesalers, and others. For details, contact the author at the address above.

ISBN: 978-1-68222-374-1

To the people of
Iowa, Russia, China, Ukraine, Italy, Malaysia,
and especially Tanzania,
who gave me a purpose in life
and the passion to pursue it.

"Shut up, Phil and just write these stories down."
– Judy Curtis-Latessa

"If you think you are too small to make a difference,
try sleeping in a tent with a mosquito."
– African proverb

TABLE OF CONTENTS

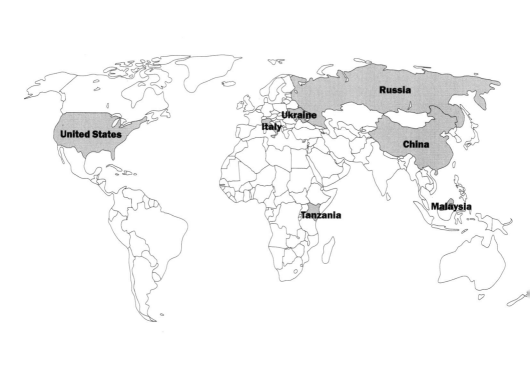

OPENING

The dim light of dawn found me standing in a paddock with Phil Latessa and about 30 cows, with a ring of thorny acacia branches encircling the enclosure to protect against marauding carnivores. We were in a groggy state from the activities of the previous evening, but it was not a typical alcohol-induced type of hangover. We had spent the night trying to blend with Maasai culture and food. With us at dawn were several young Maasai warriors wrapped in their shuka, colorful plaid robes of red and royal blue, to guard against the equatorial morning chill.

We were dutifully brushing our teeth under their supervision, trying to refresh ourselves from the long night using dental tools they made for us by fraying an end of a couple tree branches with a machete. Even with this unusual instrument, brushing our teeth was strangely comforting after the experiences with butchering, music, darkness, blood and rats of the previous night. The familiar pattern of brushing was interrupted by the sharp smell of cow dung from the patties we were dodging underfoot. I looked at Phil, who got me into all this, and the stance of his 70-year-old figure gave the impression of casual comfort as if he had done this a hundred times before.

Despite his demeanor, I knew that Phil, like me, had never had a similar experience. After all, how does one prepare for a night in a mud and daub hut with three goats, a chicken and a rat that persisted in knawing on my dried hide bed? Phil, with his round stomach, sedentary manner, and affinity for scotch (or at least a beer) is not a rough and tumble, outback kind of guy. He does; however, have a lifetime of experiences that prepared him for this and much more of what is involved in non-profit work in remote, rural Tanzania.

Indeed, it is not the rats, raw meat or rough travel conditions that are the true obstacles one encounters in this work. It is the interaction with other cultures, relationship building, and difficulties with the introduction of ncw approaches to old problems that are the most challenging. While I was focused on my immediate environment of cow paddies and tooth brushing with a frayed stick that morning, Phil was likely elsewhere in his mind, planning the proper thing to say about the night to the Maasai Chief, whose home we stayed in.

My role in Empower Tanzania, for which Phil is Executive Director, is that of an implementer. As a physician, I seek to enact programs that address medical or public health problems in the community. I am therefore constantly presenting ideas, concerns and scenarios to Phil, my travel companion on virtually every trip I have made to Tanzania in the past 6 years. He graciously listens and considers my ideas, adopts the passion, and supports the subsequent pursuit in its many potential directions. The experience feels like we are copilots in a glider, going with the wind currents of a culture, but guiding our course within those limitations. Phil has a particular talent to detect the cultural currents and shepherd the participants through them.

Understood in this ability is a high level of cultural and interpersonal awareness, as well as particular skills in communication. While some of this aptitude in Phil may be innate, certainly the scores of journeys he has made to Russia, Africa and China have allowed him to hone the talent. In the course of his career with Iowa Sister States, Iowa Hospital Association and international non-profit administration, he has dealt with the often difficult personalities of politicians, technocrats, chiefs and doctors in domestic and foreign settings. Take this eclectic assemblage of players, add vodka, beer or baiju, depending on the country, and one has the raw stuff of good stories. Add to that mix Phil's literate background, love of language and extensive practice in storytelling and you have a book of experiences that will inform, entertain and delight the reader.

Jeffrey S. Carithers, MD, FACS

INTRODUCTION: AN AVIOPHOBE

During the 23 years in which I was involved in international work, I made over 80 trips to 11 countries and flew over 1 million miles shared among United, Delta, KLM, Malaysia Air, Singapore Air, and my least favorite, the Russian airline Aeroflot. All this from a person who is afraid of flying and hates the experience of hurtling along at 500 miles per hour six miles in the sky in an aluminum tube piloted by strangers. I've managed to cope with this through what my wife calls "rituals." I always sit on the aisle (quicker escape, but I am not sure to where), take Dramamine (it could be bumpy—what a euphemism for violent movements of the plane) and 2 mg of a mood relaxer. (Don't tell me 2 mg is useless. It will spoil the magic of my "rabbit's foot.")

Many people have told me that they envy all this glamorous international travel. I tell them to consider the following:

✓ I've been through two passports, each with extra pages sewn in.
✓ Suffered through 11 bouts of travelers' distress (which has a different name in each country).
✓ Stood in line for hours waiting for a bored bureaucrat to stamp likely meaningless documents.
✓ Bribed my way into and out of Russia and Ukraine several times.
✓ Lost my luggage three times – once for one day and twice for three days. It's hard to replace personal items in a developing country.
✓ Suffered through a six-hour delay and a missed connection waiting for them to fix a minor mechanical problem on a plane—it was Bastille Day in Paris and they had to fly in a mechanic from London.
✓ Nervously watched a flight attendant pour boiling water into small plastic cups of Ramen noodles. Since I sit on the aisle, I watched her pour over me for the people in the window and middle seats. Still not changing seats though.
✓ Fought several losing battles with Customs Officials.
✓ Got lost for hours in London's Heathrow Airport.
✓ Missed two connections in the same day.

Whenever I fly to Tanzania, about 15 hours into the trip I start thinking to myself - "Why am I doing this? I'm retired and could be at home relaxing." Then we arrive in Africa and I meet those great people who do so much with so little. They count on me and others like me to help out. It's a great feeling to be doing good work in a poor place like Tanzania. That's why I do it and this is my story of a journey to purpose.

CULTURE SHOCK:
PEOPLE IN IOWA ARE GENUINELY NICE (SERIOUSLY)

OUT WEST...IN NEW JERSEY

Since I grew up near Boston in Lowell, Massachusetts, of Italian and Portuguese parents, I am what is referred to as a "captive" Iowan. Not native by birth, but an Iowan because the state is now where I call home. After moving here in 1970, I have officially lived here longer than anywhere else.

Welcome to Iowa!

When I received a job offer in Iowa City and told my family that I was moving to Iowa, I got the usual response—"Where is that anyway?" Or "Isn't that where they grow potatoes?" Or "Why are you interested in being a farmer?" Americans are notoriously ignorant of geography. I have to admit that I was pretty ignorant about Iowa until I visited and decided that I wanted to live here. So, I patiently explained the difference between Iowa, Ohio, and Idaho to my puzzled relatives. In retrospect I didn't realize my move to Iowa was an experience learning to be a stranger in a strange land. This was the initial training for the rest of my career.

The most significant illustration of how far away Iowa seems to people on the East Coast happened when visiting a cousin of my dad's, who owned a delicatessen in New York City. Just before moving to Iowa, I was in the deli with my "Uncle" Phil and while he was slicing pastrami he asked me where I was moving. I told him I was moving to Iowa and went on to explain that it is in the middle of the country and raises a lot of the food we eat.

"But where is it, exactly?" he asked. So I explained that if you go over the George Washington Bridge into New Jersey, and you just keep going for 900 miles you get to Iowa. "Is that what's on the other side of the GW bridge?" he responded, "New Jersey?"

This was shocking to me, even for someone as geographically limited as I was. "Uncle" Phil had lived in the United States for over 30 years. "You mean you've never been across the Hudson River, even to New Jersey?" I asked incredulously. "Why would I want to go there when everything is right here?" he replied in classic New York City myopia. This was not a joke to him. He was serious.

To my relatives, I was moving to a place as remote and strange as China. The going away party my mother hosted for me resembled a wake. Terra incognita was my destination and they never expected to see me again.

As it turned out, my parents visited me several times in Iowa. Actually, not me—the grandchildren. My folks thought that Iowa was charming. My mom especially liked to see the little piglets running around farmyards. Even my brother, a notorious xenophobe, made two trips here—for a wedding and a graduation. During his second trip, he was really surprised at the significant improvements in Des Moines, especially that many projects were funded by philanthropy. "You mean people gave money for the Sculpture Garden and Gray's Lake?" he asked incredulously. "Why would they do that? They aren't getting anything out of it," he said. That's just one of many differences I've discovered between the way people think in Lowell verses in Des Moines.

LOCKS? WHAT LOCKS?

When I was in Iowa City interviewing for my job, the staff took me to the Amana colonies for dinner. I rode with Roger who would be my boss. He had a new Grand Prix. When we arrived, he got out of the car but left his keys in the ignition. As I got out, I shouted to him that he had left his keys in the car. "I know," he replied. "I always do that so I won't lose them." For the rest of the evening, I was on edge expecting that his car would be stolen by someone who overheard me tell Roger that the keys were in his car. I came from an environment where two or three locks and a deadbolt at home were not enough. We often added a Fox Police Lock which fastened a steel bar to the door and attached it to the floor. We had security locks on doors and windows—even on the chimney fireplace, which made things tough for Santa.

Anyhow, Roger's car wasn't stolen and I got the job. I'm a little less suspicious now. I don't lock my car when it is in my garage—a big adjustment for me.

Then shortly after moving to Iowa, my first wife and I were invited by Joanne, a colleague, to her parents' home for a weekend. They lived in Pocahontas, a small town in northwestern Iowa. Driving into town, we passed a teepee designed to give the town's name some authenticity, although it was made of concrete. Joanne's family lived in a big farmhouse in town, the type of house which was commonly built when a farmer retired and moved to the "city." We went to the local golf course country club for dinner then returned to Joanne's family home and had a pleasant evening discussing life in small town Iowa. When it was time for bed, I was still talking to Joanne's dad. He finally stretched and said, "Time to call it a day. Sleep well." I said, "Aren't you going to lock up?" He replied, "Oh, we never lock up. I don't even know where the keys are."

I was awake for hours worrying and picturing another episode of "In Cold Blood" with us as the Clutter family. Morning came as a relief and, after I unlocked my car, I thanked Joanne's family for an educational time and we drove off. After all these years, I have made an adjustment to Iowa ways—in addition to being more liberal with the safety of my car, I no longer lock the doors while I am in the house. Most of the time.

FOOTBALL MANIA

The first place I lived in Iowa City was in a duplex across the street from what is now called Kinnick Stadium, where I was introduced to the Midwestern mania for college football. At Northeastern University where I went to college, no one even knew we had a football team until one year they went 10 and 0 and were invited to the something bowl in Allentown, PA. I passed on the chance to see my mostly unknown Huskies get clobbered in zero degree weather. Most undergraduates at NU thought we had de-emphasized football and after our drubbing, we pretty much did.

Kinnick Statium.
Photo Credit Hawkeyesports.com

University of Iowa football was one of my first culture shocks. Over 50,000 people descended on Iowa City on those football weekends. I learned that if you needed to do anything outside the home on football Saturdays, you had to do it very early or wait for the end of the game. During the game, the city was quiet, but I was trapped in the duplex because of another new thing I experienced—visitor parking. The landlord charged visitors to park their cars on the lawn and in the driveway which blocked me in. All rules and decorum were suspended during the game.

From across the street, you could hear the shouts of the fans—mostly screams of anguish because in those days, the Hawks were terrible. They had one losing season after another. Still, the fans, all 50,000 of them, came to suffer through game after game. While tailgating is not a new invention, it was not as significant an event then as it has become now. So, it probably wasn't the barbecue and beer that kept bringing people to the stadium to watch the Hawks get clobbered week after week. It must have been something else, something not visible to an outsider. It's easy to understand why football is so popular in Texas. They are ignorant rednecks in Texas and have nothing else to take pride in. But in quiet, stable Iowa with serious people, the grip of football mania is still incomprehensible to me after over 40 years here. It must be something in the water, something besides the fluoride put there as part of the Communist conspiracy.

My neighbors at the duplex were from Wyoming and went home every year where they got hunting licenses that allowed them to kill any four-footed animal. After a week, they returned with a Jeep loaded with game, even some elk haunches strapped to the fenders. They always had a game feast when they returned which was really good because they knew how to cook game, with one exception. The husband, Jim, had shot a mountain goat and decided to cook the roast. He soaked it, boiled it, and braised it and it still was tough as a board. On their next trip, they asked me to water their plants and bring in the mail while they were gone. The day after they left,

I walked into a darkened living room and nearly had a heart attack. Staring at me was a full-sized mountain goat mounted on a walnut board. Yes, Jim did taxidermy, too, and turning the goat into a trophy partially made up for the inedible roast it provided.

Anyway, now I live in Des Moines and am unaffected by football madness, unless I am on Interstate 80 on a football weekend. Then I am in a traffic jam, just like in my Boston days, but football wasn't the cause back then.

BLOOD SPORT

Before my second wife, Judy and I were married, we went to Cedar Rapids, Iowa to meet her family. She had been nervous about that, feeling that her extended Lebanese family's strong personalities would overwhelm me. She envisioned something like "My Big Fat Greek Wedding," but she had not experienced my large Italian/ Portuguese family with a lot of happy people (some of whom would not speak to each other for 50 years) all eating, talking, and hugging at the same time. So I was used to cacophony. Things went well and I was accepted into this warm, beautiful, and passionate family.

During our first holidays together, we were at a large family dinner amid a lot of joking and telling (and retelling and retelling) stories designed to embarrass at least one of them. After dinner, what had been a happy, close-linked family then played a game which showed their true colors: Pictionary. Teams were picked and, in Judy's family, it was a blood sport. There was a lot of shouting and guessing with people jumping up and down. Scores were disputed and drawings disparaged. When one team won, good sportsmanship did not prevail. Instead there was gloating and singing, "We are the Champions."

I was stunned by the blatant competitiveness and the noise of what I'd always found to be a quiet game. But my experiences with them helped explain the civil war in Lebanon. No quarter asked and none given.

WRITE A CHECK?

Iowans are amazingly honest and trusting people. For someone from the cynical East Coast, this was a big surprise. It took a while to get used to and often I found myself suspiciously waiting for the hook, the catch, or the hidden agenda.

For example, one day when I lived in a suburb of Boston, I was in line behind a woman at a grocery store who had unloaded a full grocery cart onto the belt. The cashier totaled her bill and she opened her checkbook and began writing a check. "What are you doing?" the cashier asked her. She innocently replied she was writing a check to pay for the groceries. "A check?" he sneered. "We don't take checks, we take cash." When she didn't have enough cash to pay for her groceries, the clerk called to the bag boy to put all the groceries back. Was she crazy? Who ever heard of paying for groceries with a check? I was incredulous.

Then I moved to Iowa where people paid for everything with checks. Groceries, gas, barbers, churches, anything. Not only that, if you didn't have a check, they would give you a bank check which you filled in with the name of your bank and you paid with that. Restaurants wouldn't take credit cards but would accept your check. And no one even asked for ID. Amazing.

When I first arrived in Iowa, I drove a Volvo, pretty unusual at the time. Planning ahead, I asked Roger at work where I might get it repaired. He sent me to the Joetown garage in Joetown. He said they worked on Volkswagens, so they might do work for me.

Joetown was in a very rural area about 20 miles south of Iowa City. In fact, Joetown was just a café and the mechanics garage across the street. That was it. I skeptically drove into the garage and met the two brothers who ran it. I asked if they could do work on my Volvo. They popped the hood, looked at the mighty 4-cylinder engine, and skimmed the owner's manual. "We can handle it whenever you want," they said reassuringly.

Two weeks later, the master cylinder went out. Without the master cylinder, you have virtually no brakes. So, I drove 20 nervous miles to Joetown and left it with the brothers at the garage. Four days later, they called to tell me it was ready. I hitched a ride down and looked over a very reasonable bill. Not having enough cash, I planned to pay with a check. But I had forgotten my checkbook. "That's OK," they said. "We trust you. Just send a check when you think of it." These guys let me drive off without paying and they had only met me twice.

And then one year during the Christmas holiday, I was visiting Judy's family in Cedar Rapids. We had been to the movies and as I was getting into the car, my checkbook fell out of my pocket into the snowy parking lot. I didn't miss it for a couple of days and then, after ransacking the house when I got home, was finally ready to give it up for lost. Just as I was getting ready to call the bank and close out the account, the mail arrived. Someone had found my checkbook, noted the address on the checks and mailed it to me. I looked to see if any checks had been used. None had. I looked for the name of this benefactor so I could send a reward. It had been sent anonymously. For a while I waited for the other shoe to drop— perhaps new credit cards issued in my name using my checking account for identification and billing. Or maybe paperwork on a new car loan. Or creation of another checking account and transfer of the funds in mine. But nothing bad ever happened. I was beginning to think I was on another planet.

They trusted everyone here, even me, a person obviously from the East. I don't even trust people from the East. These incidents rocked me. After I realized that they were real and that this was generally how people acted, I had to work through the culture shock. Eventually, I got comfortable with this trusting environment and began to trust people myself. As long as they were not from the East.

LONG COMMUTE TO WORK

For someone who moved to Iowa from Boston, I was amused by the complaints of my neighbors who said that rush hour traffic was getting bad. I'd smile and say, "You mean the rush 20 minutes?" What is considered heavy traffic is a subjective thing.

For example, when I worked in Iowa City, one of the staff we hired was from Los Angeles. Rick was a very capable guy and enjoyed the work environment and the cultural attractions of a university town. After a few weeks, he came into my office. "I am now acclimated," he said. "When I drove home last night, I was turning left across Burlington Street and I had to wait through two exchanges of traffic lights before I could make my turn. It took me 11 minutes to get home rather than the eight which is usual. I was very annoyed at this delay and then I remembered that in LA, I commuted an hour and a half each way to get to work. I realize I am now officially an Iowan."

I could relate to Rick's story. When I commuted to school in Boston, my 12-mile drive usually took at least 40 minutes, often longer. Traffic was so congested that the average speed was about 4 miles per hour. This turned out to be good because there were many accidents and damage to cars and people was minimal at this slower speed. Making obscene gestures to drivers who had done something stupid was a bad idea because they would be beside you for a long time because of the slow moving traffic.

IOWA STATE FAIR

I suppose that most states have a state fair, but in Massachusetts, if we had one at all, it would have been in the rural western part of the state and would have been poorly attended. I was surprised to find that Iowa had county fairs in each of the 99 counties culminating in the extravaganza in August at the Iowa State Fair. It is ten days long and draws a million people every year. In a state with only 3 million people, that is quite an achievement. It is on many lists of the top 100 things to do before you die.

Iowa State Fair. *Photo Credit Iowa State Fair.*

As a newly arrived Iowan, I made it a point to visit the State Fair. It is enormous and fittingly has a strong agricultural flavor—not to mention aroma. The horse, cattle, and sheep barns look just like barns on working farms and were a revelation to this city boy who had always gotten his meat in plastic packages.

With a million visitors in such a short time, the crowds were sizeable, but generally well behaved. After all, this is Iowa. While it had a midway just like all fairs, the focus here was on agriculture, with animal judging, exhibitions of machinery and farm buildings.

One year I brought some friends visiting from Tanzania and asked about their impressions. Their response was "Everything is big: big pig, big tractors, big food, big people." That about sums it up.

LEARNING TO DRIVE

Having grown up in Massachusetts and lived in Boston while I was a student, I learned to drive in that aggressive, dog–eat-dog environment which was complicated by streets based on cow paths from the 1600s. Whenever you met people, the first item of discussion was, "So, how did you get here?" The second item was, "Where did you park?" Driving there was dangerous and parking was frustrating, but I didn't know anything else.

Then I moved to Iowa with its geometric grid of street patterns, consistent numbering of addresses and friendly people. I had to learn the index finger wave used in rural parts of the state when meeting a farmer driving his pickup. Iowans were nice people. They took turns at four-way stops. They let you merge when the road narrowed. They stop to let a driver exit a parking lot.

But it took me a while to get used to this. I kept expecting that the person letting me turn left in front of him was going to accelerate and T- bone my car for some imagined slight. It never happened and eventually I got used to the niceness of people. Even in the big city of Des Moines, if you jaywalk, people stop their cars to let you across. Jaywalking where I grew up was a life threatening venture. You could actually hear cars speed up when they saw you.

There were a few downsides to all that niceness, though. At a traffic light, people planning to turn left do not move into the intersection but rather stay at the line. If they are unable to make their turn, they patiently wait until the next light, and sometimes the light after that. They never exceed the speed limit—at least the ones in front of me in town or even on the Interstate highways.

Even so, I'm still surprised at times by Iowans' decency, honesty, and courtesy. Lately though, we've had an influx of people from the East and West coasts because of the significant growth of some Iowa companies. These people bring their bad driving habits with them and, as a captive Iowan, I am now like most native Iowans who have to adjust to this aggressive, take-no-prisoners style. Perhaps in time these people will adopt a saner style. However, it did take me 40 years.

In contrast, my wife, an Iowa native, also had a terrible time adjusting to the driving in Massachusetts. On her first visit to Boston, we decided to visit a friend of hers in Gloucester, on the North Shore. As we proceeded on the expressway, we were merging from five lanes to two as we got ready to enter the Sumner tunnel. Traffic slowed to a crawl as we tried to merge into the next lane to the right. Judy began yelling and waving to the driver to our left, gesturing for him to let us in.

"Hon," she said. "He's ignoring me. Why won't he look at me?"

"If he looks at you, darling," I explained. "He will have to acknowledge that you are human. Then he'll have to let you in."

He kept ignoring us, but I was able to cut him off using my (rusty) Boston driving skills.

A few days later, we were driving with my brother who still lives in Lowell. He said, "Let me drive. You've lost the edge." As he drove us to dinner on Interstate 93, he was straddling two lanes. Judy was getting nervous and asked Dan if he should just be in one lane. "No," he replied. "This way, I can choose whichever lane is best."

Judy won't drive there. Probably best for all concerned.

THE FLOOD

In 1993, a series of devastating thunderstorms caused the Des Moines River to overtop its banks, cross a major street, and spill over the levee protecting the Des Moines Water Works. The plant flooded and had to shut down. I had moved to Des Moines in 1976, so this wasn't just a story on the news for me.

Flood of 1993.
Photo Credit Des Moines Register.

Judy and I had been in Minneapolis with some friends that weekend and had not been watching the news. When we dropped off our friends in Ankeny, just north of Des Moines, they found some of their other friends in their home. "We are refugees from the flood," they said, pointing to the TV broadcasting the latest information on closings. We bought some bottled water and drove home trying to remember if the suburb of Clive, where we lived, got its water from Des Moines. It did.

When Judy and I arrived home, there were 15 voicemail messages from my boss at the Iowa Hospital Association. The earliest was at 10:30 PM on the day the flood occurred. Our office building was one block away from the Des Moines River and he wanted all the staff to come to the office to move equipment off the floor. This was before cell phones and, since I was out of town, I never got this message. Nor did I get the subsequent 14 messages which grew increasingly hysterical as he became convinced I was shirking my duties.

As it turned out, our building suffered only a few inches of water in the basement. However, my boss continued to look at me with suspicion until I produced ticket stubs for the play we saw in

Minneapolis. Even then, I could tell that he believed if I were a real team player, I would somehow have learned about his frenzied drive to save the ship and I would have driven from Minneapolis to Des Moines that night to elevate computers.

In the days that followed, the weather turned beautiful as though all the possible rain had fallen and there wouldn't be any more. However, I must have turned on a faucet over 500 times with no result—just automatic behavior. Judy and I microwaved enough water each morning for washing, shaving and cooking. Like the restaurants, we used paper dishes and plastic utensils. We came close to an argument only once when she automatically flushed the toilet first thing in the morning. "Sorry," she said. I grumbled when I had to lug five gallons of water upstairs to refill the tank. Of course we cheated occasionally. We went to her sister's house in West Des Moines (their water plant was endangered, but had survived) to take showers a couple of times. We combined a visit to her mother in Cedar Rapids with doing our laundry.

In Des Moines, the National Guard stationed water trucks at each supermarket parking lot and provided free drinking water to anyone. This announcement worried me. Back in the East, these circumstances would have left people dead in the parking lots as pushing, shoving, and perhaps shooting would have been the order of the day. I should not have worried—Iowans are nice people. Since it had stopped raining, it was pleasant to be outside waiting patiently in line for water.

One concern during the weeks following the flood was that a delegation of nine Russian physicians was due to arrive soon and they were scheduled to be hosted in homes without water. I closely followed news of the water plant's acquisition of new pumps, their installation, and water quality testing. Finally, we had water again, just days before the Russians arrived.

All during this time, people showed their best behavior—no fighting at water sites, donations of water and cash to buy water from all over, including our sister state in Yamanashi, Japan. President Bill Clinton came to fill a sandbag, joining many volunteers who were shoring up the weakened levees. I regret to say, again, that this would not have been the case in my home town. The chronic air of suspicion coupled with aggression would have ensured riots and general problems during such a crisis. My home town friends may call Iowans hicks, but my adopted community did very well during this difficult period and no one killed each other in a fight over resources.

That exemplified the honest, sincere behavior exhibited by everyone during this crisis and characterizes the personality of Iowa and its people in general. It's just one more reason I am glad to have moved here and to now call Iowa my home.

WHERE EVERYBODY KNOWS YOUR NAME

One of the big surprises about Iowa is how small town it still is. Even though it is now considered an urban state, it is still mostly small towns.

While I was working at the Iowa Hospital Association, one of my colleagues was in the Nursing Department. Colleen had an appointment at one of the community hospitals in a rural part of the state. She drove to the town and, since she was early, she went to the local café for a cup of coffee. The waitress came over and asked if her name was Colleen. Surprised, Colleen looked to see if she was wearing her name badge - she wasn't. The waitress, pouring coffee, said, "You are not dressed like anyone from around here and my sister is a nurse at the hospital. She told me you would be coming." Colleen sat shaking her head. "You take it black, right?" the waitress went on. There are no secrets in small town Iowa.

On another occasion, we hired a consultant to travel to several Iowa communities to make a presentation about technical health issues. He was very capable and enjoyed the experience of working in small community hospitals. His only complaint was that the food in small town cafes was very pedestrian for someone married to a woman from India who cooked traditional Indian food for him. He was used to spicy food and since it was small town Iowa, salt and pepper were often the only spices available. After about a week on the road, he went to the local café in the next town for dinner and when it arrived, it was accompanied by a large bottle of Tabasco sauce. Surprised to see the bottle, he was even more surprised when the waitress said, "My cousin works in Waverly at the café and she told me that you wanted more spicy food. I was able to find this at the grocery store and hope that it is what you want." He replied in thanks and inquired as to how she recognized him. "Easy," she responded. "You're the only one in here wearing a tie."

It's remarkable to me that everywhere in the world, people use the same basic ingredients to make food. Meat from domesticated animals, vegetables, and fruit make up pretty much what's available. Except in China where they eat everything. More on that later. But from basically the same ingredients, a huge variety of food results, from Chinese stir fry to Argentinian grilled steaks.

I grew up in an ethnic stew of a working class neighborhood. Each culture had their own cuisine and their food was an important part of daily living. These were not precursor "foodies" trying to preserve something. Rather, these were moms cooking what they knew and what tasted good. Going upstairs in a three-story tenement, you passed all those doors from which wafted delicious smells—roasting lamb from the Greeks, split pea soup from the French-Canadians, boiling codfish from the Portuguese, and marinara sauce from the Italians.

When I arrived in Iowa in 1970, it seemed like a gastronomic desert. But there were occasional oases, like on the south side of Des Moines where there were several family-owned Italian restaurants. However, since most of the original immigrants were poor people from one particular part of southern Italy, Calabria, the cooking in all these restaurants was basically the same. Meatballs, tomato sauce, and pasta comprised the menu.

There was only one Chinese restaurant in Des Moines and it served chop suey—a dish they never heard of in China. Later a second Chinese restaurant opened and gave some needed competition to the original one. But they still cooked American style Chinese food. My guests from China said that it had too much sugar and not enough spices.

Most of the other restaurants were steakhouses, justifiably proud of Iowa beef or pork which was grilled and served with baked potatoes and perhaps some soggy vegetables. Season this with salt and pepper and sour cream for the potato and you were all set for a boring Iowa meal. The major source of competition among the steakhouses was quantity. A one pound T- bone was common and, on a special occasion, a 24-ounce Porterhouse was just the thing.

Then two things happened to change everything: refugees and a Culinary Arts program.

In 1975, Governor Robert Ray recognizing the plight of the Tai Dam, an ethnic group in Laos, invited them to come to Iowa to escape a brutal regime. This took courage for both the Governor and the Tai Dam because Iowa was nearly 100 percent white and unused to any diversity. Many Iowans opposed this humanitarian action believing that the Tai Dam would be on welfare forever, would create cultural conflicts, and would cost the local and state governments millions to provide services to them. These feelings intensified when, in 1979, Governor Ray also invited the Boat People to Iowa. They, too, had fled a repressive regime in Vietnam and were floating in small boats on the fringes of many Asian countries. When no one would accept them, Bob Ray did.

The naysayers and bigots were proved wrong. These refugees from Asia were hard working people who got jobs as soon as possible and worked to save their money to buy the houses they had been renting. They started businesses. And they paid taxes, too, and gladly. In many ways, they helped power the growth that Iowa continues to show.

In one area in particular, their contribution was widespread—they opened restaurants, exposing Iowans to authentic Asian cooking from Thailand, Vietnam, Cambodia, and Laos. Suddenly, there were several family restaurants offering authentic cuisine. Some Iowans viewed this with suspicion, but it wasn't long before many were converted and learned to appreciate food with so many spices and herbs. My first visit to a Thai restaurant was with a successful banker who emigrated from Thailand. I said that I had no idea what to choose. My host said to leave it to him and he ordered Pad Thai for me with spiciness of one star (mercifully sparing me from the Iowa spice level of zero stars). He ordered the Angry Dish which came in at five stars. After he tasted it, he frowned, called the waitress who promptly brought him a dish of chopped red chilis, seeds and all. After tipping some into his dish, he took another taste, smacked his lips and said it was nearly as good as home. I like a little spice but just looking at his plate made my stomach clench.

CULINARY ARTS

The second major impact on Iowa cooking was the successful development and expansion of the Culinary Arts program at the Des Moines Area Community College. Under the tutelage of Chef Robert Anderson, the program recruited students from across the state and from other countries. Graduates of the program began working in existing restaurants or opened new ones. They changed the landscape of dining by offering choices never before available, such as Asian fusion, country French, northern Italian, and fresh fish and seafood.

Now, each year the newly named Iowa Culinary Institute (ICI) offers dinners prepared and served by the students. The French, Italian, Chinese, Hawaiian and other themed dinners are always oversubscribed and getting on the invitation list is quite an achievement. The ICI also has a longstanding exchange program with the chefs of St. Etienne in southern France. The French chefs come to Iowa every year to teach the ICI students, and every year Chef Anderson leads a delegation of foodies on a gustatory tour of France, ending up in St. Etienne.

Despite all these gastronomic changes, Iowa's reputation as a boring food desert persists. Slate Magazine highlighted various meat dishes in each state and Iowa was noted for its loose meat sandwich. Given Iowa's training of chefs and its production of high quality beef and pork, this is insulting. When I first moved to Iowa, I was shocked and disturbed to learn that there was such a thing as a loose meat sandwich. The thought of it seemed somehow grotesque and unfinished. While I have acclimated to most things in the state, I still cannot consider the loose meat sandwich as anything but a freak of nature and not fit for human consumption.

TOO HOT, TOO COLD

Iowa's seasons vacillate between extreme heat and bitter cold, and it is a charter member of the Tornado Alley club.

For my first winter in Iowa I took my car to the Joetown garage to be winterized. As they put my car on the lift I mentioned that I needed the antifreeze changed. "Make it for twenty below," I said. Both of the mechanics started chuckling. They explained that my car will freeze solid and that they always winterize cars for down to 40 below. As it turned out, that was not an especially cold winter, but it did go below minus 25 a few times.

Then summer arrived and stretched into weeks of temperatures in the 90s with heavy humidity. Air conditioning is a blessed relief and I have learned to stay indoors or in my car as much as possible. When I grew up in Lowell, we didn't have air conditioning, but our heat waves only lasted 3 days. My mother even had a special hot weather set of recipes. Usually they revolved around salads or canned tuna in tomato sauce on corn meal. (This would now be called Ahi on Polenta and would cost $35 a plate).

INTERNATIONAL VISITORS

In addition to traveling myself, I was a part of helping to host many international visitors. The US Department of State likes to send international visitors to Iowa. Other countries' perceptions of the US are often based upon our movies and TV shows. Iowa is a lot more like the US really is than New York or LA. After I left the Iowa Hospital Association and began working with Iowa Sister States, I continued hosting groups of international visitors. Some of their observations were very insightful about the differences between our cultures.

A Russian delegation was highly interested in the interstate highway system. They were amazed to learn that there are thousands of miles of such highways across the country. They were also amazed that Russia was the cause of construction of these roads during the Eisenhower administration. There was great concern about Russia immediately after WWII and Eisenhower had been impressed by the Autobahns built in Germany. "You are welcome," our Russian friends said.

They were also impressed by the rest stops along Interstate 80 across Iowa. They thought they were wonderful and impressed that they were free. I confirmed and explained that they were very convenient to have when traveling. "But we noticed that there is toilet paper in each of the stalls," he mentioned. Puzzled I asked about his concern over this. "Why don't people steal it?" he asked.

Another group of Russians was being home hosted and after a week, they asked their host, Ron, if he was taking his gun to work. Ron had no idea what they were talking about and told them he didn't have a gun. Further discussion shed light on the fact that they thought everyone in America had a gun to protect themselves from drive-by shootings. "Have you seen or heard any drive-by shootings while you were here?" Ron asked them. "No," they replied. "We have been wondering about that."

Other times, I've shown international visitors some things we are not so proud of. A delegation of Ukrainian attorneys and judges had been visiting and meeting with their counterparts when we had an invitation to attend family court on short notice. We jumped at the chance. The judge briefed us on the case she would be hearing that afternoon. She pointed to a stack of files about three feet tall. "I assume that this is the paperwork on all your cases today," I said. "No," she responded. "That is the paperwork on just this case." The eyes of the Ukrainians widened.

She went to explain this was the latest case of child neglect in one family. The parents were drug abusers and had been in and out of prison. They had four children and three of them had been taken away because of neglect and child endangerment. It is very difficult to terminate a parent's right to raise their children, but it can be done. The judge explained that for this family, it had been very sad because the parents were irresponsible and they kept having children whom they neglected because of their drug habits. That day, she was to hear the case of their youngest child, Nicholas, who was three years old. He had been staying with his grandmother because his parents neglected him as they had the three older children. She explained he wasn't abused, just ignored.

We went into the courtroom and Nicholas was there with his grandmother. The judge asked the clerk to go out into the corridor to call the parents to appear for the hearing. No response. After five more minutes, she instructed the clerk to try again. No response. The judge then decreed that the parental rights were terminated and the grandmother was granted custody of Nicholas.

The Ukrainians were shocked. "These things happen in our country, but we never expected to see it here in the US." I explained that I had promised the State Department to show them everything and anything they asked for. That meant even those parts of our society that we are ashamed of.

From the glances they shared, I knew that they could not reciprocate if we went there. There was no such transparency in their autocratic culture.

DELAYS MUST BE PUNISHED

Laura, my associate at Iowa Sister States, was complaining one time about an incoming delegation from our sister state in Japan. "They are driving me crazy with their questions," she said. "They want to know about every meeting on the schedule, what time it will start, who will be here, what is the status of all attendees, will gifts be exchanged, how long the meeting will last." Since the sister state Governor was coming, his staff were anxious not to embarrass him and they were trying to anticipate everything. Furthermore, she had just received a request to arrange a visit at Pioneer Hybrid so their Governor could learn about genetically modified grain (GMO).

At this time, GMOs were new and there was quite a bit of controversy about them. Pioneer was one of the major companies producing this seed. Laura was able to arrange a visit with the help of Dennis, who worked at Pioneer and volunteered to arrange a tour. It was on a Saturday and Laura was unable to be there, so I volunteered to handle it for her.

The Saturday arrived and I met the Governor, his wife, and his staff of six people at their hotel promptly at 9 AM. We took our chartered bus to Pioneer's impressive headquarters in Johnston and I went inside to check in with security. They had no record of the visit.

I started panicking, and called Dennis. Apologetic, he explained he had been out of town and passed the tour to a colleague who had apparently forgotten. Dennis promised to call security and be there in 20 minutes.

I went back outside and explained that there would be a short delay and suggested we sit on the benches in the sunshine. It was a spring like day and the Governor seemed to be enjoying himself relaxing in the sun.

Dennis arrived 20 minutes later, apologized again and then took us on an extensive tour of the facility, answering all the questions asked by the Governor and his staff. The visit concluded with a walk in the corn fields where the GMO seeds had been planted. There, Dennis showed the Japanese the results of the GMO experiment. They presented him with a gift and we returned to the hotel where they rested for the remainder of the day.

Next morning, I got a call from the Governor's Chief of Staff demanding to know who the person was who made the Governor wait yesterday as well as who his boss was. I inquired as to why he was asking. "Someone must be responsible for this delay and must be punished," he replied.

"In that case," I said. "I am responsible." Not good enough for him, he was happy to blame me but also demanded the name of the person at Pioneer who was at fault and planned to speak to his superior also. I explained I would not provide him with that information because I felt it was unreasonable. I was accepting responsibility and they were aware of who my superior was. I invited him to call my superior with his complaint if he wished.

Each culture learned something about the other that day. They learned that we are sloppy. I learned that they are way more anal than we are.

SNOWSUITS, VODKA, AND MARK TWAIN

We have had several visitors from Tanzania and, during the first visit, the group asked about the seasons in Iowa. It was hard for them to comprehend our Arctic winters and rivers that really freeze. We vowed never to bring them here during the winter months. However, one year they expressed interest in attending the World Food Prize. The World Food Prize has become a major event that recognizes significant achievements in food security. It is held in mid-October in Des Moines. We figured that our colleagues from Tanzania could cope with Iowa's autumn weather conditions.

Still, the first place we took them was the Salvation Army store to buy them parkas. The weather was pretty warm for mid-October and our colleagues were enjoying themselves. Part of the time, they were home hosted by a family and attended a high school football game on a Friday evening. Because the temperature was going to be in the 40s, the host family outfitted them in snowmobile suits. They were quite a sight waddling around the football crowd. Even though they had no idea what the game was about, they enjoyed the social event—and they stayed warm.

We hosted many groups of Russians and sometimes Ken, one of our volunteers, would invite them to his cabin about 20 miles from town. This was always a good experience for them. "It's your dacha," they said referring to the country houses common in Russia. They loved this rustic setting, with its fields of soybeans, the pond, and the cabin. Ken often arranged for a wood fired barbeque and the Russians enjoyed cooking their own Iowa chops. On one occasion, after several toasts, four of them took Ken's rowboat onto the pond and while Sergei was telling a joke, his gestures were too large and the bottle of vodka flew out of his grip and sank to the bottom of the six-foot deep pond. This was their last bottle so they wasted no time in deciding what to do and immediately dove into the chilly water, searching until the precious liquid was recovered.

The pond was off limits to all subsequent Russian delegations. I didn't want to have to try to explain to the State Department how an inebriated Russian drowned in a shallow pond.

The Russians were very well read in American literature. They knew all about Mark Twain's books and his time as a riverboat captain on the Mississippi River. One group was hosted by a hospital CEO in northeastern Iowa and he took them to the Mississippi on a pilgrimage to visit a couple of the river towns described by Twain. To complete the experience, two of them jumped into the river which was running very fast due to the spring rains. Fortunately, they survived their immersion in American literature and in the Mississippi, but future delegations were kept at least 100 yards from the banks of the river.

St. Petersburg
Moscow
RUSSIA
Samara
Stavropol
Mineralny Vody
Essentuki

SURVIVING VODKA TOASTS IN RUSSIA

FLYING THE AEROFLOT SKIES

Prior to the breakup of the Soviet Union, the only airline there was Aeroflot. It served an enormous domestic need, covering a territory spanning 13 time zones. It used Russian aircraft, usually modified military ones, and they were flown by retired fighter pilots. After the breakup, each of the Republics eventually established their own airlines, or what are called mini-Aeroflots.

Before my first trip to Russia, I attended a conference in Pittsburgh with the other grantee project managers. They held an extensive orientation with us "newbies" being coached by the veterans on what to expect from our new Russian partners. During the final banquet, something puzzling happened. Our host called one of the veteran teams to the podium and gave them a certificate documenting that they had survived more Aeroflot miles than any other team. The other veterans laughed and cheered while I was overcome with a feeling of disquiet. I'll say again, I don't like flying, period. And all that cheering was ominous.

BAPTISM BY BRIBE

My first trip to Russia arrived and I was traveling a couple of days ahead of the rest of the team to plan the schedule. I landed at

Sheremetevo International Airport in Moscow where I was greeted by Joan, a member of the Moscow staff of the non-governmental organization (NGO) funding our project. She was accompanied by Leonid, who was the "fixer" for the Moscow office staff. We drove two hours to Vnukovo airport where I was to catch my connecting flight to Stavropol. When you fly into Russia on an international flight, you land at Sheremetevo International Airport and only Sheremetevo (although recently, at least one other airport was accepting international flights). To fly elsewhere in Russia, you must then transfer to the appropriate regional airport, all 10 of which are at least two hours' drive away.

When we arrived at Vnukovo, Leonid took my ticket to get a seat assignment on the flight to Stavropol. He came back a few minutes later and asked for $20. When I inquired as to why, he told me the flight was overbooked. "Just pay him," Joan said.

Antonov 24 "Accident Prone".
Photo Credit Frank Trumpy.

He returned with a boarding pass. I went through Security and was identified as a foreign traveler and taken to a separate room from the Russians. I was put on a rickety bus and driven on the tarmac to the plane. I was the first person aboard and was able to scout around a bit. It was a turbo prop Antonev 24 and it was Spartan—seats flopped over unless you were sitting in them, non-functioning seat belts, and some of the seats were not bolted down. The bathroom was a horror and I had no problem "holding it" during the two hour flight. I learned later that the Antonev 24 was "accident prone", something I am glad I didn't know at the time. I made sure to select a seat that was bolted down and a seatbelt that worked. By then, another bus pulled up with the Russian passengers. When they were all aboard, the plane was still only two-thirds full, mostly moms and children who had been to Moscow for shopping.

So, I had bribed my way onto a plane that had plenty of room and learned a lesson that was useful for all future activities and plans: Russia is still basically a peasant economy and anyone with any authority will use it to help or hinder you provided that a bribe is paid. This was so common an occurrence that we had to use line item on our expense reports to document the bribes paid during a visit. Of course we didn't call it bribery. For the accountants we referred to it as Management Services.

While it's an overstatement to describe a stereotypical Russian character, there seem to be some general attitudes that are widespread throughout the country. Invasions, revolutions, influence of the Orthodox Church, and a history of strong, autocratic leaders have resulted in a population that is suspicious, paranoid about security, and subservient to authority.

Cathedral of St. Basils the Blessed, Russian Orthodox Church, Moscow.

In 1991, when the Soviet Union broke up, the US government and NGOs established a variety of bilateral programs there to increase civil society, reduce the number of nuclear weapons, and conduct various professional exchange programs. The Iowa Hospital Association was awarded grants to conduct medical exchanges between 1992 and 2003. I managed these exchanges and traveled to Russia over 30 times during this period. What follows is a compilation of real events. These were my first experiences of working in a foreign country. The names have not been changed because no one involved is innocent.

One of the major differences I noticed was the critical role that vodka plays in Russian daily life. It is more than just a social lubricant. Rather, it is a necessary means of dealing with the serious trials of daily living and because of its liberal use, often becomes an addiction. Efforts to cut back on consumption often result in social unrest and production of bootleg booze, occasionally poisonous, leading to relaxation of these attempts at control. Regardless of lore, Russians are human beings and have essentially the same capacity to absorb alcohol as anyone else. While they may be able to increase their capacity by lots of practice, basically when they drink a lot, they are drunk. There are consequences that include disruptive behavior, domestic violence, absenteeism from work, and substandard production of work, as well as vulnerability to illnesses that capitalize on their debilitated health status, such as heart disease, tuberculosis, and some cancers.

On the morning after my medical delegation arrived in Stavropol, we met with Sergei, Chief Physician and CEO of the large referral hospital. This was mainly a social call but we also planned to discuss the general outline of the activities of our visit.

We arrived at 9 AM and were ushered into his large office. After some handshakes, he offered us drinks—either vodka or the local brandy (Cognac as he called it). Russians have no respect for international trademarks. When we politely declined, saying it was too early for us, he looked hurt. So we agreed and he poured generous shots for us. He gave a brief welcoming toast and concluded with "Bottoms up." We downed them.

Then he poured another round and said it was our turn to make a toast. The team looked at me, so I complied by expressing our thanks for his welcome and stating that we had jetlag and were tired. I closed by saying, "This is a sipping toast." "No, no," Sergei interjected. "The toast must be bottoms up." So we tossed them down again.

"Just one more," he said, opening a bottle of a brownish liquid. He boasted he had made this himself. It had herbs from Mount Struzhament and was a health drink. So we downed another shot, not feeling especially healthy no matter what the drink was made of. He inquired about our plans for the day and I explained we planned on a little sightseeing and getting some rest. I then asked about his plans for the day. "Oh, just a typical day," he said after downing three drinks at 9 AM. "I'll be seeing patients, but no surgery today." Our team exchanged relieved glances.

SECURITY AND PRIVACY

We all assumed that our visits to Russia would be closely observed by the security force which has had many names, including CHEKA, KGB, MVD. Through all the name changes, the personnel pretty much stayed the same. Once the authorities learned that we were not only harmless but had no useful information, we were pretty much left alone.

Hotel Stravopol.
Photo Credit Frank Trumpy.

Still, when we worked in Stavropol, the Intourist was the only hotel considered "suitable for foreigners," and we had to stay there. The Intourist seemed to have a large number of athletic young men always hanging around the lobby. Valentin Mezzin was the manager, a transparently oozy specimen of the worst type of security agent, and he was always there when we arrived. He offered greetings and local "entertainment" if we were interested. We were able to buy him off with jars of peanut butter to which he was addicted. In retrospect, he was probably a good example of a Matroshka doll—those famous stacking dolls with one inside another, each a little different than its predecessor. Valentin was likely a very clever agent who was playing dumb for us. However, after he learned that we were such amateurs with no information worth having, he gave up.

Much more subtle was our "physician interpreter," Vasily. He was with us continuously and interpreted many of our meetings with the Russian physicians. He was very friendly and accommodating and we took him at face value—at first.

On one occasion, he showed some of his authority. We had been stopped at a checkpoint by the police. It would have been a routine matter but one of my colleagues pulled out a camera and took a picture of the police officer with the checkpoint in the background. This violated policy and the officer was going to confiscate the camera. Vasily began talking rapid Russian and left the vehicle to continue talking to the policeman. Then, another of my colleagues took out a videocamera to film this encounter. The cop flipped out. Vasily did more talking and he and the cop went into the security building.

Five minutes later, he was back and smiling. "Just a misunderstanding. I told them who you are and about the project which has been approved by the health authorities," he explained. "They wanted your names, but I told them they were untranslatable. We can leave now, but please no more pictures of police or checkpoint." We re-evaluated our opinion. Vasily had clout.

At times, we were frustrated by how slowly things were happening. There always seemed to be a delay in getting permission to try a new procedure or to schedule a conference. Whenever we wanted to see something (pharmacy, for example) the door was always locked and the person with the key was never around. Some of this, we attributed to just the inefficiency of the Russian health system. But some we thought was deliberate and intended to slow down disruptive changes—such as more effective infection control procedures rather than relying on that mysterious sterilizing solution coming from Moscow.

We were pretty sure that our rooms at the Intourist were bugged and avoided making any offensive remarks about our hosts when we were there. However, after one especially frustrating day, our senior physician, Alex, said. "Tomorrow, I am going to talk to my shower head and I'm going to say, 'Dr. Shibkov, these delays and mixed up schedules are wasting my time. If things are not corrected, I will go home.'" At breakfast next morning, Alex reported that he had this one-way conversation in the shower and felt better just venting.

Later that day, Dr. Shibkov called me to his office to apologize for the delays and confusion in carrying out our schedule. "I promise that things will improve," he said.

When the team met, I reported this conversation and we all smiled, but no one said anything. We knew we were bugged, but we just hoped we were not videotaped.

MEET THE PILOTS

When Frank and I were returning from a visit and were in the terminal at the regional airport of Mineralny Vody (Mineral Waters) airport in the southern part of the Stavropol Region, Vasily was also traveling to Moscow. As we chatted prior to the flight being called, Vasily asked if we would like to meet the pilots. We responded in the affirmative and Vasily went on, "They are right over there, at the end of the bar. You can tell them by their uniforms. If you buy them a drink, they will invite you to the cockpit."

Tupolev 134.
Photo Credit Frank Trumpy.

Frank and I looked at each other, mentally calculating that there were already were too many people invited to the cockpit. We passed on the opportunity to see the cockpit of the Tupolev 134, the jet we would take to Moscow.

I'm sure that the pilots, like many men I have known, believed that they drove better after a few drinks. I doubt it, but at least they were not going 500 mph at 30,000 feet.

ALWAYS OVERWEIGHT

During our first Russian project, we had to transfer to Vnukovo airport from Sheremetevo. All Russian airports were dingy and dirty, but Vnukovo was in a class by itself. It looked as though it had not been cleaned since it was built. There was litter everywhere and it was crowded. The toilets were unspeakable and water ran continuously through them and the sinks. I have been in third world countries that were cleaner than the airport at Vnukovo was.

So it was with relief when I went to security to get to the departure area to leave. The security officer looked at my carry-on bag and said "Too heavy" and directed me to go back to the ticket window, pay, and get a form. I went back to the ticket counter and the agent took my bag and weighed it. "Too heavy," was the verdict. She gave me a form and sent me across the terminal to pay the fee and get the form stamped. The clerk here told me ten dollars, and I paid, she stamped the form, and sent me back to the ticket counter for another stamp on the form.

This happened every time, no matter how light or heavy my bag was. They would say too heavy and I would pay to get this over with. Just one more way that petty officials could milk the rich Americans through a little bribery, which they considered to be part of their compensation.

THE HETMAN

Dr. Tom, a retired cardiovascular surgeon, and I had joined Dr. Mikhail, Chief Surgeon of Stavropol Krai Health Department for dinner at a private restaurant.

As we arrived, Mikhail announced he was the Hetman that night. The Hetman is an old Cossack custom indicating a person who plans and organizes things. So, that night Mikhail organized the dinner, ordered the food, and managed everything. The first thing of course was to offer a welcoming toast. He poured shot of vodka and began, "My new American friends, I welcome you…" and he went on for two minutes while we stood there holding our shot glasses. Finally, he finished with "…and this is a bottoms up toast." So, we downed the shots and he immediately poured another round and indicated that it was my turn.

By now, I had figured out how this works and was determined to make the toast as long as possible. So, I invoked our collaboration in World War II, my hopes for a successful collaboration in our project, our hopes for a better world for our children and everything else I could think of. But, I was still an amateur and my toast only lasted a minute and a half. I closed with "…and so thank you,

Mikhail, for acting as Hetman tonight. This will be a sipping toast."

He looked pleased, then dismayed. "There are no sipping toasts," he said and made us drink them down. "Let me show you how it is done," and he poured himself another shot and gave another flowery toast and downed it. He gestured to me to try again and poured another round.

I was on my feet thinking desperately and saying whatever came to mind to stretch this out. I managed two minutes (about what I am still not sure) and ended with, "…and I wish good health and prosperity to all. This is a bottoms up toast." We drank again and Mikhail looked pleased that I had begun to master this important cultural matter. He got to his feet to propose another toast, but fortunately dinner arrived.

The food was very good and Dr. Tom and I stuck to the local fizzy water. Apparently, this was socially acceptable, although Mikhail looked disapproving and downed more shots. By now, he had at least six to our three but he seemed to be doing pretty well.

He said, "Do you know, Dr. Tom, that vodka is considered a health food in Russia?" We looked skeptical and he continued. "Yes, it's true. As a surgeon I have done many autopsies on Russian men and have never seen any signs of arteriosclerosis." Tom muttered to me that was probably because they all died of cirrhosis of the liver by age 35. I said nothing, lest we have to toast again or start an argument with Mikhail.

Fortunately, Mikhail didn't hear this because he was busy signing the check. "Let's have one more toast to our friendship and our work together." Before he poured out our drinks, I mentioned that I was worried that he might be driving that night. He assured me he was not driving but had a driver so he didn't have to. Tom muttered again, "I'm worried about his walking, never mind driving."

But Mikhail agreed that we should not have another drink. "I have to get up early in the morning to do surgery," he explained.

Dr. Tom and I gasped and left, hoping that Mikhail had good assistants who could steady his hands.

Russians in general are well educated. They read classic literature and poetry. They were knowledgeable about music and art and knew quite a bit about the US. They had read Mark Twain and were eager to see the Mississippi River. During one visit, their host took them to the town of Bellevue which is on the banks of the Mississippi. They visited the state park and walked along the embankment and two of them were overcome with joy and jumped into the river. Usually this would be only a little scary, but they chose to do this at Lock and Dam number 12 where commercial river traffic enters the lock and is raised or lowered between six and nine feet. This was extremely dangerous. Fortunately, no barge traffic was near the lock and the Russians survived, however, their host nearly had heart failure.

Unfortunately though, there were gaps in their professional knowledge. Much of this was due to their inability to access the medical literature or attend international conferences. However, the lingering influence of Lysenkoism also played a part. Lysenkoism is the deliberate distortion of science and the scientific method in support of an ideological goal. It is named after Trofim Lysenko who posited an alternative to evolution theory by stating that exposure of wheat seeds to extreme conditions would rapidly lead to increases in productivity. He convinced senior officials in the Agricultural Ministry and planted his "improved" seeds on thousands of acres. His theory failed and production actually declined, but he had the support of high Russian officials who had staked their careers on his work. So, they did the usual Russian thing and cooked the books and identified scapegoats or "wreckers" to explain the lack of results.

The Americans were shocked at the outdated and incorrect understanding of infection control in the Russian hospitals. One of our key objectives in the project was improved infection control. At our first meeting with our Russian colleagues, they told us that there were no hospital acquired infections. They reached this conclusion partly through ignorance and partly through fear. They did not know how pervasive hospital acquired infections could be (and are) so they did not require hand washing after seeing patients. Their sterilization techniques for surgical instruments often were limited to dunking them in some solution sent from Moscow. When we inquired about what was in the solution, they said they didn't know. Later, after gaining their confidence, we learned that they did know about these infections, but whenever they were reported to the Health Ministry, the hospital CEO was fined. So, they kept two sets of books.

We also learned about a cultural factor limiting continuing medical education. Our team had formed a good relationship with Natalia, who headed one of the surgery departments. She was willing to try some of our techniques in her department and her data was showing some success. Then we learned that her results had suddenly deteriorated. We were puzzled until one of our Russian colleagues told us that Natalia was being punished for working with us without specific permission from Sergei, the CEO of the hospital. She was being given all the worst cases and, of course, her results were bad. Dr. Alex (chief physician of our delegation) and I met with Big Sergei and apologized for failing to keep him fully informed about our plans for an infection control test in one of his departments. We said we would always let him know what we were doing and asked that he approve each project activity. Sergei was his usual jovial self and said it was not a problem and that he liked meeting with us and discussing these interesting new ideas in medicine. Things began improving for Natalia soon afterwards.

Several members of our delegation were surgeons and they were invited to observe surgeries. In fact, they were given the opportunity to perform the surgery, but declined not having any legal authority to do so and not knowing anything about equipment or procedures in the Russian OR. They did find plenty of issues for recommended changes. Anesthesia was usually done with ether, an explosive gas but acceptable with adequate precautions. However, this did not include the anesthesiologist smoking a cigarette while administering the gas. To prevent too much concentration of ether in the air, the nurses would open windows, which, of course had not been washed since the hospital had been built. The nurses tried to look their most attractive for the surgeons, so they wore full makeup, jewelry and kept their hair partially uncovered. Our team was kept busy drafting suggestions for improvements.

The role of nurses reflected the general societal bias against women. There were female physicians, but they were obstetricians, pediatricians, and general practitioners. The surgeons were men. Nurses were universally women and they had very little clinical knowledge and virtually no independent authority.

When Russian delegations visited our hospitals, they were shocked at what the US nurses were doing. They asked where the doctors were and we explained they were in their offices, seeing patients or in surgery. They then asked who monitored the patients and administered their medicines and we told them that nurses were trained to do that.

One of the chief physicians at the cancer hospital was so impressed by this that he worked with us to start a continuing education program for his nursing staff. At first, the faculty were US nurses who were models of what women could learn and do. This was revolutionary (as it had been here some 50 years ago). They also taught in an informal, interactive manner which was opposite the standard style in which the teacher talks and the students shut up and write down everything. Eventually, the nursing faculty from the local college took over and adopted some of the content and teaching style. Some real progress was made and fortunately, the hospital CEO had enough clout to keep this program going and avoid the usual punishment for coloring outside the lines.

BALD TIRES AND ENGINE FIRES

In many airports outside of Moscow, you walk out on the tarmac to board the plane. After one visit to Stavropol, my colleague Frank was returning alone and had made the acquaintance of a Russian engineer also traveling to Moscow. Since they both spoke some German, they got along well. As they walked out, Frank noticed that the plane's tires were bald. He nervously pointed this out to his new friend, who explained that was normal. He went on to say that bald tires save a lot of money because the pilots first land the plane on the side with the best tires and then slowly roll over to the poorer tires. When the good ones get bald, they rotate them to the other side and buy new ones.

By the time Frank had a chance to be shocked or even scared by this, they had boarded the plane to leave Stavropol. As they took off, Frank looked out the window and thought he saw smoke coming from an engine. Soon, it blossomed into a fire. Again, his German seat partner was nonchalant, "This happens all the time. When we climb it will go out," he said. Frank's worry continued to climb as the former fighter pilot tried to show the passengers what he could do. The steep climb to a low oxygen altitude put out the fire. Frank started breathing again until he thought about landing on bald tires.

This cavalier attitude toward safety scared the hell out of us Americans. We were used to the extreme safety measures taken by Western airlines—for instance, during one flight out of the US, our departure was delayed for an hour while a defective coffeepot was replaced. But we soon had to develop the fatalistic attitude adopted by the Russians because the alternative transportation options were even worse. Taking the trains was out of the question—"unsuitable for foreigners" which was code for robbers on the train. The highways were in poor condition and there were bandits in some areas. For the most part, Russian cars were even more unsafe than the planes. In a vehicle you would be involved in a slow motion crash as opposed to a fast one in a plane. So, we became resigned to our fate and flew thousands of miles on Aeroflot. I hated every one of them.

PAY NOW OR PAY LATER

For a while, we carried computers to our colleagues in Russia. We had a deal with Gateway to transport their computers, which at the time were the heavy monitors, hard drives, and keyboards - three bulky boxes. To avoid Customs duties, we had a letter from the CEO of our funding entity, AIHA, stating that these computers were for a humanitarian program and exempt from Customs duties.

On one occasion, Linda, an RN and member of my staff, led the delegation. It was her first trip abroad and her first visit to Russia. I had not oriented her very well. She took the three computers (nine boxes) through Customs. Or at least she tried to. Three physician volunteers had gone through Customs and were waiting for her to clear so they could carry the boxes for her out to the van.

Linda loaded the boxes on the counter and the Customs Officer said, "One hundred dollars." "Oh, wait," said Linda. "I have this letter." He looked at the letter and then the boxes. "One hundred dollars." She told him he must not understand, and explained the letter said the computers were for charitable purposes and no customs duty should be paid. He listened impassively and said, "One hundred dollars." This went on for 10 minutes with Linda getting agitated and the Customs official repeating, "One hundred dollars."

"Just pay the guy, Linda" said one of the doctors. "Phil will kill me," she replied. "There is nothing in the budget for this." I had failed to tell Linda about the virtual requirement to bribe these Customs officials.

Then, into the Customs area from outside (strictly forbidden) came Leonid, the Moscow office fixer. He was well known to the Customs Officials and he had no problem in identifying the problem with Linda standing there, surrounded by her boxes. Leonid went over to the Customs official and they had a quiet chat. Bam, bam, bam, and Linda's Customs forms were stamped.

Linda was triumphant and thanked Leonid profusely, explaining she was getting worried and did not know what to do. "OK, welcome," said Leonid with his limited understanding of English. He then took the team to the nearby Novotel where they would be overnighting before catching the morning flight to Stavropol. He took Linda into the gift shop where Leonid picked out $200 worth of perfumes and told Linda, "Pay." When she asked why, he said, "For Customs official." Leonid was a rare breed—an honest fixer. He took care of many problems for us and never cheated us. The perfume went to the Customs Official's girlfriend.

THERAPEUTIC MUD

In Stavropol Krai we typically stayed at the Intourist hotel where equipment suffered from the usual casual Russian attitude towards maintenance. Our delegations were stuck in the elevator several times and the stairwells were off limits. So, we pushed the buttons on the elevator with some trepidation each morning and evening.

We were hosted at several restaurants in the area with Continental-style cooking. Although the quality of the meat varied a good deal and was not up to US standards, when washed down with several vodka toasts, the food was surprisingly good. Most of the meat was very fatty and when we tried to cut it off, we amused our hosts who said that fat was energy food and they relished it. This was especially true of the sausages which were the usual appetizer served at lunch. They were nearly all fat and at times we had difficulty getting them down. But we did not want to insult our hosts so we did our best— and learned that in addition to being a health food, vodka was a good chaser.

After the breakup of the Soviet Union, Russians were allowed to leave the country for vacations.

So many chose to go to Turkey, Cyprus, and Croatia, that the old resorts along the southern border were deserted. These resorts along the Caucuses Mountains featured mineral springs and spas and had been the most popular vacation destinations since the time of the czars.

When we were working in that part of the Stavropol Region, we were hosted in the resort hotels which we found to be stereotypically Soviet. These were enormous hotels with over 500 rooms each and had huge dining rooms. Even though they were largely deserted, we were assigned a table and our breakfast was determined by the "nutritionist" on the staff, choice being a very foreign concept. Generally, the rooms were good and the staff pleasant, but condescending. They had developed their exercise routines and menus to deal with people coming there for the "cure," and they had a hard time accommodating independent Americans.

The Russian idea of a spa was different than ours. To them, it was a place where your visit was planned by the staff who knew what you needed to "cure what ailed you" which usually was alcoholism. They scheduled the day for you starting with your wakeup call, then the breakfast they chose for you—even the table where you took your meals and then whatever exercise program was best. Finally, they decided what your bedtime was. The real surprise for us was that there was no bar in the hotel. We thought that this was striking until we found many liquor stores within walking distance which became an important, but unofficial part of the exercise regimen.

We were working in this area (Mineral Waters region) because we had been invited to do some training of the medical and nursing staffs at the maternity hospital and the big clinic in the town of Essentuki. Two of our male physicians accepted an invitation to go to the spa. The treatment started with a warm mineral water bath— lots of little bubbles. This was followed by a brief but vigorous massage. Next was therapeutic mud. Hot mud was slathered all over their bodies and they slowly roasted until it was rinsed off with a high pressure hose.

The physicians were asked if they wanted the "extra treatment". When they inquired as to what this was, the attendant explained it was a rectal pack using the therapeutic mud. For women, they had a vaginal pack. "Very cleansing," they assured.

They were curious enough by now to ask where this therapeutic mud came from. The attendant explained that there was a lake nearby that had mud in it which was kept warm by the heat from the hot springs that fed the lake. They took mud from there, used it for two or three months, and then put it back and got some new mud. It was their way of recycling, she explained. The physicians declined, repressing a shudder at the thought of where the mud just recently rinsed off them had previously been, but promising to pass the vaginal pack option to their female traveling companions as the attendants requested.

At dinner that evening, the physicians reported on their spa experience, concluding with the offer from the spa attendants inviting the nurses for a spa visit including either the rectal or vaginal pack. "A what or a what?" exclaimed Kay. "Say that again." The physician dutifully explained the options again. Kay declined the offer to have recycled mud pushed into her body. The others nodded. Nurses are pretty tough, though, and the conversation did not spoil their dinner.

AIRPORTS AND OFFICIALDOM

Most airports around the world are congested and boring (with the exception of Asia where they are new, shiny, and interesting). But in the 1990s and early 2000s, airports in Russia had the added feature of being dingy and dirty as well as congested and boring.

The Russian policy that allowed only Sheremetevo airport to accept international flights, making you transfer to another regional airport to then fly domestically was done deliberately by the authorities to make travel difficult and to increase their control over citizens and tourists. From the moment you began walking those endless glass-walled corridors to Passport Control, you were well aware that it was an unfriendly airport. It was dirty and dark with sparse lighting and institutional dark brown everything (walls, ceiling, and broken tile floors). Finally, you and about 300 other passengers descended a wide staircase and found several hundred other arrivals, jostling for space in the "lines" for the Passport Control officials.

There was no such thing as line etiquette in Russia. You just cut in front or push your way into the mass of people. Polite Midwesterners could spend days just getting through. When you finally handed your travel documents to the official, you were greeted with a sneer and a barely comprehensible "Why are you coming to Russia?" He didn't believe whatever your response was and carefully checked every page of your passport and visa. Once, an official asked me how many times I had come to Russia. I told him about 17. He looked at his computer screen and said "Twenty-one." They keep track of all this.

After Passport Control, there was Customs. These officials made the others look positively friendly. They were surly, cynical, and distrustful—certain that you were smuggling something and it was their duty to find it. You could spend quite a bit of time at Customs because they opened everything, even your shaving kit. If you were bringing brochures or journal articles, they had to be satisfied that they were not subversive—and they defined what subversive is.

Regrettably, this supercilious, brazen, and corrupt attitude was the norm among these petty officials who exercised the power of the state over all who came under their control. While most petty officials around the world seemed to have gone to the same training in rudeness, Russians held the dubious honor of the most accomplished students.

THE DESIGNATED TOASTER

Our medical project happened through exchanges of health professionals, physicians, nurses, technicians, and administrators. Sometimes the delegations were large, up to 15 people. Our Russian hosts extended very generous hospitality—Cossack hospitality in which the guests are so stuffed with food they cannot move and so full of vodka that remaining upright was a challenge. At these formal banquets, our hosts often outnumbered the delegation.

One evening began, as always, with a bottoms up toast by the leader of the Russian hosts. Because the Americans had artfully arranged for me to be seated at the front with Nikolai, he looked to me to respond to his toast. By now, I was getting good at this, or so I thought. I began "My dear Russian and American friends…" I closed some three minutes later with the traditional "Nastarovia" (your health) and downed my shot like a man on his way to being a Cossack. Before I could get a swallow of the fizzy mineral water, the number two guy was up and toasting us and the second shot went down smoothly. Russian vodka is very good and often it is served ice cold which masks its potency. Now the number two guy—and my delegation—were all looking at me. The head of the medical team leaned over and whispered, "We took a vote and elected you designated toaster."

I wasn't in a position to get into an open argument with our chief physician about this "election", so I took one for the team and did the toast. The food blessedly arrived and I was ready for a reprieve. But this time, it was different. There were toasts between courses and the duly elected "designated toaster" had to do the deed. After the fourth one, I noticed that the team was smiling because they were dumping their vodka into the water glasses and toasting with mineral water. Because I was up front, I was unable to use this dodge.

The next morning, the team congratulated me on managing eleven toasts and still being able to walk out of there more or less on my own power. The Russians were considering honorary citizenship for me. But, all I was thinking was that those who claim that vodka does not result in a hangover are outrageous liars.

MT. ELBRUS AND THE RUSSIAN REFEREE

In Edger Allen Poe's poem, "The Raven", the narrator is driven mad by a recurring contact with a raven that responds to all questions with the word "Nevermore". I was reminded of the poem when I nearly went mad one day in Russia due to repeated sightings of a mysterious man in a striped shirt.

During a trip to Essentuki in the southern part of Stavropol Krai, our hostess, Lubov (Russian word for love), thought we were working too hard and planned a weekend for us in the southern part of the Krai in the Caucuses Mountains. Our vehicles were two old-style ambulances, the kind used by funeral homes in the US. Kay, Linda, Penny, Joann, and I sat hunched over on the wooden benches and were driven to a rustic lodge at the base of the mountains beside a rushing river. We enjoyed the spectacular scenery.

After dinner, we gathered around the fireplace and the Russians sang beautiful folk songs to us which they translated (mostly about lost love and suffering). Then they let us know that it was our turn. We were embarrassed because we didn't know any songs. They pressed us, so we sang the Corn Song, Row, Row Your Boat, Home on the Range, and 99 Bottles of Beer on the Wall. After this drivel, the Russians sang some more beautiful folk songs. We have cable television and they have playing instruments and singing as home entertainment.

Mt. Elbrus.

Next morning, Lubov told us at breakfast that we were being kicked out by some senior Party officials who wanted the lodge that night. She assured us she would find another place for the night, but invited us on a day trip to Mt. Elbrus, the highest mountain in Europe.

We arrived, got out of the ambulances, and climbed the stairs to the platform for the cable car. When it arrived, a Russian guy cut us off to get into the car. He stood out because he was wearing a striped shirt that looked like one worn by football referees and was already drunk at 9 AM.

We took the swaying cable car up to the first level. The view was magnificent, overlooking the valley and the rocky foothills and, of course, there was a bar at this level. Kay, Penny, Joann, and Linda were all for continuing on the T-bar that led to the next level, about two-thirds of the way to the peak. I noticed that there were still some bullet holes on the equipment from one of the recent raids by the Chechens. I tried to discourage the ladies because clearly maintenance was a low priority on this mountain, but they felt brave and decided to continue. I stayed at this first level and headed into the lodge with Lubov and the drivers. I had a beer or two and met some people from the US. The Russian guy in the striped shirt was there too, getting drunker and more obnoxious.

Meanwhile, my nursing friends got to the end of the T-bar line where they met some Russian guys who invited them to ride to the top in a snow cat. My brave colleagues said yes and they went to the peak. They got out to walk around and Linda promptly sank into the snow up to her hips. The Russian guys spent 20 minutes pulling her out. Kay told me about these adventures a year later, knowing that I would worry. By the time I learned about it, enough time had passed and the story was amusing rather than terrifying. After all, I "signed" for these people and had to return them. If I didn't bring them back, I would have to complete a mountain of paperwork.

The ladies eventually joined us in the bar and had hot chocolate while the striped shirt got into a loud argument with an equally drunk Russian guy. The team and I were able to slip by them as they gasped for breath. After we got down from the mountain, we met with Lubov and she told us plans for the night. We were going to stay in a Russian tourist hotel nearby. As we were getting ready to climb back into our ambulances with Vila and Sergei at the wheel, our drunk Russian striped shirt appeared in the parking lot, drinking from a half empty liter bottle that certainly wasn't filled with iced tea.

After we checked into the hotel, Vila and I were bringing in some luggage when the striped shirt arrived again with a group of Russians in a big bus. He was so drunk by then that he was barely vertical. When I got to Kay's room to deliver her bag, I found her busily swatting bugs. She had left the window open and bugs had invaded her room. I helped her murder at least 200 of them.

After a poor night's sleep on lumpy mattresses and cold showers, we met in the lobby to load up the vehicles. As we were finishing, striped shirt appeared looking grim. His stripes were crooked and he was pretty green but was working on improving his state of health by taking slugs from a fresh liter bottle.

I went with Lubov and Kay in the ambulance driven by Sergei. She had to make a couple of stops on the way back to Essentuki. Linda, Penny, and Joann went with Vila in the other ambulance. Vila was feeling very manly taking care of these American women and decided to show them what he could do. He drove along the winding, two-lane road at about 80 mph. There were plenty of hills and blind curves and the women were screaming at him to slow down. This just increased his desire to show off his masculinity and he kept going—until he came around a bend and there were 40 cattle blocking the road. Vila barely managed to stop in time and finished the rest of the trip deflated and at a sedate speed.

Lubov was furious when Linda told her about Vila's driving. "I will fire him in the morning", she exclaimed. But she didn't. No one gets fired in Russia. You may get exiled to Kazakhstan, but you don't get fired for incompetence. She just transferred him to another job where we didn't see him.

We got back to our hotel in Essentuki and everyone turned in early. I collapsed in bed and dreamed of drunks in striped shirts. And ravens. We were exhausted from our restful weekend.

THE SIBERIAN METHOD

Drs. Alex and Bill were traveling with me in the resort town of Pyatigorsk. Both of these men were retired cardiovascular surgeons and they had been invited to the hospital in this city of 100,000. They accepted the invitation because the hospital CEO was a cardiovascular surgeon who had done his residency in Greece. Drs. Alex and Bill were interested in meeting him and finding out what he had to say.

What he had to say was that he wanted their considerable assistance in starting the first open heart surgery program in Russia, outside of Moscow. As the three of them talked, (in pretty good English, but with clinical terms over my head), it became clear that there was a good chance for this happening. I reminded the Americans that our project goals were primary care, not necessarily this high level, sophisticated service. Alex reassured me that this project could be done without jeopardizing our main line of work. He went on to explain that he and Bill had good connections with the companies that make the pumps that circulate the blood during the procedure and were well connected with the University of Iowa, College of Medicine which could collaborate with additional training and use Resident physicians to help train the Russian surgeons.

Dr. Mikhail, our host, explained that currently they were limited in open heart surgeries to the Siberian method. Via this method, they put the patient in an ice bath to cool his temperature as low as possible which slows his metabolism. Then, they would open his chest, pack it in ice and remove the heart for any necessary repair. Working quickly, they then replace the heart back in the chest, remove the ice, and warm the patient.

Bill and Alex looked horrified and asked how successful the procedure was. Mikhail said about 50 percent survived the procedure and of that, about 20 percent of those succumbed to infections.

Bill and Alex huddled and agreed they had to try to help because what they were doing was terrible.

They asked Mikhail for a tour of the hospital. He was pleased to show us around. As usual, it was pretty grim--dark and gloomy, but fairly clean for a Russian hospital. Bill and Alex looked pleased. We saw the wards—very full, but with good attendants taking care of the patients. We ended up in the service room which controls electrical distribution throughout the hospital.

They asked about the backup generator and Mikhail looked puzzled. Alex explained they were looking for the generator that came on when the power was interrupted so the pumps would keep working during surgery. Mikhail said they didn't have one.

Then they asked to see the blood bank. Mikhail explained there was no blood bank at the hospital. When they needed blood, they called the blood bank in town and they sent along what they needed. He went on to explain this takes 20-30 minutes depending on traffic.

Though the backup generator could be easily accommodated, creating a blood bank at the hospital would be much harder. Other limitations quickly became apparent—inadequate lab resources, limited surgical intensive care unit, and inadequate pharmacy.

Ultimately, Alex and Bill had to apologize and explain they could not participate in an open heart surgery program in the hospital because there were too many major shortcomings. Alex regretfully said it wouldn't be right for the patients or for them.

"Too bad," Mikhail responded. "We'll have to continue using the Siberian method." The American doctors shuddered.

LUNCH IS (STILL) SERVED

We were completing a project in Stavropol when the first Chechen war was beginning. Things got pretty hot there and for a while the Russian military was using civilian aircraft to ferry troops there and back.

The rest of the delegations had left, but Bob, a hospital CEO, was staying for a few more days. As usual, he was escorted to the Stavropol airport, whisked past immigration and customs, and taken to the VIP lounge. He boarded the plane and since we usually boarded last, he was wondering what was holding things up. He heard an argument and saw that a Russian army lieutenant and a squad of soldiers were refusing to check their weapons. It was soon resolved—the troops stored their rifles in the rear luggage compartment and the officer got to keep his sidearm. He sat next to Bob and in rough English apologized for the delay. He explained that they had been guarding government sites from Chechen terrorists and were going home for some leave.

Before the door to the plane closed, a large man with two full grown Rottweilers boarded. A nervous flight attendant showed him and his dogs to their own row. The dogs soon quieted down and the plane took off.

After about an hour, it was time for lunch. At that time, Aeroflot served hot meals on their flights and the aroma of roasted chicken permeated the plane. As the flight attendant pushed the heavy cart forward and began serving people, the Rottweilers escaped and attacked the food cart. The flight attendant backed off and while the dogs' owner was struggling with his seatbelt, the Russian lieutenant was unsnapping the holster of his pistol. Bob said he moved so quickly that he barely had a chance to speak before he had the weapon drawn. Bob desperately cried 'Nyet! nyet!'while trying to think of the Russian word for decompression, when the owner finally got out of his seatbelt and got control of the dogs.

After a little shouting, the owner and dogs were back in their private row and the lieutenant holstered his gun.

The flight attendant restored some order to the food cart and continued the meal service.

Bob declined a meal after suddenly finding himself not hungry.

BOOZE IN AMERICA

When the Russian delegations made their first visits to Iowa as part of our medical exchange with Stavropol, I found a restaurant with a private dining room that could accommodate us. The Latin King is a well-established restaurant with good Italian food, both northern and southern Italian.

Before dinner, Mr. Tursi, the owner, ushered us into the private dining room closely followed by three staff who took drink orders. The order was always vodka, and it was always a double. Most times, the bar tab exceeded the meal expense by a considerable margin. Many believe that the major expansion of The Latin King was floated on all those double shots of Absolut. I couldn't possibly comment.

After a while, The Russians found that vodka was too expensive in America and wasn't very good. I asked them if they wanted Stoly. "Terrible stuff—undrinkable—and suitable only for export," they scoffed. This convinced them to bring vodka from home, usually at least a couple of liters, sometimes more. One of our visitors liked Armenian cognac and brought a bottle in his luggage. As we waited for his bag at the carousel, we could smell the cognac which had spilled from the broken bottle. His host family drove straight to the dry cleaners.

One evening, I drove a Russian physician home to his host. He had overindulged, even for a Russian, and was pretty drunk when I helped him out of the car. He wanted to show his appreciation for all that I had done. So, he stood at a slightly canted attention, made a bugle of his right hand and tooted. He then reached into his pocket and pinned a Red Army medal on my shirt. "You are now in the Russian army," he said, then hiccupped. I thanked him and steered him to the door and notified the host of his guest's condition.

I have never been asked to report for duty with my Russian Army medal. If called, I would have to decline going, even though I am a colonel.

A bewildering thing about Russian culture is keeping track of names. They have given names, surnames, patronymic names, and nicknames. A patronymic is used as a middle name and it is your father's first name with an ending denoting whether you are male or female. For instance if your father's first name was Sergei, and if you are a man, your patronymic would be Sergeivich; if a woman, Sergeiovna.

Our American volunteers who worked on the medical exchanges in Russia were casual in addressing each other by name and we confused our hosts. We all pretty much dressed alike and called each other by our first names. Russians are used to putting people in categories and knowing who bosses whom. We were too free form for them and often had to introduce ourselves, describe our education, and our jobs back home. This helped them categorize us.

They were very tolerant about the informal way we greeted them, usually by their first names. But the importance of their customs came home to me clearly when an urgent matter arose when I was back in Iowa and I needed to talk to my colleague Nikolai Shibkov in Stavropol. I asked Marina, one of our US interpreters, to make the call. As she was doing so, she asked what his name was. I replied, "Dr. Nikolai Shibkov." And then she asked what his patronymic was. "His what?" I asked. She was getting distressed and said, "I need to know his patronymic to properly address him." I was puzzled and said, "I don't know what you are talking about."

Marina made the call and spent the first five minutes apologizing for being overly familiar because I did not know Nikolai's patronymic. He told her it was Nikolaievich. So, he was Nikolai Nikolaievich Shibkov. After the call, Marina explained the social necessity of using patronymic names when addressing Russian adults whether men or women. Then I asked her about all these nicknames we heard. She replied that many Russian first names have a nickname that usually is applied. Tatiana becomes Tanya and Alexander becomes Sasha.

This was an epiphany for me and not just about relating to people participating in our project, but also in explaining some of the complexity in Leo Tolstoy's book "War and Peace." It is a classic work but I had twice failed in getting through it. I realized that it was because I couldn't get past the first 10 pages without getting totally confused with the names of the characters. After Marina's explanation, I was able to work through one of the great novels without being confused or lost in the identifications of the characters.

Finally, a cultural learning experience that had practical results and benefits.

BABUSHKAS

Babushka selling bread in Pyatigorsk.

In Russia, old (usually widowed) women are called Babushkas. The name comes from the head scarf that they inevitably wear everywhere. Although seemingly powerless, these babushkas wield great moral authority. They sit at the entrances to museums and churches that have become museums and they tell you the entry fee. No one ever disputes them and we always paid whatever they said.

Several times when I was overnighting in Moscow, I had the chance to visit church museums in the Kremlin, Pushkin, or Tretyakov museums. Always there was a babushka sitting outside. She would look at my interpreter and say five rubles. Then she would look at me and say 20 rubles. I asked my interpreter Natasha about this and she said, "You are a foreigner and should pay more." I asked how they knew that I was a foreigner even when we are not talking. Natasha told me they look at my shoes, glasses, and haircut and it was obvious to them.

If you attend church services at an Orthodox church on Sunday morning, the babushkas are there watching you to be sure that you make an offering before you light a candle. They shush people who are talking and make sure that you do not disrupt the service by taking photographs. They have moral authority and no one questions it.

On an early visit to St. Petersburg, we were invited to attend the opera, Evgeny Onyegin, at the Marinsky Palace. This was quite an honor and when we arrived at the concert hall, it was crowded (and because Russians do not have crowd manners) and we were separated from the rest of the delegation. Henry and I found a large box with seats available so we went in. Shortly after the overture, about 10 young people filed in and were seated. However, within a few minutes, they were talking among themselves and disrupting the performance for the rest of us. One of the men at the front of the box, left. A few minutes later, he was back. And a babushka was with him. She went to the young people, had a whispered conversation with them and they filed out following her like baby chicks.

YOU AND YOUR BEST TWO FRIENDS

At dusk on one visit, Dr. Alex, the retired cardiovascular surgeon, our interpreter, Natasha, and I were coming back into the city of Stavropol. As we drove by one of the many city parks, Natasha asked me what I saw. I responded that it was a nice city park with several gatherings of people.

She explained that what we were seeing was a daily ritual in the park. "You and your best two friends meet in the park and gather around a table or tree stump. One brings some sausage, another, some bread, and the third brings a liter of vodka. They talk about the day, eat the bread and sausage, and drink the bottle," Natasha explained.

I expressed surprise about the amount of vodka, approximately five or six shots per person, and inquired how they can they drink so much without getting drunk. "It's simple," she replied. "They do get drunk. It used to be only a minor problem because they would get on the bus and go home. But now, many of them have cars and they try to drive. Lots of them are killed driving into buildings or bridges."

I asked what happened if another person joined you and your two best friends. She smiled and explained they just go buy more vodka.

The major role that vodka plays in Russian life has had consequences. The average lifespan of a woman is about 68 years, while that of a man is 64 and has been decreasing during the past decade. This much drunkenness is detrimental to people's health and those around them. Productivity, already low, continues to decline. Until recently, this was pretty much a male problem. But with liberation of women, they too have been infected with this addiction. Some of our exchanges were to start classes for women who were pregnant to urge that they quit drinking at least during pregnancy so they could avoid fetal alcohol syndrome - major birth defects caused by too much alcohol.

PRICE LIST

Our interpreter, Elena, and I traveled from the Mineral Waters airport, in the Stavropol region, to Moscow to catch up with the US delegation which had left the day before. As I checked my bag, I was told the usual, "Too heavy, 100 rubles."

Elena looked the gate agent in the eye and spoke rapid Russian in a very firm voice. The agent hurried off. I asked her what was going on. Elena explained that the gate agent was trying to cheat me and she told him so. Then she demanded to see the price list.

"The what?" I asked. This was the first I had ever heard of a list of prices. She explained in Russia, a list price for all goods and services must be maintained and they are not allowed to charge more than that. But, that it was a lot of work to keep the list up to date and usually, they didn't.

A few minutes later, a smiling and obsequious airport manager arrived and apologized for the confusion. He solicitously said there would be no charge for the luggage and invited us to follow him to the VIP lounge to wait for our flight.

This resolved a potentially major embarrassment for the airport manager who had been splitting bribes with the gate agent. Everyone knew that this sort of bribery/extortion went on all the time, especially with foreigners who didn't know the game. But to provide a fig leaf for this behavior, the government required a price list for virtually everything and the list must be made available on demand. No price could be higher than on the list. In this case, the airport manager was guilty of a crime and had this escalated and the authorities chosen to make an example of him, his next stop would have been the GULAG.

"Thank you for your courtesy, comrade," said Elena, smiling as insincerely as he was. He left us and was wiping his forehead having met his match in a Russian woman, of all things.

NEITHER SNOW...

One snowy January day in Iowa, I was surprised when I got an email from my colleague, Dr. Nikolai Shibkov who almost always had his staff send email. He requested that we make a visit to Stavropol to describe our medical exchange program to the new Governor of

Stavropol Krai Province. This guy was unfamiliar with our project and considered cutting off what he saw as a waste of medical staff time.

I called Bob, CEO of a community hospital, who was always ready to go to Stavropol. Bob expressed reservations about going, considering the conditions in Russia during January would be tough. "Does Nikolai really need us?" he asked. I told Bob that his message seemed pretty desperate, so we both agreed to go.

Two weeks later, Bob and I arrived in Moscow on a windy, sub-zero day. As travel veterans, we were shameless in muscling our way to the front of the lines for Immigration and Customs. For once, the Customs Official did not try to extract a bribe—probably too stunned by anyone traveling to Russia in January.

Reaching new levels of miserable, the dingy, dirty, unfriendly Vnukovo airport was now in January, also drafty and cold. We kept our parkas zipped up while we checked in for our flight. Seasoned travelers now, we just paid the usual "too heavy" bribes right away instead of crossing the airport twice to get them weighed and then going to yet another location to pay the fee. Especially since we didn't have an interpreter with us.

Our flight was scheduled for 6 PM and we went through security to wait. By 5:30, nothing was happening and we were able to ask a fellow passenger what was up. "Delayed," he said. So we waited some more. Russia has never been consumer friendly, so no one was surprised that Aeroflot never told us what was going on. Periodically, our Russian passenger friend would give us an update. "Delayed."

Finally at 10 PM, we were herded down the steps onto a bus and driven across the tarmac for what seemed to be miles until we arrived at a small, regional type jet. As usual, the flight attendant made us wait outside on the tarmac while she said something in Russian. "Sit where you want," our friend translated. We lumbered aboard in our heavy coats and boots, struggling into the small seats of this 50-passenger jet. Bob was optimistic, pointing out that at least we were on a jet that would get there a lot quicker than the turbo prop we usually flew.

By now, we noticed that the plane was unheated, and the engines were not running. However, this was a good thing because the pilots were not yet aboard. So, we hunched down and tried to stay warm as our breath crystallized in the dark air.

After about an hour, a vehicle pulled up and the pilots came aboard. I commented that they probably needed a couple of extra vodkas to get them to make this flight. Bob told me to not be so cynical. "They were probably praying," he said. "That might be worse," I responded.

The engines started, the lights came on, and warm air began circulating. Soon, the frost on the seatbacks in front of us melted and the plane taxied onto the runway. As usual, the former fighter pilot accelerated quickly and we climbed very rapidly to cruising altitude. We dozed through much of the two hour flight since we had now defrosted.

As we descended into the Stavropol airport at 1:30 AM, I wondered out loud if they would meet us or if we would have to entrust ourselves to a Russian taxi? Bob was confident they would be there and that Galina wouldn't forget us. We coasted to a stop next to the darkened terminal building and deplaned into three inches of fresh snow. While our eyes were adjusting to the darkness, we were bear-hugged by Vadim and Sergei who had been waiting for us. The Aeroflot crew tossed the luggage onto the snow-covered tarmac and Vadim found our bags while Sergei guided us beside the terminal building to a waiting Lada.

I commented to Sergei that we were ready to get to the Intourist hotel so we could in and get some sleep. "First you meet Galina," Sergei said and drove us through the snow-covered streets. We went to the Health Administration building where 20 people were waiting for us including Galina, Deputy Director of the Stavropol Krai Health Department. We were given an effusive welcome with many kisses on the cheek. "Welcome to our friends from America," said Galina, who begun the toasting which lasted for an hour. While we exchanged toasts, we snacked on Russian cold cuts, with extra fat, and caviar sandwiches. By 3 AM, we were able to get free and went to the Intourist Hotel, where we were greeted by the sleazy KGB agent/manager Valentin Mezzin. We handed him his usual bribe/fee of a jar of Skippy peanut butter. We got into our rooms and crashed.

Four hours later, we were up and in the hotel restaurant having breakfast. As usual, there was no menu. They just brought you what they had. That time it was eggs and calling them sunny side up was a generous description. They were raw. I wondered to Bob what they were trying to do to us. Bob pointed out the metal plates were very hot and he suspected that the eggs were cooking while we waited. He was right. As I watched, the eggs slowly cooked. Great idea, but rather dangerous to bring very hot platters to the table and expect us to finish cooking the eggs, I thought.

After breakfast, two Ladas arrived and we met Galina and some of the medical staff who drove us to the Krai Medical Administration. We were ushered into Nikolai's office where he welcomed us and told us how glad he was to have us there to meet with the new Governor.

I inquired as to what we should tell the Governor. Nikolai instructed us to tell him about our collaboration and what we had accomplished both by our visits to Russia and their visits to America.

Before we left to walk over there, he looked skeptically at our parkas, boots, and stocking hats while he put on his furs and mink hat. Outside, it was clear and very cold. The sidewalks were still clogged with snow and there were frozen hillocks at each corner. Our Russian hosts had to help us up and over.

After we were ushered into the Governor's office, Bob and I began explaining the results of our project and the benefits both countries received while Nemstov listened politely. After five minutes, he interrupted and spoke for an hour about several economic development opportunities in Stavropol. We listened to three proposals that sought US investment. When he was done, we struggled back through the snowbanks back to Nikolai's office.

Both Bob and I were disappointed in the deception. We had been manipulated.

Our trip home was blessedly uneventful and Nemstov's proposals never were funded. But, on the bright side, at least I learned to cook eggs on a hot platter, proved I could survive in a Russian winter, and got some vodka and caviar home without interference from officials.

DONATIONS, PLEASE

At the end of one visit, Frank was heading home with a delegation of three other people. They were taken to the airport by local education department officials. With still an hour before departure time, an unscheduled flight arrived. The local officials went aboard and a few minutes later, four, upset people deplaned. Frank was told they had found seats for the delegation on the plane. When

Frank commented that it looked as though people were taken off to give them those seats, Sergei responded, "Not a problem. They were only Armenians."

Since it was too late to find the Armenians, Frank and his team got aboard. He asked a Russian scientist who spoke some German about this unscheduled flight. "The pilot is owed money by Aeroflot, but they were too slow in paying him, so he took this plane and sold seats for those of us who wanted to go to Moscow." Frank was incredulous and asked if there was any danger involved. "Not really," the Russian explained. "It has happened before and Aeroflot was so embarrassed that it paid the pilot immediately."

An hour later, the plane descended into a small airport. There was an announcement in Russian and Frank's new friend explained the plane was out of fuel and the pilot was landing to buy some. "He will ask us all for donations to pay for the fuel," the Russian explained. Frank realized they had gone down the rabbit hole and turned to explain things to his team.

Minutes later, the plane landed and coasted to a stop. A fuel truck pulled up and the pilot deplaned. A major argument thus ensued with the truck driver involving lots of gesturing and shouting. Then silence and the truck pulled away. Frank's Russian friend explained they might as well get off and get some fresh air until the issue was resolved. Soon, all the passengers were standing in the grass beside the runway and the pilot had walked into the terminal to continue the negotiations. The passengers took the opportunity to go into the terminal for supplies. Bad news, no vodka. But there was plenty of beer and they stocked up. In the meantime, the pilot closed the deal and the fuel truck returned to the plane.

For some reason, the passengers had to go through metal detectors before boarding and each of them set off the alarm which is sensitive to beer cans. Passengers were allowed to proceed after "sharing" a few cans each for the airport security team.

After this, the flight to Moscow was anticlimactic.

CHECHEN RAIDS

As we completed the fourth year of our five-year medical exchange project with Stavropol Krai, it was clear that our hosts had increased security for us. At first, we thought they were just keeping an eye on us, although by this point they knew we were harmless. The real reason became obvious on a side trip we made to the resort town of Pyatigorsk, in the southern part of Stavropol. We traveled in the usual convoy of small Lada cars and after our meeting, we went to lunch at the best restaurant in town. It also happened to be gated and there were security men visible at the gate and around the restaurant itself. I asked Vera, our interpreter, what was going on. She was reluctant, but eventually told me that they wanted us to have the meeting there in Pyatigorsk, but it had been getting dangerous there because the Chechens were raiding the area. Lunch was a little tense and our hosts were relieved when we were back in the relative safety of the Intourist hotel in Stavropol city.

About a month after we returned to Iowa, the news broke of a raid into Stavropol Krai by Chechen guerillas.

In 1995, Chechen rebels invaded Stavropol and were cornered in the town of Budyonnovsk where they took over the hospital with several hundred hostages. A standoff ensued when Russian military forces surrounded the hospital. After several days of negotiation, the hostages were released and the Chechen guerillas were given safe passage back to Chechnya. The hospital was virtually destroyed. All the equipment and furnishings were wrecked. Our colleagues at the Stavropol Health Ministry asked if we could help.

At the time, I was working at the Iowa Hospital Association and the CEO allowed me to make an appeal to our member institutions for donation of equipment and supplies. This quickly became a major logistical operation as the hospitals responded with radiology, lab, beds, and other equipment as well as bandages, suture, and other supplies. Iowa Methodist Medical Center generously offered storage space as this material arrived in Des Moines. Their biomedical engineering staff inspected all the equipment and converted it to operate on the 220V electrical system in Russia. Senator Tom Harkin arranged for military aircraft to bring all this to Stavropol and the Russian authorities allowed US military aircraft to enter Russian airspace for this humanitarian mission. Of course, this airlift was just a small part of the reconstruction and refurbishing of the Budyonnovsk hospital, but it was well received as a gesture of international cooperation.

A few months later, Ray Beauregard, one of the biomedical staff from Iowa who had checked the donated equipment was in Stavropol as a volunteer member of one of our exchanges. He traveled to Budyonnovsk to see the hospital and was treated as a hero by the community. He really was a hero and represented the best of our generosity and good will towards a community suffering a devastating loss.

INSURANCE IS EXPENSIVE, BUT HEALTHCARE IS FREE

When the Russian delegations came to Iowa during the early stages of our program, they always asked for information about our health insurance system as they looked for ways to reform their own system. They thought we had figured out some way of delivering high quality health services at a low cost. When I said, "Whatever you do, don't do it our way," they thought I was keeping something from them. They are naturally suspicious and skeptical, so I called Blue Cross and Blue Shield and arranged a meeting.

For these international visitors, the Blues sent their top executives who made a 20 minute presentation about rating, pricing, negotiating, and servicing their customers. The first Russian question was "If the patient dies, does the doctor still get paid?" The response was a long convoluted statement that eventually said yes. I stopped the meeting and huddled with the executives. I told them they were pitching this too high. And that the Russians needed to hear from people who set rates and make judgments about whether claims get paid or not.

We took a break and the staff who actually did the work at Blue Cross and Blue Shield came in and answered questions quickly and in words that were translatable.

At the end of the meeting, the head of the Russian delegation said, "You were right, Phil. We don't want to import your insurance system. It is too expensive and too complex. At least our system is free. All services are free to anyone."

Our interpreter whispered to me. "Yes, everything is free. But it is not always available. You can make it available by bribing the surgeon or specialist."

TOILETS

Americans are obsessed with toilets whenever they are abroad. They ask about them, talk about them, share experiences about them and take pictures of them. I have to admit the same obsession on my first trip to Russia.

On arrival, I used the public restrooms at Vnukovo Regional airport. They were dirty, cluttered with debris, and the toilets were continually flushing. This was probably a plumbing problem but I considered it a blessing because I was pretty sure that the toilets were never cleaned. Not surprising considering the airport never was either.

When I got on the turboprop plane to take me from Moscow to Stavropol, I looked into the toilet area on the plane and was glad that I wouldn't need to use it during the two-hour flight. It appeared that the last cleaning was when the plane was built.

I was home-hosted once in an apartment in Stavropol. The toilet was brownish inside and I was slightly disgusted until I realized that it wasn't dirty but that the water in Stavropol had a lot of dissolved minerals which discolored the toilet, sink, and any other porcelain fixtures.

Then I used the toilet in a new health clinic. Sparkling clean. But as I went down the corridor afterwards, the woman in charge of the restrooms was chastising me (in Russian, but her meaning was clear). It turns out that Russian toilet paper is so rough (my colleagues swore that it still had pieces of wood in it) that you did not flush it after use. You put it in a small wastebasket there to be emptied later by the matron.

One time, my wife, Judy, accompanied me to a meeting in St. Petersburg and day trips were planned for spouses. She took a bus tour with about 60 people to Novgorod, a city famous for its 1,000-year old wooden cathedrals. It was a two-hour drive and midway, one of the men asked for the driver to stop at the next rest area. After the interpreter explained this, the driver stopped the bus and pointed to a field. The men took advantage of nature's rest room but the women decided to wait for Novgorod where they were assured that there was a rest room. On arriving, they went into the small building, where a babushka made them pay a ruble. When they entered, they found a hole in the floor as the toilet.

In the rural areas, indoor plumbing was as rare as it was here 100 years ago. The outhouses were all they had. Fortunately, we never had to use them in the brutal Russian winters.

I guess our obsession with porcelain fixtures is understandable, but whenever someone shows you their Russian vacation pictures, why do the toilet pictures always have to be first?

When we arrived at Russian Customs on the way into the country, we had to declare any items of value including the cash we were carrying. At that time in Russia, credit cards were not widely accepted. So, with a delegation that could total 15 people staying two weeks, I could be carrying $15,000. If I declared more than $10,000 on the form, Customs Officials gave me another form to fill out, specifically designed for those larger amounts.

On one occasion, when I arrived in Samara after a rare direct flight from Frankfurt, Germany, I declared $12,000 and not only was I given the additional form, but I was taken to a nearby room. There, I had to produce the money and watch it being counted, twice. Russians didn't even trust themselves sometimes. After the official was satisfied with the paperwork, he stamped my forms and I was sure it was time for a bribe. Big surprise. He just ushered me back to the main Customs area and let me go.

Customs area is a misleading term. In Samara, it was a small space opening directly on the doors to the outside and people were permitted in that area. So, it was obvious to all of them that I had been taken to that little room because I had a lot of money on me.

I was greeted with especially urgent cries of "Taxi! Taxi!" from several of the bystanders. In this situation, the word "taxi" meant a brief trip to the country after which my money would have returned but I wouldn't.

Fortunately, my interpreter, Oxana, was waiting for me with a burly driver who had no compunctions about pushing through the crowd of taxi drivers who had hoped to finance their retirement. It was so out of character for a Russian official to not ask for a bribe, I wondered if the Customs Official was in collusion with the taxi drivers to split the takings if I had gone for a one-way ride.

SAMARA

Our funding organization and the State Department wanted Iowa to continue to partner with another Russian community for a medical exchange. After some discussion, I went with some Moscow staff to Samara to determine if a partnership was possible.

Samara is a city of more than 1 million people on the Volga River about 1200 miles southeast of Moscow. After WWII, Samara's main role was military manufacturing. It built planes, rockets, and ballistic missiles. Because of the focus of the Samara economy, it was a "hidden city" until the collapse of the Soviet Union. Domestic travel there required special permission and international travel there was virtually non-existent. Samara was not on any maps and, because it was on the eastern bank of the Volga River, the cruise ships that traveled on that river were required to pass by Samara after midnight.

Samara

In addition to its military focus, Samara also had several universities and technical institutes. It had specialty hospitals for veterans, maternity, and infectious diseases. As part of the effort to "open up" to the West, our request to create a partnership medical exchange with Samara was approved. Our partner entity was the Oblast (Province) Health Department, but we worked closely with the city health department which selected Polyclinics 9 and 15 for our specific activities. These institutions were large facilities with several hundred physicians and nurses on their staffs. Our focus was on improving primary care.

As a rule in Russia, women who become physicians usually are in the lower status positions such as family practice or obstetrics. The surgeons are usually men. However, in the case of Polyclinic 15, the Chief Physician (and administrator) was Lidia Fedoseeva. Her clinic was widely regarded as advanced and of high quality. On the other hand, Polyclinic 9 was headed by Valery Fattokov and his clinic was viewed as a much more traditional medical facility.

We worked with both clinics to increase the skills of their nursing staffs, improve relationships between nurses and doctors, facilitate improvements in management, and initiate patient satisfaction studies to identify problems in the clinic, and use the results to improve service.

Lidia's clinic moved quickly to initiate changes in the scope of nursing practice, in responding to patient concerns and in changing financial incentives for the staff as a whole. If costs were kept below budget, excess money was distributed to the staff as a bonus.

On the other hand, Valery was slow to appoint liaison staff to initiate activity in his facility. He was unconvinced of the value of changing the relationships among the key players at his facility, and never did conduct patient satisfaction surveys.

Lidia had more to prove and she did so. Her results were significantly better than Valery's. Ordinarily, it wouldn't have mattered because Valery would have been connected to the Russian equivalent of the "good ol' boys club." Unfortunately for him, except for the Health Minister of the Oblast, all the leadership were women.

THE VOLGA BARMAN

On weekends, our Russian friends found numerous ways to entertain us. "You work too hard," Lidia Fedoseeva said on a Friday afternoon. She informed me they would pick us up the next morning for a cruise on the Volga. This enormous river flows by Samara where we had been for two weeks. In addition to a fear of flying, I have a large aversion to boats, large and small. This caused me to have a sleepless night. I didn't realize at the time that the boat was the least of my worries.

Promptly at 9AM, she arrived with two of her colleagues and we were bundled into two Ladas (possibly the second worst car ever made, right behind the Yugo). We lumbered down to the dock where a 100 foot tourist boat was waiting. Everyone was there, except Sergei, who had to make a stop on the way. "But he will be here soon," she said, giving us baskets of food to carry on board.

Five Liters of Rodnik

Right on cue, Sergei arrived in his smoking, clattering Lada and opened the trunk to reveal the result of his important errand — a 5-liter bottle of Rodnik, the local vodka. He announced, "This is a special bottle only made for special occasions and we must finish it today." The Americans were horrified. As we got underway, Sergei opened the cap and tried to pour shots for us. But it was like getting a drink from a fire hose — vodka all over the place. He solved this by pouring from the bottle into a large bowl and from that into successively smaller containers until he eventually got most of it into a shot glass. We were secretly overjoyed at all the wasted vodka—less for us to drink.

The usual endless round of toasts ensued—interspersed with black caviar on blinis, roast chicken and potatoes, and shashlik, which are cubes of lamb roasted over a wood fire. I told Sergei the food was delicious, and asked him what his secret was. "The marinade," he replied. I asked if it had vodka in it. Sergei looked at me like I was an idiot. "Da," he said, rolling his eyes.

Three hours later we returned. The Americans were wobbly and the Russians were plastered. Only one-third of the bottle was gone and most of that was spilled during the first five minutes aboard. Drinking all of it would have killed us for sure.

HOTELS AND RESTAURANTS

Samara, which was the second community in which we had a partnership, was a larger city and more sophisticated than Stavropol. During the course of our four-year project, we stayed in three or four hotels, but two of them stand out in my memory.

The first was a small, elegant hotel in the downtown area. The lobby was attractive and the rooms well furnished. It had an excellent restaurant and we stayed there on our initial visit and two subsequent ones. The hotel was connected to an office building which, I learned later, was the local headquarters of Gazprom, the Russian monopoly that controls natural gas. During our third stay there, we were told that we had to check out of our rooms in the middle of our visit. I protested, pointing out that our reservations were good for three more days. An immovable desk clerk informed me they needed those rooms and would help us find other accommodations in the city.

Our interpreter, Oxana, explained that Gazprom often kicked people out of their hotel whenever they needed rooms for visiting politicians or other important people. "It's their hotel and they make the rules," she said, and assured me it would be better for us at a nearby Hansa hotel.

One of the rules we consistently encountered was ensuring customer dissatisfaction. This was characteristic of much of official Russia—complete indifference, even hostility, to customers. Gazprom was notorious for its high-handed ways of dealing with its customers, even national ones like in Europe. So, we were not too surprised at this treatment once we found out who owned the hotel.

On our way to the Hansa, I wasn't so sure about what we were getting into. It was located off a busy street in the central city where you turned down an alley into a dingy courtyard. Around the courtyard were some rundown looking private residences and a large wooden door with an intercom. Oxana introduced us and the door clicked open. We went down a dim corridor and entered a bright, sparkling clean lobby. Our rooms were well furnished and perfectly clean. Although the Hansa looked typically Russian (dingy on the outside, beautiful on the inside), it was owned by Lufthansa Airlines of Germany. At that time, Lufthansa was the only European airline permitted to fly into Samara. Its crews often overnighted in Samara so it bought and remodeled the hotel.

Oxana usually accompanied us to dinner to help us navigate the Russian menus and we ate at several excellent restaurants. The Sevruga (black) caviar was excellent and very cheap. Of course, there was plenty of ice-cold vodka, but they also had a very good beer from a local brewery, a Georgian wine that was too sweet for my taste, and Russian "champagne" which members of my delegation really liked.

At Oxana's urging, we tried a Mexican restaurant and it was surprisingly good. Mariachi music in the background and Corona in bottles. The fajitas were acceptable, but we were surprised to learn that you had to pay for chips and salsa. They hadn't figured out that giving them away increases beer consumption.

We passed on the new sushi restaurant, being concerned about how far we were from the ocean and lax Russian attitudes towards cleanliness.

We often went to a restaurant we all called the "hovering waiter" restaurant. It was elegant with linens and crystal. Very good menu with well prepared food. But the waiter we always got believed in a very intense level of service—quite the opposite of most places. He was never more than four feet away from us and after you took a sip of mineral water, he was right there filling your glass again. He replaced flatware after each course and generally made himself a nuisance. He completed the picture with an obsequious attitude that was either sincere, which was off-putting, or fake, which was infuriating. We ate there less often than we might have, just because of him. Too much of a good thing.

For a change of pace we went to the restaurant operated at the Zhiguli Brewery which was a local institution and one of the few places in town where you could order a beer with your dinner without the waiter asking you why you weren't ordering Rodnik (the local vodka). The beer was very good and they served it cold. It was a busy place with basic Russian food and while the waiters were attentive, they didn't hover. We went there pretty often and one of our Russian colleagues, Dr. Pavlov, seemed to know when we would be there. He would show up, let us buy him a beer and then he would tell us about all the good appetizers available there. He would order most of them, taste them, and then leave before the bill came. He was fond of Jim Beam bourbon and I would bring him a bottle which he would reciprocate with a bottle of Armenian cognac. Again, another example of how Russians don't care about trademarks or international conventions on names. But whatever you call it, I got the better of the trade. The brandy from Armenia was really good.

Author and team, Basement Restaurant.

Just down the street from the Hansa hotel was a restaurant that we often patronized. It was down a few steps from street level, so we called it the Basement Restaurant. The caviar was excellent and always available. Three hundred grams of ice cold Rodnik vodka was the perfect complement. Staff were good and understood enough English so we could order from the menu and give Oxana a night off. In preparing to write this portion of the memories of Samara, I googled restaurants in Samara and found a link that mentioned the Basement Restaurant. There was a photo on that page, and when I magnified it, there I was with two other companions. It has been over 10 years since I went to that restaurant. But my photo is still there—looking a lot younger and with more hair. It's either the proprietor's favorite photo or none of the locals wanted their picture taken, I guess.

A CLASSLESS SOCIETY

Scientific Socialism (Marxism, Communism—take your pick) posits a society in which there are no class distinctions—no rich, no poor. "From each according to his ability, to each according to his need." In fact, what they developed was a very rigid class structure based upon Communist Party membership and your position in the party ranks.

Our delegations dealt with senior Regional Health Department officials and we saw evidence of these "class" distinctions every day, including official vehicles with drivers, access to the best apartments, international passports, and the freedom to travel internationally. While the average Russian stood in line to buy whatever groceries were available that day, high party officials went to stores restricted to them. The stores had fresh produce and meat and were stocked with imported goods.

The realities of this "classless society" were driven home during Russian visits to Iowa. We often took them to buffet restaurants to allow them maximum choice and to avoid the complex task of translating a restaurant menu. They were very impressed with the fresh fruits and vegetables in November. "This restaurant must be restricted to high officials," said Svetlana, head of the delegation. After deciding that she wasn't joking, I said "Svetlana, look at the clientele. Do they look like high officials?"

In the Russian "classless society" money is not a motivator. Salaries are determined by the central planners in Moscow. Recognition by your peers and party officials replaces the capitalistic invention of bonuses. However, after two or three Orders of Lenin for exceptional production, it became clear that these motivations were ineffective. Mostly, the result was indifferent performance, doing the minimum necessary to avoid punishment, and above all, avoiding blame for poor results. "It's not my fault," was the refrain we heard whenever we tried to understand and fix a problem. In explanation, my Russian friend, Ivan, said. "What's another name for a person who stands out in a crowd? A target."

One day in Samara, the streets were very crowded and buses were full at mid-day. I asked Oxana who these people were and where were they going. She explained that most of them were professional people, like lawyers or doctors. They were all going to their second jobs. They were not paid very well and they needed to have second jobs. So, they worked at one job for a few hours and then went to the other to work for a few hours. Regrettably, many people in the US have to work at two or three jobs to make ends meet. But very few of them are lawyers or doctors.

TAXI!

When we began our work in Samara, we contracted with the local government office of transport. After a few visits, Oxana, was confident enough in our relationship to tell me that we were being cheated. This was more than the usual skimming of 10 percent off the top, an accepted cost of doing business in Russia. Rather, we were being charged nearly double the official rate.

We terminated the relationship and Oxana began contracting with other local transportation services. Sometimes, our delegation was divided, with the clinical team working at the big clinic and Oxana and me going to meetings with health department officials. When that happened, we left the vehicle with the clinical team in case they needed to go to the hospital. When I asked Oxana how she and I would get around town, she replied that we would take a taxi.

However, there are no "taxis" that we would recognize in Samara. People used their personal cars to ferry people around. Oxana told me that even the Chief of Neurosurgery at a Moscow hospital took off two days per month to use his car as a taxi for tourists. She said that he made more money during those two days than his monthly salary. This may have just been a rumor, but I believed it.

So, Oxana would go into the street and raise her right arm while I waited on the curb. Being a very good looking woman, Oxana had cars stopping immediately with offers of a ride. She would negotiate a price with the driver and then gesture me over.

The drivers' expressions quickly changed from great pleasure and anticipation to resignation and despair as I appeared. I didn't blame them. Only once, did one of them drive off in disgust.

PAY EVERYONE!

At the end of one visit, our large delegation—15 people plus interpreters—arrived at Moscow's Vnukovo airport and piled into a pretty old looking minibus. We began the two-hour drive downtown to our hotel for an overnight stay before catching our flight back to the US. As we drove, we noticed that the streets were very quiet and that there were a lot of security police visible. Someone remembered that President Clinton was in town for meetings at the Kremlin which explained the security and nearly deserted streets.

After about 10 minutes, our bus was pulled over by Russian police. While we were clutching our passports, the policeman engaged in a heated argument with the bus driver and then left. I was sitting next to Elena and I said, "What's this all about, Elena?" She nervously shushed me and whispered that she would tell me later.

We were released to move on and very shortly arrived at the hotel. While the group was checking in I cornered Elena in the quiet lobby. "Tell me what was going on," I told her. She said she had just been worried because she left her internal passport at home and was afraid she would have to present it to the officials and that they would not understand why she did not have it. I sensed there was something more so I pushed her, "Are you sure there was nothing else?"

She hesitantly admitted she didn't want to tell me in advance, but with President Clinton in town, all the buses had been hired. I looked puzzled and asked why this was a concern. She went on to explain that the bus we were on was rented from the mafia. Before I could shout "The mafia...??" she put her hand on my arm to keep me quiet. I asked her what that had to do with the stop and subsequent argument with the police.

She replied, "Leonid did not pay off all the other mafias and they wanted their share. Fortunately, President Clinton is here and they do not want a ruckus, so they didn't shoot anyone."

"Next time," I said. "Pay everyone."

She tried to assure me there wouldn't be a next time. Oh, yes there would, I thought to myself.

NOT SO FAST

One Friday, three of us had finished a visit to Samara. This was a good place to work. It had good hotels, restaurants, and its own distillery and brewery. It also had a direct flight to Frankfurt on Lufthansa, which helped us avoid Moscow when coming and going. Frank and I were going to meet our spouses in Amsterdam for a long weekend. Doreen was heading back to Iowa.

Or so we thought. When we got to the Samara airport that Friday morning, we learned that a selective Lufthansa strike had selected our flight as the one to eliminate. Quick thinking led me to call the AIHA (our funding organization) Moscow office to ask for help. They called back with reservations on an Aeroflot flight from Samara to Domodedovo airport in Moscow where a driver would take us across town to Sheremetevo airport for our international connection to Frankfurt and then the short flight to Amsterdam where we would arrive only three hours later than originally planned. That sounded great and I thanked the AIHA staff person. We would still be there ahead of our spouses and all would be well.

Or so we thought. A combination of Aeroflot (retired fighter) pilots and poor equipment maintenance meant all the bad pilots were dead. You had to be good to keep flying the never-change-the-oil Tupolev 134. But the pilot on our flight to Moscow must have been to advanced fighter school and wanted to show us what he could do. Our takeoff was practically vertical, but we should have a smooth, quick flight to Moscow after that.

Or so we thought. There were thunderstorms in the area and our jock pilot just flew through them. Bumpy is not the best description for the ride. Near death experience is closer. We landed at Domodedovo a few minutes early with carry-on bags scattered all over the plane and the powerful odor of vomit permeating the air. I hate to fly, and after this trip I was especially glad to be on solid ground again.

Boris, one of the best AIHA drivers, met us and hustled us to the vehicle, and took off for Sheremetyevo International Airport, about two hours away. Normally very easy going, Boris seemed irritated. Of course this was Friday afternoon and he had planned to leave work early. Instead, on very short notice, he had to ferry three Americans across Moscow in rush hour traffic. Doreen, Frank, and I settled in for the standard two-hour drive.

Or so we thought. Boris wanted to salvage as much of his long weekend as possible. Moscow drivers are very aggressive, but Boris set new standards that afternoon. Not only did he speed, make dangerous lane changes, cut people off, and run red lights, but at one point, he drove on the sidewalk to bypass a line of cars, causing the people who were there waiting for the bus to scatter. Later, he drove on the shoulder, but others had tried the shoulder short cut route, so instead he cut across country, dodging telephone poles. Doreen turned pale and Frank and I told her to close her eyes. If we crashed, at least Frank and I would know it a millisecond before she would. I tried to show a brave face, but I was terrified. It was the most dangerous drive I had ever taken. Later, I told Frank that my sphincters were like knots. He replied, "Better that way than the opposite."

Boris got us to the Sheremetevo airport in 90 minutes, shaving 30 minutes off the previous record. He grabbed our bags and pushed us to the front of the line. Immigration stamped our passports and we were free.

Or so we thought. In Russia, you go through Customs when you leave the country as well as when you enter. Frank and Doreen were ahead of me and got their forms stamped without problems. As I was getting my form stamped a uniformed official ambled up and asked me how much money I had. I told him I had about eight hundred US dollars. He asked how much I had arrived with and I told him two thousand. He was now holding my passport and asked to see my financial form. I explained I didn't have it because they kept it at passport control. Invariably, Immigration people look at this form to be sure that you are leaving with less money than you entered with. After checking it, they throw it on the floor. I was now seeing my chances for making Amsterdam quickly fade.

He wanted to see my money, so he took me to a screened off area where I had to strip down to my shorts so he could make sure that I only had one money belt, which he took. "Eight hundred US dollars," he said. "But where is your financial form?" While trying to maintain dignity in my un-pantsed situation, I again explained that the Immigration people had taken it. He instructed me to wait and left with my passport.

So, I dressed and waited. I could see Doreen and Frank nearby getting nervous as flight departure time approached. That made me nervous and I started thinking about how they would abandon me here like a dog. Then I'd have to face the fury of my wife who would never believe this explanation. Or worse, they'd take me to Lubyanka, the KGB prison, and then send me to the GULAG for being an enemy of the state for improper paperwork.

I started to sweat. I had recently read part of the GULAG Archipelago and knew that living there would be unpleasant, at best.

Ten minutes later, the uniformed official returned with the form. Somehow, he found it amidst the mounds of discarded forms. "You are OK," he said. But he was still holding my passport. I gave him $20, explaining it was a small payment for all the trouble I caused him. "Safe travels," he said.

I rejoined Frank and Doreen who claimed to be relieved and said they would have waited for me. Fat chance, I thought cynically, as I was now practically an alumnus of the GULAG. We boarded the flight to Frankfurt which was typically uneventful and we knew we were home free.

Or so we thought. The flight from Moscow to Frankfurt arrived late and Frank and I had to sprint for our connecting flight to Amsterdam.

We made it huffing and sweating. Again, we were relieved to finally be free.

Or so we thought. Ordinarily Customs in the EU is cursory at best. You pass through a large gateway to baggage claim. Usually, there is a Customs Official standing there, just looking off into space.

Except this time he singled me out from several hundred passengers to stop. He asked where I had been and I told him Russia. He countered with asking how much vodka I had in my bag. Without missing a beat I said two liters. He wanted to see them so I opened the bag and right on top were two, one liter bottles of Rodnik's finest. He indicated I was OK and could go. I closed the bag quickly, hoping he wouldn't see the other two liters nestled below.

SKEPTICAL

In addition to being paranoid, Russians are also skeptical. They have been lied to for so long about so many things that they doubt anything you might say. While the lying has been in overdrive since the Revolution, it has even deeper historical roots.

When Catherine was Empress of Russia in the late 18th century, she took many lovers, among whom one was Grigori Potemkin. One of his duties was to travel ahead of Catherine whenever she was visiting parts of the Russian Empire. He would create false facades on the buildings of the villages through which she would pass and he would populate them with actors who portrayed beautiful, happy people who were singing joyfully as Russian peasants under her rule. Because of this, "Potemkin villages" became part of the Russian vocabulary indicating the phoniness of officialdom.

Outwardly, Russians were very supportive about decrees from Moscow about industrialization, achievements in agriculture, and consumer goods. But inwardly they were saying, "Potemkin village." This carried over to their visits to Iowa. When we took them to visit a hospital, they were very impressed by the equipment and the clean environment. But, they said, "This must be your show hospital, the one you take your visitors to see." So, we arranged to take them to a small county hospital where they saw similar equipment, nurses responsible for patient care, and the network of emergency services.

When we took them to a buffet restaurant, at first they thought it was restricted to high government officials. (See observations under "Classless Society" above). After we convinced them that these places were open to the public, they said "Broccoli in November. This must be the only restaurant like this and you show it to visitors." We had to take them to three other places before we overcame their natural skepticism and their expectation that anything good was a Potemkin village.

SEPTEMBER 11, 2001

On September 11, 2001, five of us were in Samara preparing for a three-day conference on domestic violence that we would host. We had completed our final planning sessions and were back at the hotel getting ready for a dinner with the local interpreters and staff. Each of us had BBC TV on while we changed clothes. And each of us was horrified as we saw the second plane fly into the World Trade Center.

We were shaken when we met in the lobby. At the nearby restaurant, we shared our shock, grief, and anger and tried to determine what we should do

We all were distraught and could not believe this terrible thing had happened and that so many people had died in the disaster. It was horrible to feel cut off and powerless so far away from home. Allan suggested we call our families later to let them know that we are okay and to find out what was happening.

I agreed that was about the best we could do at the moment. We all decided to stay focused on why we were there and not let the tragedy back home interfere with what people here were coming to see.

Next morning, we were grim when we went to the conference center. As we arrived and began setting up, many of those in attendance came up to us to express their sympathy. It was hard to keep from choking up. Dr. Pavlov, Deputy Director of the Samara Health Department, opened the conference with words of sympathy and support. Allan extemporized and told the audience that we appreciated their sympathy, but that we had made a commitment to them and to keep it we had to stay focused on the conference objectives. After that, the conference went well, although some of us needed to leave the room to recover our composure.

After the three-day conference ended, planes were still not permitted to fly into the US. The AIHA staff told us that since we were not able to fly home, we should accompany them to Moscow where they could take better care of us and could make flight reservations for us as soon as possible. We agreed and tried to act like tourists for the three days we had to wait.

Finally, when flights were again permitted to the US, the AIHA staff booked us through Frankfurt. We got there and found a huge crowd of business people and tourists anxious to get home. Security was very tight but no one was complaining. We got home and our families were greatly relieved, as were we.

AMERICAN DOLLARS

The currency in Russia was the ruble. The central planning economists pegged it at 1 ruble to 1 US dollar, and since the ruble was not traded internationally (it was illegal to take rubles out of the country), this rate was accepted by the Russian people with some pride. However, once it was possible to exchange rubles for dollars, the rate plummeted. In the short term, this didn't matter much to the average Russian since all the prices were in rubles. It was illegal to use any other currency in Russia—only rubles were allowed. However, money is more than a medium of exchange—it is a store of wealth. Whenever possible, people asked us to pay in dollars which they hoarded (just like gold) because they expected that the ruble would continue to decline in value compared to other currencies. In fact, we were often accosted on the street with requests to exchange our dollars for rubles at better than official rates.

I asked Oxana if she preferred being paid in rubles or dollars. She looked at me as if I were crazy and said, "Dollars, of course." I asked why the interest in dollars since she couldn't spend them to buy things. She explained she would keep them safe as they are a store of wealth and she could always sell them on the black market.

During the course of our visits, the ruble kept sinking in relation to the dollar and we were getting big stacks of rubles at the currency exchange. This reflected international concerns about the strength of the Russian economy now that it was competing with other countries' production. The distortions caused by the central planners became obvious.

Without warning, the Russian government devalued the ruble by 90 percent. Old rubles had to be exchanged for new ones at the rate of 10 old ones for 1 new one. The impact on our Russian friends was devastating. Their savings were virtually wiped out. A few of them had been able to establish bank accounts in foreign countries—an illegal practice—and they were able to weather the storm.

But it explained Oxana's desire for dollars as they were worth more than ever.

CELEBRATING VE DAY

On a beautiful day in May, Frank, Doreen, and I were at one of our favorite restaurants in Samara. We were having dinner by ourselves because we felt comfortable at this place which had a menu in English, more or less. The staff also spoke a little English so we gave Oxana the night off.

We were just completing a good dinner when the waitress brought us a round of drinks—shots of vodka, of course. We started to say we didn't order them when some Russian guys at a nearby table said, "Welcome, Americans. Today we celebrate the victory in the Great Patriotic War." We had forgotten that this was VE day, the day that WW II ended in Europe. It is a major holiday in Russia which bore the brunt of the Nazi invasion and fought them to a standstill. After D-Day, some of the pressure was off the Russians as the Nazis moved some troops to oppose the landings at Normandy. This allowed the Russians to attack the Nazis and eventually enter Berlin ahead of the Western Allies.

During the course of the war, Russia lost millions of its men, virtually wiping out a generation of people. Celebrations of this victory are a major event in Russia and these men wanted us to share in them. So, we offered a toast to them, the Russian people and the allies who defeated the Nazis. They more or less understood us and were pleased.

We tossed down our drinks. Then, it became clear that the celebration was going to continue for a long time as the waitress delivered two liters of vodka to their table. Sensing that this was going to be a problem, we began edging our way out of the restaurant. We had to pass the table of the celebrators and we stopped to shake hands, express our appreciation for all that Russia had done in the war, had one more drink and were then able to escape.

Two of my American colleagues and I went for a walk in St. Petersburg during a break from our conference meetings. I noticed the small glassed in phone booths we had been passing and asked my colleague, Ed, about the lack of phone books in the booths. Ed explained there were no phone books. The idea is if you didn't know the person's phone number, then you had no business calling them.

Several months later, we were working in the Samara Region and Doreen asked for a copy of the map of Samara Region that she had seen on an office wall. Like many people from Iowa, Doreen was very spatially oriented. She needed to place herself in space according to a map or compass setting. If she could not do this, she was disoriented. Or as the Iowa natives put it, she speaks "compass". Ivan, our host, promised a copy of the map the next day. Next day, there was no map but there were apologies for forgetting to get it. Next day, no map either and no excuses. We finally dropped it and my colleague, Alex, explained to Doreen and me that maps were not available. If you don't know how to get there, you had no business going there.

Later, after our Russian friends were confident in our discretion, they explained this strange behavior (like so many "oddities") with an anecdote—probably true, but if not, it should be. The story goes that in the 1930s, Josef Stalin began a major road building program to the West, toward Europe. He hired engineers to oversee this construction project through dense forests. At the end of the year, they reported "Comrade Stalin, the forest was so impenetrable that we built only 5 km of road instead of 50." He had them shot and hired another team of engineers. At year's end, they report, "Comrade Stalin, through heroic efforts we exceeded our goal and built 75 km." Of course, nothing had been done. They had just learned from the experience of the first group of engineers. The new "road" appeared on all official military maps, showing yearly progress toward Poland. In June 1941, the Nazis invaded Russia using stolen military maps. However when they arrived at the border they were confronted by virgin forest instead of a highway clearly shown on their stolen maps. So, the Russian road building engineers as well as the military helped to defeat the Nazis.

Russia has been invaded so many times over the centuries that they are realistically paranoid about maps. Even now, they are not available. In fact, a team of Australian technicians was caught using GPS technology to locate future cellphone towers. They were arrested and their equipment confiscated.

I had the good fortune of participating in several meetings and conferences in St. Petersburg, easily the most sophisticated and beautiful city in Russia. Many Russians wanted to move St. Petersburg, but the authorities strictly controlled access to the city.

When I arrived (carrying about $8,000), I cleared Passport Control quickly and on my way to Customs, I read the new sign that described the conditions under which you could go through the Green Zone (no inspection). Everyone else had to go through the Red Zone, answer questions, and possibly have your luggage inspected.

I was tired and misread the sign, thinking it said if you had more than $10,000 you had to go to the Red Zone. Having less than that, I went through the Green Zone. Actually, the sign said $1,000, not $10,000. But since there was a soccer game on TV, all the Customs Officials who could have stopped me were preoccupied. So, I went through the Green Zone unimpeded and out the door.

The conference was very informative and we had a great time sampling some of St. Petersburg's cultural venues.

When it was time to leave, my colleague Allan and I went to the airport and got through Passport Control. Allan went through Customs without incident and waited for me at the nearby Lufthansa counter where we would get our boarding passes.

Just as I was about to clear Customs, a uniformed official came up to me and asked to see my documents, which I handed over. He asked how much money I had and I told him about $1,000. When he discovered I had brought $8,000 into Russia he told me I had the wrong paperwork and that I should have gone thru the Red Zone to declare the amount when I entered Russia. He pointed to the sign describing Red Zone/Green Zone requirements. He was right and I apologized.

Allan and the Lufthansa ticket agent were looking at this developing scene. I learned later that Allan started to come over, but the agent grabbed him by the arm and told him to stay out of it.

The Customs official looked me in the eye, and said the official policy is that they confiscate my money and in 60 days I could come to the airport and claim it. I protested and said I was going home to the US and wouldn't be there in 60 days. He repeated the official policy and now, with sweat now running down my back, I repeated that I wouldn't be there in 60 days. He looked at me and speaking slowly in the tone you use to talk to a 3-year old, said once more, "The official policy is that I confiscate your money and in 60 days, you can reclaim it."

In my growing desperation, a light bulb finally went off and I said, "Is there an unofficial policy? Can I pay a fine?" He gave me a look that said, "Finally, you get it, you idiot," and instructed me to follow him.

We walked across the terminal (and saw Allan still restrained by the Lufthansa agent and looking concerned). We entered a room that was clearly intended for staff. Several of them were at long tables, eating lunch, and paying no attention to me. There were no signs of waterboarding or rubber truncheons so I was starting to feel a bit relieved.

He brought me over a massive book and opened it to a page in closely written Cyrillic. He pointed to a paragraph and said, "Official policy." I cannot read Cyrillic and looked puzzled. He then pointed to another paragraph and said, "Unofficial policy." Clueless, but knowing where this was going I ask how much the fine was. He told me one hundred dollars.

I started to hand him the hundred dollar bill and he stopped me, instructing me to instead put it in the book. I complied and he closed the book. I ask if we were done and could I go. He said yes. As I turn to leave the room, he asked, "Do you want a receipt?" A receipt? He had brass ones, even for a Customs agent.

ART AND CAVIAR

Russians claimed to be concerned about some of their historical treasures leaving the country and their Customs agents were vigilant about preventing this.

On a visit to Samara, my colleague, Allan, had gone shopping at a store specializing in antiques. He was entranced by an icon in a silvery metal frame. After negotiating a price, the shop owner produced a document stating that the icon was not a cultural heirloom and had been legitimately purchased. The owner explained this would allow Allan to pass through Customs. A week later, he and I were going through Customs and the Official looked at the letter and called over his supervisor who said the paper was not an official letter from the Ministry of Culture. Allan apologized and while handing over $20, asked if they could help him get such a letter. Ten minutes later, the Official returned with an official looking letter with stamps and seals. We went back to the Customs line and a frowning agent told Allan his letter did not look official. Another $20 and suddenly, it was official and we got our stamped passports. Later, Allan explained, "When you buy art here, you have to figure in the price of the bribes you have to pay to get it out of the country. This was about average."

On another occasion, we were leaving Samara and going through the Customs exit. Mary was the last one in line and the Customs Official asked her how much caviar she had. She told him four jars. He responded that the limit she could take out of the country was three. Agitated, Mary asked him if he was sure because the last time she was there, they said she could take home as many as she wished. Starting to get agitated himself, he repeated that the limit was three.

This was rapidly becoming a test of wills—a test that Mary was going to lose. One of our colleagues, Penny, told her to just leave one behind. Mary was getting feisty and was threatening to give the fourth jar to Oxana who had appeared in the Customs area, which is against policy.

A level-headed Oxana told Mary to just give him the jar because she didn't want it and if she kept arguing, they would take everything. Mary grudgingly handed it over and joined us still grumbling. As we waited in the departure lounge, she said. "It's a good thing I brought six of them. I still have five."

RUSSIA IN 2015

I had the privilege of working in Russia during what turned out to be a brief respite between autocrats. Stalin was followed by a series of incompetents who drove the empire into the ground, resulting in the breakup of the Soviet Union in 1989. By 1999, Vladimir Putin was Premier of the Russian Federation under Yeltsin who resigned in favor of Putin. This began an unbroken period of rule by Putin as President, Prime Minister, and President again. His reign effectively ended any progress toward democracy and individual freedom in Russia. Putin declared that the breakup of the Soviet Union was the biggest catastrophe of the 20th century and he has continued to press for restoration of the territory of the former Soviet Union.

Many of my Russian friends told me that Russia had never been able to decide whether it is European or Asian—code words for democrats or autocrats. I think that perhaps that was what they want to think, but the reality appears to be that they need what they call a "strong" leader. That means someone who gives orders and expects obedience. Civil liberties are unimportant, although given lip service as an international fig leaf.

During the 1990s, there was a brief flowering of a civil society in Russia with free elections and an openness to the world and a willingness to learn from others. That door has been closed. Not perhaps as obvious as an Iron Curtain, but just as effectively. The brief period of "free enterprise" was characterized by the Oligarchs who robbed the Russian people of the country's resources. They were tolerated by an increasingly centralized government which allowed corruption to flourish provided that it maintained control while it re-nationalized much of what had been privatized.

Putin has kicked out all NGOs that supported a civil society and has done all he could to re-establish Russian power on the cheap. He has ignited ethnic tensions in Georgia and Ossetia to create pretexts to re-absorb these parts of the former Republics. He is now doing the same thing in Ukraine which is being invaded by Russian soldiers thinly disguised as "volunteers." In Moscow, his opponents are murdered in broad daylight and Putin declares he will supervise the investigation personally. The cynical and hypocritical cult of personality did not die with Stalin. It has reappeared dressed in new clothes, but it is the same autocrat in charge.

In the long run, he will fail. Russia is a fossil. It is too dependent on extraction industries which have not been modernized and which will soon be non-competitive. That is virtually the entire Russian economy and with the current state of corruption at all levels, chances for any modernization are slim. In addition, the population of Russia continues to decline. More abortions, fewer births, and increasing alcoholism among women as well as men means further declines in productivity. Military readiness continues to decline and it is only effective against much weaker opponents or threats of the use of its thermonuclear weapons.

Further disruptions in Russia can be expected as it attempts to regain its stature as a superpower. But these efforts will be frustrated as the weakness of the country becomes apparent to everyone. The Russian people may eventually get the democratic, representative government that they deserve and with the freedoms they cherish. But first, another collapse will be required, followed by a realization that a mature society with educated people does not need a "strong" leader.

CHINA

CHINA:
THEY EAT EVERYTHING

The US has had a complex relationship with China for a long time. In our eyes, they have been either good honest peasants or dangerous, inscrutable Asian hordes. We've vacillated from Pearl S. Buck, (The Good Earth) to Mao Zedong (Communist Leader).

Sine Mao's death, the United States has engaged in direct trade with China and has created strong mutual economic linkages. Both countries have tried to strengthen these ties though both have differing views on many topics. A small part of this complex relationship is the link created between the state of Iowa and the Province of Hebei.

Iowa Sister States began a relationship with the Hebei province in China in 1983. During my time at Iowa Sister States, I had the opportunity to visit China several times and to host many delegations to Iowa from Hebei in northeastern China. Hebei and includes the capitol, Beijing, and the port city of Tianjin. Hebei has over 60 million people and is a mix of urban and rural communities— although many of the rural "villages" contain over 200,000 people. Its capital city is Shijiazhaung (hereafter called by SJZ), which has only 5 million people and is about a two-hour drive from Beijing.

My visits to China were confined to this general area and, because of my very limited exposure to this large and complex country, my observations are not comprehensive or even particularly accurate descriptors of Chinese history, culture, or its people. Rather, these are personal observations from my direct experience with these remarkable people.

China has a long continuous history of dynasties, warlords, civil wars, and efforts to unite the country. In the 1930s, Japan invaded China and conducted genocidal actions against the population. After the end of WWII, the Communist Party of China established the People's Republic of China in 1949. Mao Zedong (or Mao Tse-Tung) led the Chinese Communist Party and was ruler of the country from 1949 until his death in 1976. He led the Great Leap Forward, a plan for a major increase in agricultural production. This failed and the crops that had been harvested were sold to Russia for armaments. An estimated 40 million people died of starvation.

Depite the excesses of the Great Leap Forward and the Cultural Revolution, the people generally support the government and are patriotic. Partly this is due to their strong desire for stability and partly because they believe that China's rightful place is on top of the world. It should be noted that this characteristic is not limited to China, but rather, it is a First World phenomenon. In the 18th and early 19th centuries, the French believed that this was their destiny; in the late 19th and early 20th, it was the British and Germans who thought they were at the apex; and in the late 20th and early 21st, the US is the only superpower. For some time, we were worried about this Chinese expectation and that accounts for the "Yellow Peril." This was the code word for American racism against Asians, especially Chinese, beginning in the 1870s when they were brought to the US to help build the railroads. Quotas and exclusionary legislation against China was our policy until the 1960s.

It can be difficult for Westerners to understand why the Chinese people put up with some of the government's harsh policies that limit their freedoms. My friend, Will, was born in China, came to Iowa to study, and stayed. He explained that the Chinese people will put up with a lot in order to have stability. After all they've been through, I can see why.

HOW IS THE TEA?

My first official visit to China occurred in 1996 when I was still working for the Iowa Hospital Association and was invited to join a delegation as someone who could investigate possible health care exchanges. Jane Van Voorhis, as Iowa Sister States board president, led the delegation and at 6'2", she towered over all of the rest of us, not to mention the Chinese. We toured the Forbidden City one morning and were a major attraction for Chinese people and their kids. Jane good naturedly squatted down to the kids' level, held up two fingers, and said "two meters", answering the question they were too polite or too awestruck to ask.

Forbidden City

The Forbidden City was remarkable for the magnificent buildings. The detailed artistry both on the exterior decorations and carvings and on the interior paintings was a sight to behold. But one thing struck me as an insight into the Chinese mindset: the buildings were not enclosed and nothing was protected from the weather. Beijing gets hot and humid in the summer and cold and snowy in the winter. Preservation of these antiquities was a high priority but they were not put under glass or protected the way we would. Rather, they were left in their natural setting even though there were subtle signs of deterioration as some of the paint was fading and some of the fabrics were fraying.

Of course, with air pollution continuously reaching record levels, the phrase "natural setting" is very different from the time of the Emperors. It will be interesting to see how the Chinese resolve this conundrum. So far they haven't changed their approach to preservation, or lack thereof.

I was invited to visit one of the large hospitals in SJZ, to tour the facility and determine if an exchange was possible. My guide was Dr. Zhao, the Chief of Cardiology, who had done his residency in London and whose English was very good. The hospital was large and very well equipped with the latest radiology gadgets and plenty of electronics.

After touring the extensive pharmacy, I asked Dr. Zhao if the hospital offered traditional Chinese medicine. When he replied in the affirmative, I asked how they decided whether to treat a patient with Western medicine or Chinese medicine. He told me the patient decides. There was a traditional medicine pharmacy on the hospital campus and he offered to show me.

We walked across the campus to a two-story building and after we entered, I saw a large sign in Mandarin, which my guide told me was the price list for procedures and treatments. We looked

Modern Medicine.

in on a patient being treated with acupuncture then descended to the traditional medicine pharmacy. It was a large room filled with cabinets, bins, and tubs containing roots, herbs, dried plants, and other items that to my Western eye were unrecognizable. "After the patient sees the traditional medicine specialist, he is given a prescription," Dr. Zhao explained, showing me a prescription form in Mandarin. "He presents the prescription here and the technicians fill it." We watched as a technician went to several drawers and bins, collecting bits of roots, flowers, and nuts and wrapped them in a square of cloth. I asked how the patient administers this medicine. Dr. Zhao said they usually make a tea.

Traditional Medicine.

This was fascinating to me and I told him that our physicians would love to see this and study the data on the results of this traditional medicine. Dr. Zhao smiled and said, "We don't have data. All we have is 4,000 years of history showing that these teas really work." I pondered this as we walked back to the main hospital thinking about the FDA and clinical trials versus 4,000 years of anecdotal history.

We returned to the CEO's office and met with hospital executives and talked about the tour and prospects for an exchange program. I told them that I was very impressed with their facility and fascinated by their traditional medicine, especially how they offered both traditional and Western style treatments. I described how the hospital association operated and was talking about difficulties in developing a useful, cost-effective proposal when I noticed that some of the executives were exchanging glances. One of them finally one of them asked me how I liked the tea I had been served. It was then I noticed an ornate cup with a lid on the table next to my chair. I removed the lid and tasted the tea. I said it was very good. Everyone then removed the lids on their own cups and drank their tea. "This is very rare tea," the CEO explained, "just reserved for special guests. We are glad that you liked it."

He was much too polite to call me a barbarian, ignorant of basic manners, while I chattered away instead of drinking the special tea which they really appreciate but rarely get to have. This was the first of many faux pas that I committed in China, a very subtle and complex culture. Each time, they were very polite and forgiving, but I tried never to make the same mistake twice and quickly learned that it is better to ask what is appropriate rather than to blunder ahead in my usual American manner.

CHINESE FOOD

My friend, Will, has lived in Iowa for many years, but he still visited China frequently and was very valuable help when he accompanied us. Once, he went to China ahead of the delegation to visit family there. I arrived at the hotel in Beijing late in the afternoon, one day before the rest would arrive. As I was studying the display in the lobby advertising the Italian restaurant in the hotel and trying to decide if I really wanted Italian food, Will and his wife, Kathy, saw me. Kathy was also born in China. Both she and Will have adopted American names. This is a common practice among Chinese people who tell me that their Chinese names are too difficult for Americans to pronounce.

After greeting me, Will and Kathy invited me to a good Chinese restaurant across the street. Now "across the street" in Beijing was often a challenge, to say the least. Eight lanes of traffic was the norm and drivers did not have any respect for pedestrians. It was a 10-minute nightmare getting across during which we provoked a lot of screeching brakes and horn tooting. After my heart rate slowed down to 90/minute, I reflected that these guys were good enough to drive in Boston.

The restaurant we entered was a gothic masterpiece. Twenty-foot ceilings, pointed windows, shields on the walls, and heavy dark furniture. I asked if we were at a German restaurant, but Kathy assured me it was a Chinese one. As soon as menus were delivered, it became very clear this was not a tourist destination. They were only in Mandarin. I closed mine and asked Will and Kathy to order for me as I could not read the menu. Will said no problem and carefully turned the pages of the bulky menu.

A few minutes later, the waiter arrived and there was a rapid exchange of Mandarin, immediately followed by a guffaw of laughter from

Kathy. I asked what was so funny. Will didn't look amused and Kathy just kept laughing. Finally, she subsided and explained that Will had ordered cashew chicken, which was what he always got, even at the Chinese restaurant at home in Ankeny, Iowa. "I happen to really like cashew chicken," Will replied looking a little miffed.

I asked what they ordered for me and again that sent Kathy off into gales of laughter. Will didn't respond and when Kathy was gasping for breath and able to speak again, she told me I was getting sweet and sour pork. "Will is the Chinese version of the meat and potatoes Iowan," she continued chuckling.

Later, Will and I agreed that the cashew chicken and the sweet and sour pork were the best we had ever had. But he promised to be more adventurous next time.

YOGI JOINS THE CIRCUS

On one trip, we completed our official business a few days early and our hosts planned a visit to the community that trains acrobats. Will and Dr. Yogi, a physician volunteer who had also visited medical schools in Tianjin with us earlier in the trip accompanied me. Yogi had a warm and generous personality and people were drawn to him. He was also pretty fearless.

We watched two motorcyclists drive their bikes inside a cylindrical wire enclosure, going in rising circles, faster and faster until they were at the top. It was very exciting and noisy.

Next we went to the sleight-of-hand magician who was doing the classic game of three walnut shells and the pea. Yogi was a good sport and kept trying and failing to guess where the pea was. He never thought to guess the magician's palm. Good thing he didn't wager on his guesses.

Then they took us into the big top and, as honored guests, put us in the front row. We watched a thrilling slack wire performance and some excellent tumbling. Then, a young woman came in along with furniture that let her recline and keep her legs in the air. She looked to be about 4'10" and could not have weighed more than 95 pounds.

Her assistant began tossing her items to be juggled with her feet - rings, Indian clubs, small vases. She finished by spinning a large, hollow wooden container about four feet long and two feet in diameter. She spun this in a circular fashion and then lengthwise.

We applauded her performance. One of the circus staff came over and invited Yogi to enter the ring. Yogi is 5'11" and weighed about 160 pounds. The asked him to climb into the container and I can still see him peering out with his hands clutching the lip of the container. They lifted the container up and over to the juggler who promptly began twirling the container with Yogi inside. When Yogi got out, he was a little dizzy but was excited at having participated in the act.

I kept a close eye on Yogi during the rest of the night. He was having so much fun that I worried he would run away and join the circus.

VERY SUBTLE

I participated in an official visit with Iowa Governor Tom Vilsack and a group of business leaders. The US Embassy had arranged an official meeting for us with one of the Vice Premiers of China. Our Chinese liaison staff told us to be ready to leave two hours prior to the meeting because of traffic. Beijing was surrounded by 10 ring roads (maybe more by now) and we needed to cross two of them and travel a few kilometers along the next one. It is unforgiveable to be late to an official meeting, so we left very early and arrived about half an hour early. The Chinese are masters of protocol and being early was nearly as bad as being late.

We got past the gates into a large, park-like compound. It was very surprising to see this in such an overcrowded city like Beijing. We strolled on the grounds until summoned. At the door, Governor Vilsack's security team was barred from the meeting. Very unusual, but Vilsack didn't seem to mind. Still, I began feeling uncomfortable that the honorable guest was denied his personal security in an official meeting.

We entered a large, ornate room with seating around the walls for the rest of us while Vilsack and his interpreter sat up front with the Vice Premier and his interpreter. I noticed that there was no tea on the table next to my chair, which was unusual. While I puzzled over this, the meeting began.

The Vice Premier made the usual type of welcoming speech, thanking us for coming and wishing us a successful visit. Then Vilsack began his speech—again the usual, formal type of thanks for the meeting. After a couple of minutes, the Vice Premier interrupted him with a comment. That was surprising. Vilsack started again and was getting ready to conclude when the Vice Premier interrupted him again. Now, I was getting suspicious. Interruptions like this never happened. When Vilsack concluded, the Vice Premier got up, thanked us and left. Meeting over.

"No gifts?" I thought. We had just been insulted by the Vice Premier of China. The Chinese don't make these protocol mistakes. It was deliberate. I was really pissed off and angrily explained why to Vilsack. He just blew it off.

The next morning, we had a meeting with the US Ambassador and Vilsack was reporting on what we had done so far. I described the insulting way we had been treated by the Vice Premier and the Ambassador agreed with me. "I'm very sorry that this happened. I think I have an explanation. The US Secretary of Commerce is coming here next week to discuss the possibility of some tariffs on Chinese textiles that will be imported into the US. The Vice Premier was letting you know that they are unhappy about this and was using you as an instrument to let me know."

Wow, I thought. My suspicions were correct. They did this on purpose. They never make protocol mistakes and they are too subtle for me. They could have just called the Ambassador and told him they were pissed off.

BEIJING OPERA

A traditional form of entertainment in China was stylized telling of famous stories. Like European opera, it featured drama or comedy, dancing, ornate costumes, and singing. With electronic translation of the story on a screen overhead, we were able to understand and enjoy it all—except for the singing. It is a high falsetto accompanied by strings which were played in a fashion I was unaccustomed to. It was very unnerving but eventually I got used to it and enjoyed it.

My first exposure to Beijing Opera was not a positive one, though. Sarah, who was then Executive Director of Iowa Sister States, and I had just arrived from the US on a 13 hour flight and we were tired. When our colleagues met us and told us they had purchased tickets for the Beijing Opera for us, we couldn't refuse.

Right after we sat down and ordered some tea, the lights were lowered and the performance began. I sipped my tea in the darkness and learned that all tea in China is loose tea and the tea leaves usually float on the surface. I got a film of tea leaves on my teeth

Beijing Opera.

with every sip and slowly learned how to blow the leaves to the other side of the cup before sipping. This took several tries in the darkness and I ended up rolling the tea leaves removed from my teeth into a napkin. I am sure later the staff was convinced that another Western barbarian had arrived. Not only that, but I was so tired that I nodded off a couple of times during the performance. A poor beginning for what later became a great source of entertainment for me.

THE LUNCH REBELLION, RED CARDS, AND THE KITE MAKER

In 2002, I led a delegation for Iowa Sister States to Hebei for their celebration of all the international relationships that they had established around the world. Iowa sent about 20 people, including former Iowa Governor Robert Ray who had signed the original agreement. As the official head of the Iowa delegation, he and his wife, Billie, traveled from Beijing to SJZ by limo while the rest of us were in a coaster bus. Because of the large number of delegations, our liaison, Mrs. Wang (pronounced Wong), of the Foreign Affairs Office, could not be with us but sent a bi-lingual college student, Ms. Li, to take care of us. Ms. Li was nervous and wanted to do a good job. She had been told by Mrs. Wang to keep us on schedule and that everything had been planned for us.

One member of our delegation was Wade, a TV reporter from Cedar Rapids who had hosted some young Chinese journalists the year before. These journalists tried to ride with us on the bus, but Ms. Li firmly refused. So, they shadowed us in a car, talking to Wade through the open bus windows while we traveled through the congested Beijing traffic.

Following instructions, Ms. Li told us we would have lunch at a Western style hotel before leaving town for SJZ. Wade announced that his young journalist friends told him we were going right past a "vertical mall" with an extensive food court where we could have some great Chinese food. At first Ms. Li stood her ground, but we insisted that we would be offended if we didn't change plans. She relented, but with ill grace.

We stopped at a ten story building and the journalists took us to the food court on the fifth floor. All around the walls were food stalls each selling Chinese food from the various regions of China. Overwhelmed with all the choices, we told the journalists to pick out things they thought we would like. So, instead of club sandwiches on china plates, we ate delicious Chinese food on Styrofoam.

Back on the bus, Ms. Li talked about how much more emotional Americans were than the calm Chinese and reflected that this was due to the culture of patience that was part of Chinese society. We listened with interest. However, when the bus stopped at a traffic light and the journalists tried to sneak aboard she whirled on them and angrily chastised them and tossed them off the bus. We didn't understand her words, but there was no mistaking her tone. She was pissed. I wasn't the only one on the bus grinning at this "calm, patient" Chinese woman.

The next morning, we traveled to the auditorium to begin the ceremonies welcoming all the international delegations. SJZ has 5 million residents and our route had us traveling downtown during rush hour. I was concerned about being late, an unpardonable sin for an official function. But I noticed that as we drove through the heavy morning traffic that there were police at each intersection and they were stopping traffic for us. At least they were for Governor and Billie Ray ahead of us and our bus driver stuck to the limo's bumper. This happened all the way across town. I asked our Ms. Li what was happening and she explained that in the windshield of the limousine, there was a small red card. The police know that was for a VIP and they stop traffic to allow them through. I was incredulous that a policeman standing in the sunlight in the center of a busy intersection could see that little red card and would stop traffic for us. "That's right," she said. I told her that would never happen in the US unless there was a police escort. She just smiled enigmatically.

During the interminable opening ceremonies, I reflected on the little red card and my discomfort at the special treatment we received during our trip. Growing up in America, I developed strong feelings of egalitarianism and I was very aware of the status differences while I was in China. We were not just guests, but were treated with the same deference as senior officials. This was hardly the classless society we were told existed here. The same had been true in Russia where your membership and position in the party determined your status and privileges.

That evening, we witnessed another illustration of Ms. Wang's efforts at controlling us. On a previous visit to Hebei, Sarah (my predecessor as CEO of Iowa Sister States, who was with us on the trip) had met a kite maker and she and Jane wanted to visit him to buy some kites for their kids. We learned later that the kite maker had done something to offend the authorities—we never learned what it was—and Ms. Wang was determined to keep us from meeting him. She arranged evening activities for us after a full day of business. She cut off our official transportation in the evening, claiming that the vehicle needed maintenance or that the driver's wife was ill and needed him. But Sarah and Jane were determined. They avoided an evening activity and took a taxi to the kite maker's residence. When they returned, I was in the lobby with Ms. Wang. Since the kites were six feet tall with paper wrapped around the sticks, it was obvious that they had defied Ms. Wang's efforts at control. She was torn between her professional responsibility and anger at this defiance. She hesitated, then continued talking to me in a tightly controlled voice while ignoring Sarah and Jane.

The atmosphere was chilly for the rest of the visit, which fortunately was nearly over. Sarah and Jane had a hard time convincing the flight attendants to store the six-foot kites somewhere on the plane besides the overhead bins, but they did get them home safely.

THE ICE CREAM AND PIZZA REBELLION

On several occasions, we were able to plan incoming exchanges from Hebei province. One of the most memorable was a two week visit by 30 primary school children and two of their teachers from Tianjin. The children had prepared a one-hour program of singing and dancing while wearing charming costumes. We arranged a tour for them to six Iowa communities. They were to be home hosted, except for the teachers who insisted on staying in hotels. We hired a West Des Moines school bus and driver and started out for Burlington near the southeast corner of the state. We met their home hosts who took them by twos to their homes to settle in and then returned them to the middle school auditorium for their first performance. They were poised and charming. The audience loved it and local television featured them that night.

Prior to their arrival in Iowa, I had received detailed instructions from their parents through my colleagues at the Hebei Foreign Affairs Office. The children must do their studies every day. They must eat only Chinese food. They must get plenty of rest.

I dutifully passed on these instructions to the host families in each community and was promptly ignored by both the families and the Chinese children. They bonded with the American kids who hosted them, ate pizza and ice cream, and stayed up late playing video games. Each morning, when they gathered together, the teachers would question them and I would get chewed out for laxity in forcing the host families to obey instructions. The kids were unfazed, slept on the bus, and continued their rebellion throughout the visit. I just gave the teachers my best impersonation of a Chinese enigmatic smile. This was payback for the many times when I was in China and asked an unanswerable question and received an enigmatic smile as a response.

The kids were a roaring success in Davenport after which we proceeded to Osage, Iowa. When they weren't sleeping, they were amazed by Iowa's open spaces and all the crops growing in the fields. Osage is a small, rural community in north central Iowa. It has a population of 3,609. These kids came from Tianjin which has over 12 million people and they couldn't believe that they were in such a small place. They performed at the high school auditorium and both high school and middle school students attended. The warm reception and the exceptional performance were the highlight of the visit. Afterwards, we walked across the street to a park and had ice cream, one of the forbidden foods according to the parents. The Chinese claim that they are lactose intolerant and perhaps there is some truth in that. Nevertheless, the kids loved the ice cream and by now, the teachers were pretty worn down and did not object. The kids then ran around the park with their American counterparts before leaving for Charles City, a metropolis of 7,812, compared to Osage.

The rest of the trip continued to be just as successful and many Iowa families gained a first-hand exposure to children of a very different culture. These cultural visits always pay dividends for the US. Sometimes in very specific ways. Twenty years ago, Xi Jinping visited Iowa as part of an agricultural exchange. The time he spent in Iowa clearly was important to him. Just before he became President of China, he came to the US for consultations in Washington, DC. Then he came to Iowa for a four-day visit. He stayed in the same home with a family in Muscatine where he had lived when he was here the first time.

This extraordinary visit shows the depth of feeling he had for his first visit. Staff and volunteers of Iowa Sister States made efforts to recreate his time here. He stayed overnight at the same home in Muscatine. His driver, formerly a staff person at Iowa Sister

States and now an executive with a multi-national company, took on those duties again. Visits were arranged with many of the citizen diplomats who had been with him. He met with the Governor and other senior officials and pledged close cooperation in trade agreements and future exchanges.

All of the Tianjin kids will have good memories of the US and someday one of them could be President of China, equipped with a better understanding of us than those who never came here. This is a critical lesson for us. Our own kids must travel internationally more—and should go to places other than England or Italy. They need to see other places and cultures and develop a broader world outlook as a result.

THE GREAT WALL

The Great Wall stretches 5500 miles from Northeastern China along the defensive border of inner China. Built to keep out the barbarians, it is now a tourist attraction for camera toting barbarians who buy plastic versions of the Great Wall to take home. At its closest point to Beijing, the Great Wall has been repaired and is a colossus. To get to the Wall from the parking lot, you walk a long way through a gauntlet of shopkeepers who have every type of souvenir junk for sale—all of it "made in China." You then have the choice of walking up several flights of stairs to get to the top of the wall, or riding a conveyance like a small open train through a tunnel to the top.

On my first trip, I climbed the stone steps to the top and walked

Great Wall. Left to Right: The author, Wade Wagner, Jane Van Voorhis

out on the Wall. I was pretty winded from the climb and vowed never to do it again. A few years later I accompanied Iowa Governor Chet Culver's party and agreed to follow him into the modern way to the top. The ride began underground where we climbed into little cars, like the toy railroads at theme parks. Culver was a big guy, but he squeezed in and we took off in the tunnel. I quickly noticed that there wasn't much headroom in the tunnel and I hoped that Culver would keep his head down. While looking at the roof of the tunnel, I noticed a lot of wires visible there. Some were bare and a few were even sparking. When we were free of the tunnel and the car stopped, we scrambled out as quickly as possible.

On top of the Wall, the scene was spectacular. This part of the Wall was in hilly country and you could see it rising and falling for vast distances in either direction. We walked uphill toward one of the guard towers and climbed to the top. It was an overwhelming vista that left us truly gaping in astonishment.

Perhaps the bare wires in the tunnel were just there to encourage passengers to disembark rapidly so the train could take more trips. If that was the goal, they certainly achieved it. Traveling in a dark tunnel at an undetermined speed, it was impossible to know how close we were to those wires and how much of a risk the Chinese were taking in potentially electrocuting a visiting official. One thing is sure, they don't have OSHA over there.

THEY EAT EVERYTHING

Two important things to know about Chinese cuisine are, first, they have a long complex history of learning about the best ways to serve food. Second, they have suffered through many famines so, as Will told me… "They eat everything."

To prepare for my visits to China, I practiced with chopsticks using Cheerios. I got pretty good at it. Even though the Chinese will give you Western utensils, they prefer that you use chopsticks whenever you can. The food I ate there was the best Chinese food I have ever had, as you might expect.

BREAKFAST

Breakfast at our hotels was a mixed Western and Chinese buffet. Omelets, waffles, and pastry alongside soups, steamed buns, and vegetables. Rice or noodles were not served, as they were considered poor people's food. Although I had practiced at home with chopsticks, my skills were pretty rudimentary. Eventually I learned to pick up steamed buns and take bites rather than trying to stuff the whole thing in my mouth.

I tried eating a fried egg with chopsticks and found it was impossible to cut off a piece small enough to bite. A staff person arrived with a fork and I used it without shame. I'm not sure what the Chinese do about fried eggs. Perhaps there is an advanced chopsticks class that teaches a technique. Mostly, I resolved this by avoiding eggs—scrambled were worse than fried—and stuck to steamed vegetables.

The soups came with small porcelain spoons, but most of the soups were too sour for my taste.

LUNCH

Lunch was a more social and official event. Our colleagues usually took us to restaurants in hotels. On one occasion, we were entering a 5-star hotel and I noticed a brass plaque affixed to the wall. It said "Reserved for Aliens." Martians, I thought? No, they mean me.

We went to a private dining room and sat at a round table. The staff began bringing dishes which they placed on a large, glass, lazy Susan in the middle of the table. My colleagues began using chopsticks to grasp items from the dishes—items like green beans, peanuts, shrimp, pieces of chicken, beef, and fish. Some of the dishes had those little porcelain spoons with which to serve yourself. But for the most part, you used chopsticks. As I watched my hosts efficiently grasping a green bean or peanut and putting it in their mouths, it suddenly occurred to me that this was very unsanitary. The chances for cross contamination were very high as all these pieces of wood that had just been in someone's mouth, plunged into a dish and grabbed a piece of something and put that in their mouth. It appeared to be the Chinese version of double dipping. I decided not to worry about it and did my best with my chopsticks. As often happened in China, my ignorance led me to the wrong conclusion. At these lunch events when food is served on lazy Susans, there are "Sharing Chopsticks"-larger versions of what we ate with. They are used to select food from the dishes and transport it to your plate, where you use then your own chopsticks. I had overlooked that everyone was using them except me and my hosts were too polite to tell me. So, they risked my Iowa bacteria out of courtesy. The next day, I did better.

Even with my newly acquired skill from picking up Cheerios, I was still very awkward and slow with chopsticks. Often the lazy Susan was stopped in front of me for a long time while I tried to get something with the sharing chopsticks. Peanuts in sauce were the worst. Although they tasted good, they were so slippery that I gave up trying to corral even one of them. Despite my clumsiness, I never went hungry and what I did manage to grasp with chopsticks was delicious.

The staff continued bringing more and more little dishes and stacking them on the lazy Susan. Most of the items in the little dishes were familiar, like vegetables, shrimp, and peanuts. Some were familiar but not acceptable as food to us, such as chicken feet. Will was sitting on my left side and occasionally, he would lean over and whisper "that dish is not suitable for Westerners." Usually that meant something like tree fungus (although we eat mushrooms), sea cucumber, or jellyfish. Sometimes Will was busy talking to someone else while I was selecting something—usually I felt safe eating small pieces of meat in a brown sauce. But twice, he asked me how I had enjoyed something that had just passed down my gullet. I told him it was OK. "Camel," he replied the first time. "Donkey," the second time.

DINNER

During our trips in China, our hosts arranged two types of dinners. One type was at famous restaurants and the second was a formal banquet in a hotel.

The restaurant food was excellent and the one I remember the best was the Peking Duck restaurant in Beijing. Secretary of State Henry Kisssinger allegedly dined here when making the diplomatic opening to China. His boss, Richard Nixon, probably would not have enjoyed this since his favorite lunch reputedly was cottage cheese with ketchup. Two perfectly fine things but taken together are a gastronomic nightmare, especially in a food conscious country like China.

Peking Duck is a famous dish from northern China and is a complex recipe taking nearly a day to complete. A simplified version online explains that the duck is air dried, then air is pumped between the skin and meat, boiling liquid is poured over it, it's air dried again, roasted, then served carved in slivers with flesh and crispy skin rolled into little pancakes (like blinis) with some scallions and hoisin sauce. It was outstanding.

Some of the general principles governing Chinese cooking include color, aroma, taste, and texture. They also balance four natures: hot, warm, cool, and cold. And then they consider five tastes: pungent, sweet, sour, bitter, and salty. Finally the food must be visually appealing with the right mix of colors.

On several occasions, our team was invited by a local official to a formal banquet. This is where the Chinese truly showed off their culinary art. Incorporating all the elements in everyday cooking is challenging, but when managing a banquet with all those courses, it requires skill of a high order. On one occasion, I sat next to our host and saw the list of courses we would have. Here is the menu:

Chinese Appetizer

Hot Dish

"Cantonese" Style Soup

Sautéed Beef Tenderloin with Pomes Mustard

Stuffed Pan Cake with Goose Liver

Deep-Fried Australian Scallop with Thai Chili Sauce

Sautéed Eggplant with Japonic Sauce

Braised Bean Curd with Abalone Sauce

Stir Fried Vegetable

Fried Rice with Prawn Oil

Wonton Small Soup

Fresh Fruit Plate

Every banquet was a phenomenal evening—except for the toasting. This wasn't toasting with shots of vodka like the Russians. In fact, the Chinese mocked the Russians for overindulgence and loss of control. Rather, we had small cordial-size glasses filled with Baijiu, which the Chinese consider good quality Chinese "wine." Toasts were offered and they were to be bottoms up toasts. This was just as well because the Baijiu hooch tasted terrible. Whatever grain they used to make it tasted like it still had kerosene in it, too. After each toast, young ladies in traditional dress holding metal pitchers came by and filled us up again. You had to get the stuff past your tonsils to avoid the awful taste. As a parting gift, my host gave me a ceramic bottle shaped like a dragon filled with that stuff. It is still unopened.

Later I questioned one of our hosts who kept calling this stuff "wine." He confirmed it was distilled and when I asked about the percentage of alcohol he said about 60%. That's not wine, it's liquor. More like moonshine. No wonder all the guidebooks strongly suggest that you curb your consumption. That was easy enough because it tasted terrible.

VODKA MARTINIS

On one of our trips, we visited Tianjin, the port of Beijing. It had 12 million people of its own and was very congested. We stayed in the Astor Hotel which had a rich history. Before Herbert Hoover became President, he was a mining engineer and traveled the world rehabilitating mines and making them productive again. Early in the 20th century, he and his wife lived at the Astor Hotel. Their suite has been preserved, although in the best entrepreneurial Chinese fashion, you may rent it for a much higher price than the other suites.

At the time we visited, the Astor was getting pretty bedraggled. It needed new fixtures, furniture, and a more attentive staff. It had a tea room that provided high tea as well as two bars. One was called a Japanese bar and the other was a typical Western style bar of the early 20th century with heavy furniture and overhead fans.

Four of us went in for a cocktail and quickly learned that the bartender was hopeless. He couldn't even make a vodka martini. So, we asked him if we could make them. He looked relieved and turned the place over to us. So, Frank and I became mixologists at what was once the most famous hotel in Tianjin. By the time we were through, that bartender knew how to make martinis.

IOWA CHOPS

Iowa Sister States also hosted professionals from China many times. One group in 2003 was home hosted and were taken to a Chinese restaurant for dinner. I was stunned by the poor judgment of my fellow Iowans in taking the Chinese out for American Chinese food. The next morning, I asked the delegation what they really thought of American style Chinese food. They said they thought it had a lot of sugar in it. I agreed and offered to take them wherever they wished that night. And they all said they wanted to eat some Iowa food.

That evening, we dined at the Machine Shed which recaptures the early settlers' farm experience. The atmosphere is 19th century with pine floors, checkered tablecloths, and old agricultural tools hanging from the walls. They loved that ambiance and were ready to order Iowa food. Chinese people eat a lot of pork so they were curious about how we prepared it. Two of them ordered Iowa chops, which are 1½ inches thick and were stuffed with a bread dressing. The others ordered fried chicken and they all wanted mashed potatoes. They were shocked when the food arrived. Machine Shed specializes in very large portions and their plates were stacked high with food. They spent 10 minutes taking pictures of their dinners, much to the amusement of the nearby patrons. Of course, they couldn't finish more than half of what they were served. They learned about doggie bags and how we spoil our pets. Taking the leftovers to their home hosts was not necessary because more than enough food was prepared for them. So, they also learned that we waste a lot of food. The Machine Shed became a standard stop for future delegations but we recommended they split their dinners between at least two people.

HOW MUCH IS...

Several Chinese delegations chose to stay in hotels but expressed interest in visiting an American home. Often it was mine.

When they would arrive at our home, a 1700 square foot ranch with a finished lower level, the first question they asked was always, "How many people live here?" They always looked shocked when we told them just the two of us. Then they would start looking around and were especially interested in the kitchen with its big refrigerator and dishwasher. They turned on the taps and tested the hot water. The toilet was very interesting to them and they took a lot of pictures and flushed it a couple of times. So, the Chinese obsess about toilets just as we do! Perhaps they showed their American toilet photos to their friends first after they returned home, too.

The highlight of our finished lower level is a print given to me by a Chinese artist who visited here in 2005. He is news director of the Hebei TV station which has an audience of 60 million viewers. Like others on his staff, he is also an accomplished artist. During his visit, I helped him arrange displays of the artwork he had brought. One delegation knew this artist and was quite impressed that he had given me this artwork.

They typically thought our workout equipment, treadmill and elliptical, was very interesting, but didn't seem to understand why we had them in the house instead of going to the gym. We explained that with both people working long hours, this was the easiest way to get our exercise. They sniffed at that and we continued to the storage area of the basement and hit gold. They were always fascinated that we had our own furnace and not only asked many questions about it, they took more pictures of that than anything

Padua O O Venice

ITALY

ITALY:
WET FEET, SHAKY LEGS

Italy's history stretches from the Roman Empire as the center of Western Civilization to the present center of Christianity's Holy Roman Catholic Church. The city of Venice in northeastern Italy was built on 117 islands in a lagoon to ward off attacks by other city states and the armies of the popes, but it was eventually conquered by Napoleon. Venice now has 177 canals connected by 409 bridges and is the capitol of the Veneto Region which includes the city of Padua and the winemaking region surrounding it.

Iowa Sister States has had a partnership relationship with the Veneto Region of Italy since 1997 including exchanges in sports, cuisine, winemaking, art, and trade. While I was Executive Director of Iowa Sister States, I made several trips to Veneto. The recollections below are based on my experiences and observations and, of course, should not be taken as anything else.

It is important to note that in the 19th and 20th centuries, immigrants from Italy settled in Iowa. The south side of Des Moines is still home to many of their descendants. However, most of these immigrants were from the southern province of Calabria (capital is Catanzaro) and they reflected old country resentments of the southerners towards the northerners. This resentment was not apparent until the Sister State relationship with (northern) Veneto was established. This resulted in a strong effort by south side Italians to create a

Sister City relationship with Catanzaro. This was done in 2006. Relationships between the two groups of volunteers are cordial but separate.

WET FEET

On my first trip to Venice, my wife, Judy, joined me for a few days before the delegation was due to arrive, so we had some time to be tourists in one of the most beautiful cities in the world. We wandered through the narrow streets and across bridges following the signs for Piazza San Marco (St. Mark's Square) and entered the square, which was dominated by St. Mark's Cathedral. The other three sides of the square had classical style buildings with shops that had raised entrances, about a four inch step up from ground level.

Judy noticed that there were tables in the square and a string trio playing for people having lunch and suggested we have a romantic lunch there. I tried to tell her it was too touristy. "Come on," she insisted, "Let's live a little." Clearly she hadn't traveled with me enough to know about all the "living a little" I had already done.

St. Mark's Basilica.
Photo Credit Frank Trumpy.

She was right, though, and we ate a wonderful lunch on a beautiful day in gorgeous surroundings while musicians played Mozart. It was perfect. Even the legions of pigeons left us in peace. We were so intent on our conversation that we didn't notice when the musicians stopped playing and left the square. Not only that, but all the other people left as well. I looked at St. Mark's Cathedral and saw some workmen assembling staging three feet high across the entrance. "Hmm," I thought, "Perhaps a choir will be performing there soon."

Then I looked down and saw that water was bubbling up through the tiles in the plaza. This seemed impossible. Water is supposed to drain down through these perforated tiles, not rise upwards.

I immediately signaled for the waiter to bring us the check. By the time he arrived, our table was a little island in the midst of a very wet plaza and the water was rising. We paid and left the plaza in a hurry, sloshing through two inches of rapidly rising water. When we made it to the covered walkway for the shops, the water was over three inches deep and still rising. That explained the high thresholds for the shops.

A combination of high tide, a full moon, and offshore winds had resulted in an exceptionally high tide that morning and everyone in Venice, except Judy and me, knew about it and took shelter. Our lovely romantic lunch had a soggy ending.

We continued to wade through the rising water to visit the shops and no one seemed to notice that there was a flood in the square. Our shoes were squishy, but eventually dried well although my trousers were wrinkly at the bottom three inches. Judy commented if wrinkles were the worst thing about Venice, she'd take it. Scientifically, Venice is the subject of a continuing controversy – is the city sinking or the sea rising? Whichever it is, the result is the same—sometimes Venice floods.

PACK YOUR OWN BAGS

Dale and Anita accompanied Judy and me on that first trip to Italy. Dale worked with me as the deputy director of the data processing department and was the only person in that department who could talk to people as well as computers.

A few days into the trip, we asked another couple with us to find a local restaurant for dinner. They did and we arrived at 7:00 PM at a small, family-owned place near our hotel. We ordered the usual three courses. The antipasto was excellent, followed by a penne pasta with an oil and herb sauce. Italians believe food needs to be prepared to order and should be savored, so we had been there about 90 minutes. Before the veal with asparagus came, Anita began getting anxious. She explained that she and Dale needed to leave soon to do some shopping at a nearby store.

I pressed them on why they couldn't wait until the next day. She explained that the store closed at 9 PM and she needed to buy some pants for Dale. Come to find out, she didn't like the ones he had, so she just didn't pack any of them. So, they really needed to buy more because he had been wearing the same pair since they left the states.

We were stunned and Dale looked sheepish. However, he did look smart in his new trousers the next day.

Venice is famous for its canals, but until you go to the only major city in Europe that has no "streets", you do not realize the complexity of just getting around and daily living. There are several ways to move within the city: on foot, which accounts for the slender population despite their high carb diets; by Vaporetto, the water buses which travel on schedules and standard routes through the canals; by Water Taxi, which will take you a specific "address"; and, of course, by gondola. But there are no cars.

Grand Canal.
Photo Credit Frank Trumpy.

For the most part, you walk and you cross innumerable bridges, traverse many embankments along one side or another of the canals and walk up and down steps leading to bridges. Shopping for clothes or groceries can be difficult. The shops and markets are small and people buy their groceries daily. Most people have small carts and they muscle these up and down the stairs, onto the Vaporetto, and then along the embankment and up the stairs to their apartment. There are very few elevators in Venice.

The Vaporetto (plural vaporetti) runs like wheeled buses elsewhere. The boat holds about 40 ticketed passengers. Passengers get on and off at the various stops around the city. Many of them are pushing their carts with grocery shopping or luggage by recent arrivals. For the most part, it is an honor system, but there are transport police who occasionally board the Vaproretto and demand to see your ticket. If you have one that is expired, there is an immediate fine (not to mention the embarrassment of all your fellow passengers smirking at your misfortune).

Water taxis are personal modes of travel. They take you at very high speed to whatever destination you may choose within the city. If you take one from the airport to your hotel, you pass over the lagoon which separates Venice from the mainland and you can witness the defenses the city used to defend itself over the centuries from invasion. There are buoys and other channel markers showing the safest route through the marshy lagoon. Whenever Venice was threatened, fishermen simply removed all the buoys and markers. That, and mosquito borne infections, took care of many invaders until Napoleon. Water taxis are convenient, but more expensive than the

Vaporetto. They do, however, give their drivers the chance to show their skill as water borne Formula One racers for the Ferrari team.

Gondolas are mostly for tourists. However, at a few locations along the Grand Canal, they are used to ferry people across the canal to avoid the long walk between the bridges over the canal. On the infamous "wet feet" visit described earlier, Judy suggested we take a romantic ride in a gondola. I grumbled about this being "very touristy", to which she replied with unassailable logic, "We are tourists, after all." So we boarded a rocking, narrow gondola propelled by a man in the traditional striped shirt and kerchief. We floated out into the Grand Canal and were rocked by the wake from large commercial motorized boats, which dampened the romance a bit. We did get to see some of the gorgeous Venetian palaces and churches from the water, by far the best way to enjoy them. And I think I paid extra for the gondolier NOT to sing any Rossini. I had not taken any Dramamine which I often do on boat rides, so by the time we got back to the dock, I was getting a little nauseated.

My aversion to boats had not improved since that morning cruise on the Volga River with Sergei pouring shots of vodka. I think part of my dislike for boats is because I don't swim. However, in Venice, swimming from a capsized boat would be deadlier than just drowning. Venice was the first city in Europe to have a "modern" sewage system. Its inhabitants dumped their chamber pots into the street just like people in London or Rome. But in Venice the streets were canals which were regularly "flushed" by the tides. This worked very well in the 16th century. But now, it is not especially effective. Many tourists complain of the odor—although the locals deny any unpleasant smell. But no one goes swimming in those canals, a Petri dish of bacteria.

YOU CAN'T GET THERE FROM HERE

On my first business trip to Venice, I traveled alone and when I got to Amsterdam, I went to the KLM Transfer Desk to get a boarding pass for my flight to Venice. After a few minutes, the helpful KLM attendant said, "You are not going to Venice." I replied that of course I was going to Venice. I explained I had a reservation on the KLM flight and just need a boarding pass.

She looked at me patiently and said, "Sorry, but you cannot go to Venice because the airport is closed." I was baffled. Was there a fire? An international incident? How an airport could be closed? She went on to explain that the staff at Marco Polo airport were on a one- day strike and they had closed the airport. I was stunned.

She went on to tell me that the flight would leave on time and would land in Treviso, a town near Venice. She didn't know what I would do then, but she said they would "figure something out" while we were in the air.

I was not really comforted by this, but I couldn't think of any alternatives, so I boarded the plane. An hour later, we landed in Treviso at a small airport, but one with a runway big enough to handle a 737. As we deplaned, I noticed several other planes parked nearby and a row of buses to which my fellow passengers were going. I asked the bus driver where we were being taken and he told me Marco Polo airport.

As I have since learned, one-day strikes were routine in Italy. In fact, unless people were directly affected, no one even noticed the strike. Somehow, civil society continued and chaos was averted.

WHERE THE LOCALS EAT

All guidebooks tell you to eat where the locals eat. This way, you avoid all the tourist traps with mediocre food and high prices. However, the locals don't want to tell you where they eat because then all the tourists will go there and the food will become mediocre and the prices high.

We were blessed with having Paolo with us in Venice. He was a native of Milan who immigrated to Iowa and often led the Iowa Sister States delegations to Veneto. He knew a place where the locals ate and took us there. On one cold and damp evening in November, his friend Alessandra came to join us for dinner. She was a public official in the town of Padua, about 20 miles from Venice.

We followed Paolo and Alessandra like little ducklings along embankments, over bridges, up and down stairs until we were hopelessly lost. "I hope they know where they are going," I told the rest of the delegation. I couldn't believe that we had walked so long in such a small place as Venice. It was too late to drop breadcrumbs, so we just stayed close to Paolo and Alessandra who were chattering away in Italian. Finally, we crossed another bridge and went down an alley to a blank storefront. There was no sign, but as soon as we opened the door, delicious smells wafted out.

"Alessandra and Paolo," shouted the proprietor, a hefty Italian, who gave us all hugs and invited us to please come in and have dinner, and seated us around a big table.

He soon bustled over and gave us menus, which fortunately had the English translation of the Italian dishes. I tried to order the Bronzino grilled, but was stopped by the owner. "Not very good today," he replied. One of my colleagues asked about the ravioli with cream sauce. "I wouldn't recommend it," responded the owner. Alessandra finally told the owner to choose for us, bringing us whatever was good that day. The owner beamed, took our menus and hurried off to the kitchen.

He chose well. We began with antipasto—sliced meats, cheese, olives, fried peppers, and tuna. This was followed by an outstanding seafood risotto. Then came veal piccata with green beans, and finally, sponge cake soaked in Marsala with mascarpone cheese.

We thanked him for an excellent dinner. He was very pleased that we were happy and said that he was leaving to go home to his family, but the restaurant manager would take care of our bill and that we should come again.

He was no sooner out the door than the manager appeared with Italian cookies and dessert wine. He instructed us to soak the cookies in the wine, and promised that this would be delicious. We protested that we were too full to do this, but he insisted. He was correct. They were delicious and somehow we managed to demolish all that he had brought.

Then he came back with Grappa and limoncello. "A digestive," he said. "Very traditional." We groaned a collective groan, but sipped our cordials. He told us these were on the house and invited us to come back again. The bill was shockingly reasonable.

We waddled happily home and though I did my best to memorize all the twists and turns, the bridges and embankments, I was soon lost again. Perhaps with a GPS, I could find the restaurant again, but otherwise, the restaurant where the locals eat remained safe from the incursions of tourists.

One of my volunteers on the Veneto committee was interested in wine making. So, our colleagues in Veneto arranged a wine tour for us. After learning too much about why Prosecco was such a wonderful sparkling wine, we finally left the Prosecco Association and went to a winery. The leader of our group, Eleanor, was allergic to sulfites, a preservative added to wine, so she politely would hold her glass of Prosecco while the winemaster explained his secrets. When I looked around again, Eleanor's glass was empty. I paid closer attention when the winemaster poured us all yet another version of Prosecco. As before, she stood listening attentively and holding her glass. Beside her was a discreet battle going on between Paolo and Chef Robert, two of the members of our delegation. Each was trying to get next to Eleanor to take her full glass and exchange it for an empty one. "How childish," I thought. "Grown men vying for another free drink." But it was delicious wine, so I joined my two colleagues in jostling to be beside Eleanor at the next two wineries we visited.

That evening, Judy and I sat across from Chef Robert at dinner. He was head of a culinary arts program and during the four course dinner, he repeatedly made little noises of appreciation, clearly enjoying his food. When dessert arrived, he was euphoric. Judy asked what it was, as it resembled vanilla pudding. He smiled and told us it was Pannacotta, an Italian dessert made from heavy cream, gelatin and flavorings. She took a bite and made the same euphoric noises as him.

From then on, we always sat next to Chef Robert and waited for him to review the menu and order. Then we said, "We'll have what he's having." We were never disappointed. He was a very good sport about this and we became friends. But he never let me get close to Eleanor at any of the other wineries again. Friendship only goes so far.

RAGBRAI

For over forty years, the Des Moines Register newspaper has sponsored a bicycle ride across the state. (RAGBRAI stands for the Register's Annual Great Bike Ride Across Iowa). It travels from the Missouri River to the Mississippi River over a six-day period. Over the years it has grown to over 10,000 riders. Small towns along the route welcome the riders (and their entourages) with housing in public facilities, tent sites, food stations, and entertainment. It is a traveling carnival with lemonade stands, beer tents, pork chops, corn dogs, and all sorts of gustatory challenges along the way.

After our sister state agreement was signed, the Italians sent a bike team to Iowa for RAGBRAI. They came in full regalia with super bicycles, spandex costumes, and space age helmets. We provided them with maps and home hosting arrangements along the way, as well as transportation to the beginning and ending of the rides back to Des Moines.

The first day was quite a surprise to them. It was about an 80 mile ride along rural highways to the next town. They got up early and took off, arriving at the next town by 9 AM when most of the other riders were just getting to breakfast. Our Italian friends thought that this was a race rather than a two-wheeled feeding frenzy. They soon adjusted and got into the spirit of the event. They did meet the team from the US Air Force Academy and conducted several races against that team so that both groups could blow off some steam and burn off some pork chop calories.

After the traditional dunking of the front bicycle tire in the Mississippi River (having dunked the rear tire in the Missouri River at the beginning of the ride), we met them and drove them back to Des Moines for a pool party at Elizabeth's home. She had arranged a buffet lunch and when I arrived, many of the Italians were splashing around in her pool. Shortly afterwards, two women who were part of the team arrived looking elegant in silks and high heels. Clearly they wanted to show us that they could dress up. However, no one told the men in the pool who promptly grabbed them and tossed them in. This could have been a tragedy, but we quickly hid all the knives and poured more wine. Thankfully, these women had experienced this camaraderie before and forgave all.

I thought this was amazingly tolerant for Italians who are noted for passionate outbursts. Still, as they say, "Revenge is a dish best served cold," and I worried about these men after they returned home.

MARRIOTT PROPERTIES

On one of the trips to Venice, the state Economic Development Director was going to join us there, make a presentation about Iowa, and then travel on to Germany for more meetings. A week before departure, his very efficient secretary called me to say, "Mike likes to stay in Marriott hotels." I explained there weren't any Marriott hotels in Venice. She went on to ask about Marriott properties, like Fairfield Inns or Courtyard Inns. I apologized and said there were none of those either. Then she responded that he preferred to be above the sixth floor in any hotel. And again I burst her bubble, explaining that none of the buildings was over three stories high and he would have to tough it out with the rest of us in a nice hotel with only two stories. She sighed, defeated.

The Santa Chiara Hotel had one big advantage over all the others in Venice. It was the only hotel in Venice to which you could drive. It was in the Piazzale Roma, right on the Grand Canal. On our first trip to Venice (the eventful wet feet trip), Judy and I had arranged to stay at the Mozart Hotel. We got in a cab at the Marco Polo airport and told the driver our hotel name. He drove into the big square that is the Piazalle Roma and stopped the cab. He then pointed to a kiosk where tickets were sold for the Vaporetto, the water buses, and said "Two stops". At the ticket counter, the clerk verified, "Mozart Hotel, two stops."

So, we stood on the dock with our luggage and waited for the Vaporetto to arrive. When it did, we jumped aboard a thirty foot long boat stuffed with Italians going somewhere. Several confirmed, "Two stops for Mozart." So at the appointed stop, we got off and dragged our luggage down the street. And yes, I mean dragged because even though our luggage had wheels, the "streets" are all cobblestones. We felt a little foolish dragging our luggage, but then noticed that a lot of other people were doing the same thing.

On future visits, I chose to stay at the Santa Chiara, just because it was easier. Then I could move about the city pretending to be a local and smugly watching the tourists dragging their bags. I think the Economic Development Director was pleased by that convenience, since there were no staff people with him to carry his bags.

GRAPPA

I've had a long , mixed history with Grappa, which is an alcoholic drink made in Veneto from what is called pomace—the distilled result of leftovers from winemaking including skins, stems, seeds, and pulp of grapes.

My first exposure was on the same trip with Judy and the pants-shopping Dale and Anita. We had a long day touring in Tuscany and I was getting ready to turn in. Dale had seen a little café at the bottom of the hill from our hotel and said he wanted a coffee. It was too late for coffee for me, but I said I would join him for a drink. When we got down to the café, Dale ordered his cappuccino and while I was thinking over my choice, I noticed several locals drinking a clear liquid from small glasses with a twisty stem. "I'll have what they are having," I told the waiter. "That's Grappa," he said.

It arrived in one of those curious glasses and was colorless and odorless. I took a sip. Wow. It was like barbed wire was being pulled out of my throat. After some gasping and downing a glass of mineral water, Dale and I decided that the Grappa was probably all of two days old.

Two years later, I was at a dinner in Venice when one of my Italian colleagues suggested a Grappa after dinner as a digestive. I mentioned it was hardly a digestive, as drinking Grappa required surgery on your throat from the harshness and abrasiveness. He told me I was mistaken, and that I must have had cheap, poor quality Grappa. He insisted I try the one he offered.

With some reluctance, I took a sip and found it to be very good! I assured him it was a world of difference from what I had my previous time.

A year after that, at the end of a long day of meetings and delays, Michael and I walked back to the Santa Chiara hotel. Michael was an executive chef and restaurant manager and we had been trying unsuccessfully to arrange a chef exchange. The Italians had too many requirements which prevented the simple exchange of chefs through their association.

We were ready for a drink, but as often was the case, the bar at the Santa Chiara was closed. So, we walked along the embankment beside the Grand Canal looking for a bar. The first one we entered was too full of tobacco smoke. The second had loud Europop music playing. The third place we entered seemed good, but I needed to go to the bathroom, so I told Michael to just order for me. When I returned I noticed that we were in the Westin and it was gorgeous. The bar was elegant and quiet.

"I ordered you a Grappa," Michael said. "It should be a good one because it will cost 20 Euros." That was the equivalent of $30. I savored it and developed a new appreciation for good Grappa.. When I got home, I had an extended duel with the accountant about the price of this drink. "But it was really good Grappa," I said. She was unimpressed and we split the difference. Money well spent.

HOW DO YOU SAY, "DOUBLE-WIDE" IN ITALIAN?

Through the offices of Iowa Senator Tom Harkin, the Italian-American Society of Des Moines received a grant to refurbish a building into a museum documenting the life experiences of the Italians who immigrated to Iowa. Exhibits were created showing their work in the coal mines in southern Iowa, their work as tailors, and as restaurant owners. Wedding pictures and gowns and the celebrations of special occasions were shown with pride. A volunteer member of the society made a series of signs in Italian describing the exhibit.

On one occasion, Iowa Sister States was hosting a staff person from the Chicago Italian Consulate. We had a productive morning of planning future visits and we ended the day with a visit to the museum. She politely moved through the exhibits and asked questions of the volunteer staff. She expressed her thanks to the staff for a useful representation of life in the late 19th and early 20th centuries for Italian immigrants in Iowa.

As we were driving her to the airport, she said. "Please accept this feedback in the way it is intended. The museum is quaint and interesting, but the signage is all wrong." She went on to say that the person who made the signs used poor grammar and worse spelling. She said she believed in English we would say this was trailer park English and that clearly this person learned Italian from uneducated people. She told me we needed to do the signs over in proper Italian.

I discretely mentioned this to the chief of volunteers and she was embarrassed, but told me she didn't dare do anything about this. Angelina, the volunteer who wrote the signs was their biggest donor and was very proud of her heritage.

I told her I understood, but thought to myself that Angelina's ancestral estate must be a double-wide.

Coming home from a late November visit to Tanzania, I had to make a side trip to Venice. I was invited to a post-Thanksgiving dinner by two of my colleagues, Amy and Tom, who had the good fortune to own an apartment in Venice. November is cold and damp in Venice, so I walked quickly to their apartment building on one of the side canals.

We had a delightful dinner punctuated by interesting conversation as they described the tribulations of foreigners trying to buy property in Venice and then remodel it using Italian contractors, who make the US variety look speedy. While removing an old drop ceiling, the contractors uncovered beams from the 14th century which necessitated a halt to construction until the Venetian antiquities officials could make an inspection. They then required that the beams be preserved and not covered again. This created an interesting contrast with the ultra-modern décor of stainless steel and birch paneling in the rest of the apartment.

Then they explained the many issues encountered in trying to get a boat. But the wonderful Venetian environment made up for all the hassle—at least they thought so.

After dinner, Amy told me that Tom had taken up rowing a gondola for exercise and was planning to go out after dinner. They wondered if I would like to go along and he would drop me at my hotel. Trying not to be ungracious, I agreed.

Again of course, nothing is simple in Venice. The only way to get into the gondola was through a French door on the lowest level of the building. Tom was already in the gondola and was giving me instructions on how best to get in without capsizing it. Not a fan of this ride in the first place, I wasn't comforted to see this wasn't a normal tourist gondola. It was kid's boat that was only about eight feet long and three feet wide. "What had I agreed to?" I worried to myself.

Meanwhile Tom was repeating his instructions. "Put your right foot on this center board and while you are bringing your left leg over, pivot on your right foot so that you are facing forward. Then sit down carefully on the center board and don't make any sudden moves." Good grief. When we were both in the boat, we were only about six inches above the surface of the water. I thought about the cesspool we were floating in and wondered if bacteria could fly.

Somehow, I accomplished gymnastic maneuvers even while encumbered by heavy shoes and a thick raincoat with liner. The boat (gondola is too kind a word) rocked a bit, but steadied and Tom began working the oar at the stern of the boat. As we glided away into the canal, he said. "I like to travel on the back canals, especially at night. It's more mysterious." I was afraid to speak and contradict him for fear of him capsizing the boat.

Side Canal.
Photo Credit Frank Trumpy.

He rowed into one of the side canals which was very dark with just an occasional lamp casting a dim glow on the black water. The cold November night was getting foggy, lowering the visibility even more. As Tom was energetically rowing, it occurred to me that boats were parked in this canal alongside the homes of their owners—and there were no lights or reflectors on those boats.

I was convinced we were going to hit one of them and I tried not to squirm. I could see the story in the Des Moines Register – "Executive Director of Iowa Sister States drowns in eight feet of water after crashing into parked boat and being held under by heavy shoes and overcoat." Or, perhaps several days later, the story would read, "Executive Director of Iowa Sister States dies horribly from an unknown and untreatable bacterial infection. 'Never seen anything like it,' said Director of the Centers for Disease Control."

Somehow Tom could see all these boats, or he was just very lucky, because after 20 minutes of sheer terror, while I was frozen in place, he said, "Well that's enough I think. I'll get out onto the Grand Canal and take you to your hotel. Okay?"

My teeth were chattering when I meekly responded, "Okay." Could have been the dampness or could have been fear—maybe both. But I was relieved that we would soon be on the Grand Canal where there was light. We drifted out of the side canal into the Grand Canal which is the water equivalent of entering an interstate highway from a gravel road.

Even at that late hour, there was a lot of traffic. Vaproetti, cargo boats, speed boats, and all sorts of craft are busily churning the waters of the Grand Canal and our little boat was bobbing like a float. "Try to stay still," Tom said needlessly. I was frozen to the spot with fingers and legs cramping—not to mention sphincters tightening.

Now the story in the Des Moines Register read, "Executive Director of Iowa Sister States drowns in 20 feet of water after his tiny boat is struck by a motorized craft. 'He sank like a stone' said the skipper of the craft."

After another nightmarish 10 minutes of bobbing and rolling, I saw the dock for the Santa Chiara Hotel. Tom bumped us against it and although he was trying to give me instructions on how to disembark ("Put your hand on the side and stand up slowly..."), I had already bolted, springing onto the dock. Legs trembling, I turned and thanked him for an eventful ride. He waved and started rowing back onto the Grand Canal in the wake of a Vaporetto. He bobbed and rowed into the darkness while I stumbled up the steps to the hotel, grateful for a solid surface under my feet.

I rushed in the front door, ready for a large drink, only to learn that the bar had closed. Just as well. The ethanol would have probably send me into cardiac arrest. To this day, when people ask me why I am afraid of boats, I just smile and tighten my sphincters.

SNOWFALL

On another cold, dreary winter afternoon in Venice, my team and I were finishing lunch with the staff of the Veneto foreign affairs department. We had just finished a spectacular meal when I looked into the courtyard and asked, "Is that a snowflake?" My Italian colleagues turned around and said it couldn't be because it almost never snowed in Venice. Having lived in Iowa for over 30 years by that time, I knew a snowflake when I saw one.

As we went outside, another snowflake drifted by, and then thousands of them appeared. I made it back to the Santa Chiara Hotel and met with the rest of the team while it continued snowing. We decided to cancel the dinner reservations we had at a restaurant on the other side of Venice, opting for a restaurant closer to the hotel. While we walked there—over a bridge, along an embankment, down an alley—we enjoyed the snow falling into the black water of the canals. By that time there were about three inches of snow on the embankment. We were used to walking in snow and just trudged along, making minor adjustments when we begin to slip. But the Venetians had no experience with this situation and several times, we had to stop to help someone up who had fallen. Just like in Alabama when it snows, they keep driving like always and crash into each other. The big difference was that Italian curses are more melodious than the English ones in the Deep South.

We arrived at the restaurant and found that the door was locked. It was 7 PM and it should have been open especially for early diners like Americans. Some knocking produced the maître d' who said they were not open as there was no staff and no food.

I asked why there was no staff or food. The snow hadn't stopped the Vaporetti and it was only a few centimeters deep. He explained that none of the staff lived in Venice because it was too expensive to live there. The snow was causing big problems for the commute, and many couldn't make it in.

I pleaded with him to let us in, promising we would just drink wine and eat bread. He reluctantly opened the door and the six of us powered our way in, in case he changed his mind. He brought us wine and bread and we speculated about how Venice will deal with the weather. A few staff began trickling in as we talked.

The maître d' returned and said they would offer a reduced menu that night. "Bring us everything," we said. Even the limited menu was great—antipasto, seafood risotto, broiled fish from the lagoon, pasta with an oil and anchovy sauce, pannacotta for dessert, and Grappa or limoncello as digestives.

Of course, since we were close to the hotels and the Grand Canal, we paid a premium price for our dinner and I had to do some explaining when I returned to Iowa and submitted my expense report.

Part of my explanation was that in addition to the dinner, we had participated in a show—watching the Venetians cope with a snow storm. This made no impression at all on the accountant. I guess you had to be there.

LOST IN TRANSLATION

Eventually, we were able to arrange a chef exchange and the fundraising events arranged by Iowa Sister States with chefs from Veneto were always interesting, and sometimes, even profitable.

The first chefs' exchange was led by the head of their association along with two of its leading members. These chefs, we learned later, worked at the highest levels of cuisine in Italy and primarily participated in various exhibitions and contests. They were prima donnas and we spent a lot of time catering to them and smoothing over a lot of irritated people with whom they worked "with" at a well-known club managed by our friend, Michael. The idea was that the visiting chefs would make a dinner for a fundraiser, so Michael gave them the run of his kitchen. It was his staff that had to deal with these temperamental chefs who kept changing their minds about what the menu would be.

Chef Amadeo demanded pigs' blood to make sausages for the dinner. One of Michael's long suffering staff explained he could not have pigs' blood as it was illegal to use in making food. "Don't you have pigs in Iowa?" Amadeo persisted. "Just go to where they are killed and get some blood for us." The staff apologized but said sorry, they couldn't do that. "Savages and barbarians," the chefs muttered.

Iowa Sister States had sold 100 tickets at $100 each for this dinner and Michael had generously promised that after deducting for the food, we would receive all the proceeds. We were happy about this, but didn't know the chefs would keep dithering about what would be served.

The dinner was a great success and the chefs came out to a standing ovation. Later, Michael told us that our net from the dinner was $200. We were shocked and he said he was sorry, but that the chefs had decided two days before the dinner to cook a veal dish and the veal had to be flown in from Chicago on such short notice that they blew through the budget.

As a parting gift, the chefs gave us translated copies of the recipes they used. We were thankful and planned to distribute them to the guests as a reminder of the dinner and a suggestion to join us again next time.

However, as with everything else they did, the chefs refused help in translating their recipes from Italian into English. They used one of the earliest computerized translation programs with results that were incomprehensible. We decided that the name of their association must be Accademia Internazionale de Chefs Arrogante et Pain en Bottome.

We tried to be smarter when we had the next chef exchange—we invited just one person and avoided the showboats who only worked at international competitions. Mario was a pretty down-to-earth guy who asked us to take him to an American steak dinner on his first night here. We complied and he was complimentary about Iowa beef, although he thought there was too much of it on his plate. He even liked the California cabernet sauvignon that we picked to accompany his dinner. Or was very gracious and said he did.

As before, we planned a fundraising dinner and Michael was again generous and offered to let us use his club's kitchen and restaurant. This time, a member of the Italian delegation volunteered to be sous chef. Gino was here as a business representative from Vicenza but was also an accomplished cook.

The first course of the dinner was to be an onion based soup and Mario put Gino to work chopping the onions. I dropped in to see how things were going and stood by Gino who had a mountain of chopped white onions on the butcher's block. They were small cubes, about one-quarter inch per side, so all that chopping had taken a long time.

While we chatted, Chef Mario came by to check on progress. He pushed some of the onion cubes around and picked up a few of them. He frowned and told Gino they were not all the same size. With a hint of desperation in his voice, Gino said they were for a soup and that no one would know. "I will know," Mario responded sharply and swept all the onions into the trash. He told Gino to start over.

As I left, Gino was softly weeping. And it wasn't from the onions.

UKRAINE: STAY OUT OF THE WATER

Iowa Sister States established a relationship with the Cherkasy Oblast Province of Ukraine in 1996. It is a largely agricultural region but with was some chemical industry in the Oblast. Several exchanges have been conducted with Iowa, including farmers, students, and health care workers.

The population is largely Slavic but by 1922, it was part of the Union of Soviet Socialist Republics (USSR) and the Ukrainian language and culture were suppressed for a heavy emphasis on industrialization which put great pressure on the peasants to provide increasing food supplies. Stalin began a forced collectivization of agriculture during this period. Resisters were deported or shot. Quotas were imposed and productivity collapsed. If the often unrealistic quotas were not met, there would be no grain for the collective farm—its entire output would be seized. Starvation became common and in 1932-33 and over 10 million died in the Great Famine.

Ukraine was heavily damaged during WWII and afterwards, Stalin embarked on ethnic cleansing in Ukraine and deported hundreds of thousands of people to Siberia and Kazakhstan. In 1986, Soviet authorities tried to suppress news of the Chernobyl nuclear disaster there.

In 1991, the Soviet Union collapsed and Ukraine became a sovereign state again. The history of invasion and domination by Russia helps explain the ongoing struggle for independence by its people.

Even after my several years of experience in Russia, I was still surprised by some things in Ukraine, despite Russian attempts to Sovietize them.

GOING TO CHURCH

The end of the Soviet Union made going to church respectable again and in Russia, it became fashionable though many of them had been destroyed or converted to warehouses during Soviet times. We never had the opportunity to attend church services while we were in Russia, but we did when we went to Ukraine.

The church we went to was very crowded and smoky. This was due in part to a lot of lit candles but also to the extensive use of incense by the priest. Since there were no pews, we stood crowded against each other as the service progressed. There was also no music, but occasionally we heard chanting from a choir. People were coming and going during the service although the priest seemed unaware or unconcerned about this. In the Orthodox service, communication is between the priest and God. The congregations are observers, not participants, so if they come and go, it makes no difference. This illustrates the importance of the individual, or the lack of it, which fits nicely into the secular attitudes of communism which also considers the individual unimportant except as a member of a group.

However, during the service, we were not totally unobserved. Older women (babushkas in Russia) were present and watched us closely. I presume they were making sure that we paid to light candles and that we avoided boisterous behavior during the service. As in Russia, the babushkas here wielded a great deal of moral authority.

Typically, Orthodox services were long—at least two hours. The length of the service didn't seem to bother anyone—mainly because most people left after having made an appearance. The babushkas didn't mind, as long as you paid for the candles.

LINE ETIQUETTE

IIn general, there was no such thing as line etiquette in Ukraine, just like in Russia. People had no compunctions about pushing ahead of you to get closer to the bureaucrat who would stamp your visa, passport, license, or whatever document you had.

However, when in line for a boarding pass at the airport, behavior was pretty good since most of us were westerners who had manners. Monty and I waited to check in and get boarding passes for our trip back home. There were some computer failures and power blackouts, and we were getting bored standing there. I had been looking at the line behind us and noticed an elderly woman near the end of the line. She was about five feet tall, skinny, wearing all black, and carrying a cane or umbrella.

A few minutes later, I looked again and she was closer. Somehow, she had bypassed several people in the line. I told Monty about her and he glanced over my shoulder to see her. We continued our chat about the visit and when he looked back again, he said she was still moving up. "How is she doing it?" he puzzled.

Being bored and pretty desperate for entertainment I suggested we try and block her. I told Monty when she got close to us, we should both move sideways to stop her. Monty, who was just as bored as I was, agreed to this plan.

As she approached, somehow getting by people, I moved to the right and Monty to the left. We looked at each other and smiled. But when we looked forward, our smiles disappeared. Somehow, she had passed right by us effortlessly. Having been outfoxed by an elderly widow, we watched her continued progress. She would sidle up to people and when they looked away, she would slip by. Sometimes, she would use her umbrella to gently tap someone who shrank from the touch and she would slip by them. She was amazing and while we could not understand why she was doing this (maybe she was bored too), we were entertained by watching a pro at work.

When it came time to produce boarding passes, she was first in line.

STUDENTS

Iowa Sister States received a grant from the US Department of State to conduct exchanges of high school students from Iowa and

Cherkasy Ukraine. High schools in Urbandale and Marshalltown were paired with two high schools in Cherkasy. Monty, an Urbandale biology teacher agreed to accompany me to Cherkasy to select the students for the exchange and to manage details of the project.

Requirements for the Ukrainian students were set high. They had to be fluent in English, have exceptional grades, have recommendations from their teachers and write an essay in English on why they wanted to participate in this project. For the US students, we required good grades, recommendations from teachers and an essay. Fluency in Ukrainian was not feasible. Because both Ukrainian high school principals were reluctant to make the final choices (for fear of outraged parents), Monty and I did this.

We spent a day at each school interviewing the students and reading their essays. Each school had about 25 finalists and it took all day to review their materials and discuss why they wanted to be part of the project. We had to select six from each school and it was a difficult task because so many of the students were exceptionally qualified. We made our choices, explained to the disappointed finalists, and met with each of the principals. They were pleased with our choices stated that those would likely have been their selections.

While at High School #1, the principal, Sergei, asked Monty and me if we would like to meet one of his recent graduates who had landed a very good job. We agreed and he took us across the street to the McDonald's. Monty inquired of Sergei why he thought McDonald's was such a good job. Sergei explained it paid in US dollars, was clean, provided free food, had good rest rooms, and taught American style management.

"All this at McDonald's?" I wondered. While I tend to be snobbish about McDonald's as a fast food restaurant, there is no denying its success as a company offering a standardized, reasonably priced product. It has a successful management training program that assures consistent, effective management and it is clever enough to add local items to its menu to accommodate local tastes. Their corporate policy worked worldwide. No wonder Sergei was impressed.

THE TASTE TEST

Monty and I interviewed 25 finalists from High School #2 where Nadezhda was principal. It was a long day and the students were all excellent. Eventually we made six choices. She agreed with our choices and then invited us to her home for dinner. This was quite a compliment because in Ukraine, most hospitality was done in restaurants. So we gratefully accepted.

We arrived at her huge apartment building, characteristic of Soviet construction since the Revolution. As usual, the front yard was beaten dirt and the entrance door was broken. The rickety elevator clanked to the eighth floor and we stumbled down a dark, dirty hallway. All the light bulbs were broken or stolen. The floor hadn't been swept since the building was occupied. Then we entered her apartment, brightly lit, perfectly clean and well cared for. No one owns the public spaces, so no one takes care of them. But you have possession of your flat and you take good care of that.

Nadezhda greeted us and said that dinner was not quite ready. She ushered us into her dining room and said that her husband, a retired Russian general, would entertain us. We met a distinguished looking gentleman in his 60s who greeted us with a strong handshake and instructed us to sit by him and drink the vodka shots he was pouring. "Bottoms up," he said needlessly. "What do you think?"

Monty and I agreed that it was very good. He then poured a shot from another bottle into our glasses and again we agreed it was very good.

In a vain attempt to shift the conversation to another topic, Monty asked to hear about the retired general's military career.

Ignoring Monty's attempted diversion, the general asked which drink was better, the first or the second. We looked at each other. Both of the vodkas were excellent and we couldn't tell any difference. So we guessed the first one. "Wrong answer," the general replied. "Try again," and he poured out two more shots. We tasted again and after another round, I said the second one. "Wrong again," he said with a ghost of a smile. "I switched them. One is Ukrainian vodka and one is Russian."

Just as he was unscrewing the caps for another taste test by the hapless Americans, Nadezhda appeared with the appetizers. "Sergei, have you been bothering our guests with your vodka tasting?" she asked sternly. Sergei just smiled and Monty and I dug into our caviar sandwiches having failed the vodka taste test.

My guess is that the general would fail the Coke or Pepsi taste test.

Our selected 12 students and two principals came to Iowa for three weeks and were home hosted by the US students who would later go to Cherkasy. The Ukrainian students accompanied their hosts to classes, to sporting events, and to school dances. The Ukrainians were amazed at abundance and at the newness of things. Most things, anyway: they tested the US McDonald's and approved, saying it was the same as they had in Cherkasy. Some things never change.

POST 911 MADNESS

After the terrorist attacks on September 11, 2001, Homeland Security significantly increased the difficulty of getting any kind of visa to enter the US. Considering the abuses of the past which allowed the terrorists to enter freely and overstay their visas, this response seemed reasonable.

However, like most policies, especially those developed under pressure, it went overboard. Iowa Sister States had a good reputation as an organization that welcomed international visitors and gave them a reasonable view of America, rather than what is shown in movies that we export. To do our job, we had to have international visitors and they had to have visas.

Under the new rules, a potential visitor had to complete a questionnaire about the reasons for the visit and obtain a date for an interview with staff at the US Embassy in their country. It often appeared that the Visa Control Officer required the visa applicants to prove that they were not terrorists, that they planned to return to their own country, and that they had good reasons to return home. It wasn't enough to say that there was family were waiting for them. The Visa Control Officers were afraid to make a mistake leading to granting a visa to a person intent on doing harm to the US. So, they made the interviews as difficult as possible with the intent of tripping up first timers and the unwary. The Visa Control Officer had tremendous authority and there was no appeal of his decision. You could appeal to the Secretary of State to determine if procedures had been followed, but the appeal would not include the actual decision itself.

On a State Department funded program for Ukraine, the high school students got visas but their principal was rejected. Turned out he had the same name as a terrorist on the no-fly list. Fortunately, State Department staff cleared this up for us. But on another occasion, nothing helped. We had invited a high school basketball team from Tianjin, Chibna to come to Iowa to play exhibition games against high school teams here. We carefully explained the visa application process to the students and their coaches. When the day came for their interviews at the Embassy, only half the students and half the coaches were granted visas. Half the team and half the coaches came and played mixed team exhibition games with Iowa schools. So we had exhibition games with half a team, thanks to our half-brained government.

AQUA MASSAGE

I've had massages before, and I really like them. They reduce my stress and alleviate aches and pains. So, one day when my Ukrainian hosts didn't know what to do with me for a few hours, they suggested a massage at the local sanitarium. After they clarified that this was not a mental or TB sanitarium, I accepted.

My massage therapist was Marina, about 25-years-old, five feet six inches tall and maybe 115 pounds, but muscular. She asked "Swedish type?' I said yes. "Firm pressure?" Again, I said yes.

Firm is one of those words that can mean a lot of different things. Firm pasta is al dente. Firm mattresses have some flexibility. Firm pudding means a thin film over a semi solid mass.

In Ukrainian massages, firm means crushing, unyielding force applied with phenomenal leverage by a 115 pound girl. She only gave me a couple of minutes of what I considered "firm" before charging ahead into torture land. My moans and groans urged her on to new heights or depths. After this bruising (literally) workout, she briskly rubbed me down with oil.

Thinking I was done, I started to slide off the table and wrap my sheet around me. "No, no," she said. "Must rinse off oil." She pointed to an oddly shaped tub—something like a large urinal on stubby legs. I squatted in it with a towel over my shrunken genitals. (No need to give her any more amusement after all the moaning and groaning, I thought). Then Marina came back with what appeared to be a garden hose.

"Rinse off," she said and turned on the fire hydrant. I was blasted back into the wall of the tub/urinal and globules of oil were flying into the air in a sort of mist. My muscles were shuddering like I was experiencing G forces. "Turn over", she commanded and I was too numb to object. A few more minutes of intense pressure and it was suddenly over.

I gasped for a few minutes, gathered my senses and somehow found the strength to dry off with a big Turkish towel, and got dressed.

"Thank you, Marina," I said in my creaky Ukrainian.

"It was nothing," she said in perfect English, smiling.

"Nothing indeed," I thought. My answering smile was a grimace. After I returned home, I told this story to Jill, my massage therapist in Iowa. She laughed so hard that she had to stop the massage she was giving me at the time. Then she asked if I wanted her to continue with firm pressure or Ukrainian pressure. I maintained a dignified silence while she continued chuckling.

THE ROWBOAT AND THE YACHT

On one of my trips to Cherkasy, it was unusually hot, even for summertime Ukraine. We had finished our morning appointments and my hosts were talking in Ukrainian deciding what to do with me. "Too hot to go back to the hotel," they said. "No air conditioning."

They suggested a ride in a boat on the river. By now you know that I don't like boats (even cruise ships for that matter). I flunked the YMCA swimming class in the 8th grade and have been averse to any water over three inches deep ever since. Usually it takes several ounces of ethanol and peer pressure to get me into a boat. This was a peer pressure moment but, not wanting to disappoint them, I agreed to go, tensing up at the mere thought of it.

We went down to the banks of the Dnieper River and I realized that this was a really big river, maybe not Mississippi size, but big nonetheless. It looked even bigger when I saw the "boat." It looked like a kid's toy, maybe 10 feet long. Too late to chicken out, I gingerly stepped aboard and we (they) rowed out into the middle of the Dnieper. Of course, it was hot out there too and the sun was reflecting off the river. Sunglasses were not much help. We drifted around for a few minutes and then one of my hosts got out some fishing tackle. I worried that he actually might catch something and that we would have to eat it. I frantically tried to remember if the Dnieper flowed past Chernobyl. If it was a two-headed fish, I decided, I would make them throw it back.

As I sweated and worried about radioactive fish, I discovered the Dnieper is navigable when some rather large barges and ships came by. We rocked and rolled in their wake and a few of them said things to us in Ukrainian that were probably not pleasant greetings.

Just as I was about to plead for mercy, they decided to go back to shore. We arrived hot but fishless.

The next morning, I told my colleague, Sheri, about this unnerving experience and she said, "Oops, I accepted a ride this evening on a yacht." I got pale, but then she explained that it was a 12 meter racing yacht and they wouldn't go out until sunset. More peer pressure.

At sunset, we boarded what looked like a pretty nice 12 meter yacht—into which could have fit three of my rowboats of the day before. The skipper casted off, raised the sail, and we glided into the Dnieper. I had begun to relax my grip on the rail when it started to get cloudy and the wind picked up.

I asked Sheri what the Ukrainian word for thunderhead was. She looked astern and said, "Uh oh." Just then the storm hit us with heavy rain, lightning, and thunder. It also got very windy and the skipper sent us below deck. This clearly was not a luxury yacht. "Below" was about six feet in diameter and surrounded by sailing gear. Sheri and I were talking quietly by flashlight—no electricity on the yacht either—when we noticed that even though the rain and wind were still raging, the yacht was not rocking as much. She climbed up the ladder and peeked out, then reported that the skipper had tied us up to some trees on an island in the river.

We continued to talk about whether the yacht had lifejackets (it didn't) or how long a person could float in the Dnieper (no comment). It was too discouraging so we traded life stories for a while, fully expecting that the stories would end that evening.

Finally, the skipper's head appeared and he said the storm was over and we could come on deck.

He was right. The storm had moved on and the wind and waves were dying down. He looked at Sheri and me and asked one of the dumbest questions of the decade. "Should we go on or go back to the dock?"

One look from us was sufficient answer for him and we motored back to shore.

Our ancestors left the water world long ago. I feel we should respect the evolutionary pressures that led to that momentous decision and stay on dry land.

THE COGNAC SWORD

Monty and I were at the end of a successful visit to Cherkasy and were thanking our hosts for their hospitality when one of them presented each of us with a parting gift—a glass sword about three feet long and filled with cognac. We were speechless, but managed to croak our thanks. What I was really thinking was that there was no way I could get rid of it, so I would have to find a way to get it home.

Like the Russians, Ukrainians don't care about international conventions and produce a brandy that they call cognac even though real "Cognac" is limited to brandies produced in the Cognac region of France. And like everything else, there is a range of quality in these "cognacs" produced in the former Soviet Union. Armenian cognac is the best. What was in these glass swords was probably not the best quality since its primary function was to provide a nice light brown color in the transparent sword.

The drive to Kiev was uneventful and Monty and I clutched our swords and hoped that the bumpy road would not shatter them and spill Ukrainian cognac all over us. Our first flight was on Lufthansa to Frankfurt. The flight attendants were very accommodating and agreed to store our swords in the rear of the plane. When we arrived at Frankfurt, we looked pretty dangerous with our glass swords, but the young German security police merely regarded us as foolish tourists.

When we boarded the United flight to Chicago, the flight attendants came to our rescue and took our glass weaponry to the rear of the plane. Seven hours later, as we approached O'Hare, one of the flight attendants appeared with one of the swords, apologizing profusely explaining that the second sword had broken. "You take it Monty," I shouted before he could say anything. The flight attendant went on to say how bad they felt and that we should please accept the two bottles of wine she handed us. I said thanks and assured her that these things happened and there were no hard feelings. What I was thinking was that two bottles of wine from the first class cabin in exchange for a glass sword filled with indifferent cognac was a very good deal. I could tell that Monty was thinking the same thing.

We got through Immigration and Customs without a hitch. The Customs official glanced at the sword and waved us through. I figured he'd probably tasted the cognac in those swords and wasn't interested in any more of it.

Finally, when we were at Security, I went through first with no problems. I noticed that Monty was doing a lot of explaining to a Security official who was holding the sword. In another minute, there were four additional Security officers at the scanner. I could see Monty and he didn't seem concerned, just annoyed. Finally, he came out with the sword in hand. According to Monty, they had never seen one of the glass swords before and each of them wanted to see what it looked like going through the scanner. "I should have given it to them as a training device," he said. I thought to myself, "They would never have accepted it."

Ten years later, I ran into Monty at a fund raiser for Iowa Sister States and inquired about the sword. "Holding up just fine," he said. I asked him if he had ever tried the cognac. "I'm waiting for it to eat its way through the glass," he replied.

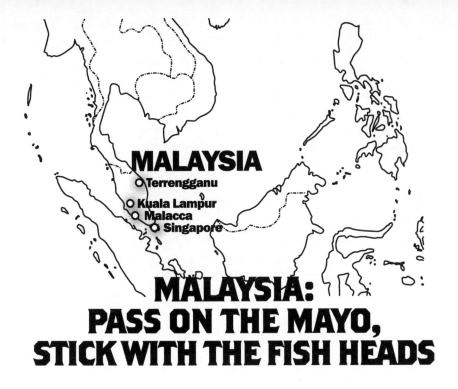

MALAYSIA:
PASS ON THE MAYO,
STICK WITH THE FISH HEADS

Along the Straits of Malacca, Malaysia occupies some of the most strategic geography in the world. The two-mile wide, 500-mile long strait separates Malaysia and Sumatra and connects the Pacific and Indian oceans. For centuries, trade between China and India and later Europe passed through the straits to avoid the long detour around Indonesia. And, for centuries, pirates infested the straits. As the European countries began trading for spices, they sought ways to protect their ships from the pirates.

After independence in 1957, the government has retained a constitutional monarchy with a British style parliament and legal system. Recent discovery of significant oil and gas reserves as well as booming electronics manufacturing and tourism resulted in significant economic growth for Malaysia. They have planned to achieve first world economic status within the next 10 years. However, to join the club of first world nations, Malaysia must solve its historic problems of discrimination of minorities.

Unlike many Muslim counties, Malaysia is forward-looking and pursues economic development. There are occasional clashes with Western culture. Beyoncé had to cancel concerts in 2007 and 2009 because of protests that her costumes and choreography would be immoral.

On my first trip, I was amazed by the beauty of Malaysia—its verdant forests and the profusion of flowers. Its beaches are world famous for the brilliant white sand and deep blue waters and the scuba diving opportunities are among the best. The people were beautiful, friendly, and well educated. The shopping malls were modern with the latest stores and much of south Asia's people come here to shop. The future looks bright for Malaysia.

CYCLONES

Because of our partnership with the Olympic Council, we were working with some very influential people and they arranged things for us that ordinary tourists did not experience. We ate dinner at the restaurant at the top of the television tower for instance. Thankfully alcohol is available for tourists in Kuala Lumpur (It is referred to as KL by the locals), even though Islam forbids it. So after a couple of martinis, I was able to appease my vertigo about the location. In addition to hating airplanes and boats, I'm not crazy about heights, either.

Petronas Towers.

On another occasion, we were taken to the Petronas Towers. These two, round skyscrapers were owned by the national oil producing company which had a lot to do with Malaysia's economic success. The towers were beautiful twin buildings which were connected on the 41st floor by an enclosed bridge. Our friends at the Olympic Council had arranged for us to visit the towers and cross between them using the bridge. This is a two-level bridge, with the upper level open to tourists. The lower level was for official business and special guests and was all glass on the bottom with only three inches of plexiglass is between you and the ground, 41 stories below. It was breathtaking, and for me, absolutely terrifying.

My colleagues just scooted out onto the bridge and began taking pictures of the scenery below and of each other. Meanwhile, with no martinis in sight, my vertigo had me rooted to the spot while I calculated how fast I would be going when I hit the ground after plunging through that flimsy looking floor. (Very fast with acceleration of 32 feet per second per second, excluding air resistance). Our young Malaysian tour guide came up to me and asked if I was OK. I looked at her, 5 feet tall, weighing about 95 pounds and dressed in her blue blazer, white blouse, and gray skirt and shakily said that no, I was not OK. And I was thinking about going back down and meeting the team on the ground floor of the other building.

She agreed I could to that, but perhaps she could take my hand and we could walk to the other side together. Trying not to seem like as big of chicken as I felt, I agreed to try.

I have no idea what the conversation was or what I said, but I do remember her English was perfect and she was beautiful the way so many Malaysians are. I was able to maintain some sort of conversation with her as we walked what seemed like 100 miles of glass over 10,000 feet high.

When we got to the other side, I thanked her profusely for helping me get over my serious acrophobia. She said she was happy to do it. I mentioned that her English was perfect and without the British accent we heard so often there. "I was an undergraduate at Iowa State University," she responded. "There are enough of us here to have an alumni association."

It's true. Cyclones are everywhere.

STEAMBOAT AND THE COLONEL

We spent much of our time in KL. It is a sprawling city with a modern veneer over a very old Asian city. The rapid growth of the economy is shown in all the new construction and the modernization of the society is reflected in many women walking alone and without covering their hair. Such brazenness is more or less accepted in foreign women, but even Malaysians are adopting these new ways of dress. However, there is ongoing discrimination against the Indian and Chinese minorities. Quotas that restrict the number of ethnic Chinese still exist for admission to the best schools and many professions. Still, Malaysia is one of the more tolerant of the Muslim states with a philosophy that embraces modernity and seeks to succeed in the current world environment.

With such a diverse population, cuisine was complex and varied. Spices permeate all cooking, of course, and seafood was pervasive in recognition of its extensive seacoasts and long history of sailing and fishing.

Part of the grant project included a visit to Iowa by the coaches we had trained in KL. They were astonished by the usual things—how big everything was, how much space we had in our homes and how we were able to get hard working people to volunteer their time to organize and supervise sports in their neighborhoods and communities. It was a very successful visit except for one thing—the food. It was boring and incredibly bland for people coming from a culture with complex spicy food. I remembered the consultant who came to Iowa to work in small community hospitals and had been presented with a bottle of Tabasco by the waitress whose cousin (a waitress in a different café) heard him say he wanted more spicy food. So I took a tip from her and saved the day by presenting to each of them a large bottle of Tabasco sauce which they used liberally to make our cooking palatable.

In KL, we found most menus were much more Western in the places where we ate, but the quality was always very good. On one visit, I met with some local men for dinner at a restaurant where the "locals" eat. It was in a basement with plain checkered tablecloths and wooden chairs. The specialty was Steamboat. We were brought a container of boiling water on a charcoal brazier. Into this we dropped vegetables, noodles, fish, and shrimp, fishing them out with chopsticks and draining them onto plates of steamed rice. We seasoned everything with chili sauce (which I had to dilute with water—too hot for my developing taste).

Another time, we drove to a large building in a park. Our hosts told us how happy they were to invite us here. It was once an exclusive British dining club and Malaysians were not permitted there, except as waiters. Now the Malaysians own it and they permit British guests to enter without requiring them to be waiters. They were very proud of this accomplishment, but I found the atmosphere still pretty stuffy, probably a holdover from the British period. And the food was only mediocre—probably another holdover.

As we drove through the crowded, traffic jammed streets of KL, we saw many different kinds of restaurants—even McDonald's. I was apologizing to our hosts for inflicting this American food on them when they said that this was popular with their children.

The most popular Western restaurant is Kentucky Fried Chicken. All cultures, except vegetarian Hindus, eat chicken and statues of Colonel Sanders are everywhere.

Halfway around the world, extra crispy is available.

SPORTS AND FISH HEAD SOUP

Since independence in 1957, Malaysian sports have been focused on finding and training elite athletes who would complete in the Olympics and Commonwealth Games. Also during the rapid economic development of the country, parents and teachers placed major emphasis on studying. Although education was critically important to success, it became clear there were negative effects of a lack of physical fitness, in addition to the missed educational opportunities that come from sports participation itself.

The Prime Minister began a program that encouraged local athletics and sports programs. He had sports facilities built across the country, but few attended. So he turned to the US government for support. Iowa Sister States was awarded two grants by the US Department of State to conduct projects in Malaysia, in cooperation with Iowa statewide and community level park and recreation directors, to facilitate the development of Malaysian community sports programs. Our partner in Malaysia was the Olympic Council.

For our first trip, I led a group of several community park and recreation directors and the director of the statewide association. It was a long tiring flight—thirteen hours from Chicago to Tokyo, then another five hours to Singapore where we overnighted before taking the flight to KL next morning. Kuala is the Malaysian word for river. So the city is Lumpur River, named for the river that flows through it.

There were five of us traveling together and one more person arriving the next day. This latecomer was Dave, a prima donna who managed the park and recreation program in a large Iowa city. He claimed that he was too busy to travel with us, but our consensus was that he just wanted to make an entrance.

Our colleagues from the Olympic Council were very gracious and had even found us a better hotel at the same local government rate and took us there when we arrived. Of course, Dave didn't know this and when he arrived, the original hotel knew nothing about where we were. After several frustrating hours for him, he finally tracked us down and moved in.

The main problem with the sports issue seemed to be that Malaysians were accustomed to the national government taking care of things. But its strategy of build-it-and-they-will-come in regards to the sports facilities had failed. We were there to show how local community volunteers could organize and conduct sports activities in their towns at very low cost. Surprisingly, Malaysians were not used to volunteering for things and we had quite a bit of work convincing the local officials that this was feasible.

Our team trained the local officials in techniques for creating interest in local sports and in facilitating participation by adults as volunteers. We also had to develop strategies for making sports interesting and fun so that students would forgo some of their study time to get some exercise and fresh air. This went well and we conducted two exhibition matches in different parts of the country.

Malaysia is a largely Muslim country with very strict rules about women in public. But we found that girls were eager to participate in sports. In Terengganu, one of the most politically conservative parts of the country, our sports exhibition drew a girls' netball team which included three Muslim girls who played the game in full burkhas. They said they were hot, but they loved the exercise.

Throughout our stay, Dave proved to be a real pain. He was often late and rambled in his lectures. His biggest complaint was lunch. We were teaching the sports directors in the building owned by the Malaysia Olympic Council. It had good teaching facilities and many athletes stayed in its hotel rooms and ate in the training table cafeteria. We did too. The food was Malaysian and was excellent, although quite different from the Midwestern US diet. Dave was unhappy about what he called "fish head soup" and said so on several occasions.

The day before we left, Dave came to lunch late and started with his fish head soup complaints again. One of the staff overheard him and offered to make a club sandwich which seemed to placate him. The sandwich arrived, three decks of toast with lettuce, tomato, sliced chicken (but no bacon) slathered in mayonnaise. Dave wolfed it down, having forgotten to thank his hosts for their extra effort on his behalf.

The next day we had a late departure from the Kuala Lumpur International Airport, so we planned to spend the day touring Putrajaya, the new capital city of Malaysia. Like many developing countries, the original capital city of Kuala Lumpur was old, crowded, and not suitable for a growing country with an expanding bureaucracy. So, they built a new capital city using local architects to design spectacular buildings. Like many other such changes, the government officials were fighting a rearguard action to avoid moving out of Kuala Lumpur to Putrajaya.

Dave was unable to join us for the tour. He had been up all night sick, and skipped the tour to rest. When he arrived at the airport he looked pretty grim and he was pretty miserable on the long flights home.

We found out that mayonnaise for his club sandwich had been aging long past the expiration date. It would have been kind of us to be empathetic and try to help. But, we were human and gloated about the delicious fish head soup we had had the day before. Revenge is indeed a dish best served cold.

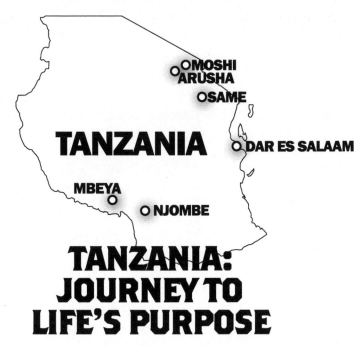

TANZANIA: JOURNEY TO LIFE'S PURPOSE

For the geographically challenged, Tanzania is located on the East Coast of Africa by the Indian Ocean. It is one of the oldest sites of human settlement in the world. Four degrees south of the equator and about four times larger than Texas, Tanzania has a population of 45 million.

During the 19th and 20th centuries, the area that is now Tanzania was under typical colonial rule. This meant minimal development and little preparation for the independence that came in 1961. It should be acknowledged that of the colonial powers, the British were among the better ones. They gave Tanzania its political structure and its legal and educational systems. On the other hand, at independence, there were only fourteen physicians for the entire country.

After independence, Tanzania embarked on an experiment in socialism, mostly in reaction to the depredations of colonial capitalism. The experiment was largely unsuccessful and gradually a free market economy was established.

However, one component of socialism remains—the government owns all the land. Colonial policies in Zimbabwe that allowed white farmers to keep their land after independence were disastrous. Eventually the farms were expropriated, often by force and violence and agricultural productivity declined significantly. By contrast, in

Tanzania, the government owns all the land, and the people can lease the land for up to 99 years and can leave the lease to their children.

Working with American volunteers in cooperation with Tanzanians has changed the lives of Tanzanians—but it also changed the lives of the American volunteers, including me. We have become much more conscious of our wealth and our waste. We value our relationships more and have become deeply empathetic to others. The following experiences illustrate my observations and understanding of Tanzania and its people who are some of the warmest and most resilient people I have ever met.

IN THE BEGINNING...

Tanzania is one of the poorest countries in the world with an average annual income of $360. It has one of the highest HIV/AIDS infection rates in the world and many tropical diseases are endemic there. It needs just about everything to develop.

My involvement in Tanzania began with a chance reading of a notice that the American International Health Alliance (AIHA) was now working in Africa. I had managed two medical exchange projects in Russia for AIHA, so I went to their website to learn more. One of the countries participating was Tanzania, which faintly rang a bell in something I had heard in church. I called my church office and asked about Tanzania and was referred to the Bishop's office.

In a few minutes, I was speaking to Bishop Philip Hougen of the Southeast Iowa Synod of the Evangelical Lutheran Church of America (ELCA) who told me that he and Bishop Msangi of the Pare Diocese, Evangelical Lutheran Church of Tanzania (ELCT) were partners in establishing relationships between congregations in Iowa and in Tanzania. He explained that he and Bishop Msangi had been trying to find a health project without success so far and would I be willing to look into this.

Who can resist a Bishop? I made a few calls and learned from my colleagues at AIHA that faith-based organizations were eligible for funding from the President's Emergency Plan for AIDS Relief (PEPFAR). When I called Bishop Hougen back and told him this news, he asked if I would draft a Palliative Care Project proposal for the Southeast Iowa Synod and the Pare Diocese. Again, I couldn't resist the Bishop and I agreed.

After some backing and forthing, the proposal was approved by AIHA. Bishop Hougen told me that he and Bishop Msangi wanted me to manage this project. I explained that I already had a job, but he was insistent. "We know that you can do it," was his response.

My board of directors at Iowa Sister States agreed I could do this provided I did it on my own time and used my vacation when I needed to go to Tanzania. So in 2006, I started managing the Palliative Care Project from Iowa Sister States. When I retired in 2008, Empower Tanzania (ETI) had been created and I transferred it there. The project has now phased out of the PEPFAR program into local support.

This initial project focused on palliative care (end of life care) for terminally ill HIV/AIDS patients. The Tanzanian health system cannot do anything more for these people, so they are sent home to die. We trained over 200 Community Health Workers (CHW), giving them basic skills to provide comfort care to the dying and to train their families on how to keep them as comfortable as possible. Our trainees were the types of people who would volunteer to take care of their neighbors anyway—we just taught them skills and gave them some basic materials to do this better.

This work connected me with other people in the SE Iowa Synod Lutheran churches who were partnering with churches in that same Pare Diocese in Tanzania. The original covenants focused on spiritual relationships, but once Americans had traveled to their partner church, they thought of many projects that would help improve the lives of the people there. However, the Americans soon became frustrated with legal restrictions that prevented church groups from qualifying for governmental or private foundation grants to do these projects.

So, a group of us did the American thing and formed our own non-profit, non-governmental organization, Empower Tanzania, Inc. and obtained tax exempt status (501c3). We continued the PEPFAR project, absorbed and expanded several church projects, and created new programs. Our focus is improving the life of Tanzanians in rural areas through programs in education, health, and development.

A key element in Empower Tanzania's successful work is developing relationships with the Tanzanian people. Nothing lasting ever happens there unless this close relationship exists. We always begin by meeting with local officials, stakeholders, educators, and village leaders and listening to what they say their needs are. Then we listen some more before we begin to offer suggestions on dealing with these needs. We try to arrive at a solution that is satisfactory to everyone and is sustainable. This approach doesn't always work, but the alternative of Americans parachuting in with solutions and then going home—that never works.

HOSPITALITY

Despite being exploited as a colony for over a century by countries predominantly white, Tanzanians seem to bear no grudges against Wazungu. Wazungu is a Bantu word that literally means, "People who wander about aimlessly." It initially referred to the European explorers in Africa in the 18th century. It is often used by children and from the mouth of a child who has never seen a white person before, it is a term of wonder. From older more cynical kids, it probably means "whitey" or even "honky." Adults never used this word with us, fearing that we might take offense. However, at times, people from Tanzania used that word to emphasize that the visitors were from the US. Now, it means just about any white person. We think that that is how people mean it when they describe us. Perhaps there are still some disgruntled people, but we have seen no evidence of this.

Visiting a terminally Ill AIDS patient.

Visiting a mother who has AIDS and child who is HIV positive.

Everywhere we went, we were greeted warmly and with great hospitality. Even the poorest villages fed us rice, chicken and vegetables—foods that were so expensive that they could not afford it for themselves. We were met with the same hospitality from individual families. We were always made to feel welcome and that our visit was a blessing even to desperately poor, terminally ill AIDS patients.

After we built relationships with these small communities and developed mutual confidence, Rev. Joas, who manages the Palliative Care project, was able to convince the villagers that these were business meetings and that our budget should pay for them without violating their customs of hospitality.

Pastor Joas Mpinda is a key member of the team that manages Empower Tanzania's projects. He was a Tanzanian agricultural engineer before he got the call to become a Lutheran pastor. When the person serving as Tanzanian Coordinator for the project left, Rev. Joas took over. His warm, engaging personality endears him to everyone and he knows most people by name. His skill and understanding of cultural and political problems and helping find ways to resolve them has been of immeasurable importance to the success of our project.

PALLIATIVE CARE

The initial PEPFAR funded Palliative Care Project that ETI was involved in began in the Same and Mwanga Districts of the Kilimanjaro Region by training health care professionals that palliative care was useful even though they don't have time to provide this care, and that lay people can do it instead.

When we started, I put the word out for volunteer physicians, nurses, and other health care providers in Iowa. I was inundated with applications. Health care providers are suckers for things like this. All they had to do was arrange to go with us. They did this without any compensation. We just bought the plane tickets. I tell them that they can go to where they are needed, and that they can do their training or practice without any paperwork. They jump at the chance to effect real change where it is needed. It is in their DNA to do this. Still, many of the US volunteers were nervous and asked, "How can we teach them anything? They know more about HIV/AIDS than we do."

Small Group Session.

Once there, the US team faced some additional obstacles. It was hot and, of course, no air conditioning—just some inadequate fans. It was crowded and the Americans had to get used to the fact that Africans tend to come into our personal space when they greet you. It was also noisy, because the training center was downtown and un-muffled motorbikes kept going by. The power would go off at unpredictable times and Power Point presentations became useless, so they improvised: low tech flip charts saved the day.

The US faculty was also concerned about some of the teaching methods they planned to use, such as breakout groups and role plays. The British style of education that Tanzanians were used to is very traditional - mainly the teacher talks and the students listen and write down everything. Despite these concerns, the 60 Tanzanian health providers who came to Same for the first training session took to these new ways of learning very well. They managed the breakout sessions without problems and loved the role playing exercises.

But even before the training began, Todd Byerly, a US missionary Empower Tanzania works with, and I were next door discussing the next day's schedule when two of the trainees approached us. They were the President and Secretary of the class. Oftentimes, in training sessions, these officers are elected to maintain order and to report on the previous day's work. They explained that the trainees complained that the per diem payments for lodging and meals are not enough and they wanted sitting fees.

Sitting fees are payments for attending a training class, in addition to per diem payments for transportation, lodging, and meals. Our donor agency had a policy forbidding paying sitting fees since the attendee's employers were still paying their daily salary.

Todd and I met and agreed the per diems were too low because all the guest houses had raised their prices in anticipation of the training conference. The next morning, we apologized for the mistake in the per diems and said we thought the adjustment was fair. Heads nodded. Then we explained that our donors would not pay sitting fees and we agreed with this policy. We explained that most of our project money should go to help their neighbors suffering from AIDS. This had the desired effect. We told them we understood if some of the trainees could not accept this decision and any that chose to leave should see Todd for their reimbursement for travel. It worked and things went along smoothly.

We did the second training in the Mwanga District. Todd, Frank, and I went a day before the US team arrived to set up the hall. It was big enough for the 45 we expected, but Todd had to buy lumber and build a frame for a flip chart. The wood was too hard to nail and he had to drill holes for screws. Then we started setting up and testing the video projector for the Power Point presentations.

Although we had tested the projector when we arrived, an hour later it didn't work. Todd is an electrician and Frank a community college teacher in physics and math. They tested the connections on the projector and the linkage to the computer, looking for the problem. After an hour, Todd and Frank were frustrated and starting to worry. Just as they were ready to disassemble the electric plugs, the headmaster appeared and apologized, saying he hoped we were not inconvenienced that the power had been cut off for the past hour. We looked at him and at each other thinking, "How stupid can we be that we hadn't thought of that?"

Frank admitted that was the last thing he would have checked. I told him I should hope so, because if he kept looking after finding it, that would be stupid. The look I got from Todd and Frank are unprintable except in symbols.

Our third and final, training was held in the Lutheran Cathedral in Same again, the only building big enough to handle the 96 attendees. This time, the US faculty included Dr. Yogi, a very warm and friendly person who charmed the entire group. Things went well, even with such a large class. Dr. Yogi had to leave before we finished because he had a commitment elsewhere in Tanzania. We were able to complete the training without him, but he was genuinely missed. Before he left, one of the team members arranged to take a photo of Dr. Yogi smiling with his right hand extended.

At the conclusion of the training, we had a graduation ceremony during which the faculty lined up to hand out certificates of completion and shake hands. Bishop Msangi was able to attend a few of the training sessions and came to the graduation ceremony to shake hands and thank the graduates. Behind the spot where he stood, we had set up the screen and projector to show Dr. Yogi's image. When the image appeared, there was cheering and shouting. Bishop Msangi had never had such a reception before and was flattered by the attention. Then he turned around and saw Dr. Yogi's image.

He took it in stride.

Mt. Kilimanjaro.

At the end of my first trip to Tanzania, I was trying to absorb the hundreds of impressions I had received during my two week visit. It's a cliché but Tanzania really is a land of contrasts. There was the great natural beauty of the land, from the plains which looked like Eastern Colorado with low bushes and flat topped Acacia trees, to the Pare Mountains, not so tall, but very steep, rising from the plain like the Tetons do in Wyoming.

On the other hand, poverty is always in your face. The houses are poor quality mud brick, and usually without electricity or plumbing. Women are always seen carrying something on their heads: water, firewood, or farm tools.

Yet the people are warm and giving. They want help to develop their country, but it's hard for them to know what to do first. Everything is a priority because they need everything.

We drove from the city of Moshi to the Kilimanjaro International airport on a clear day and Mount Kilimanjaro, usually hidden by clouds, was visible. In fact, both peaks were visible, a very rare occurrence. Kili, as the locals call it, looked magnificent. It is the highest mountain in Africa and the glaciers at the peak were clearly visible. While I was mesmerized by the view, I noticed that there was a pickup truck parked on the shoulder and the driver was standing outside looking at Kili. I thought to myself, "Isn't that great? They see it every day, but still stop to look at it and marvel at it."

Actually, no. As we pass his truck, I saw that he was urinating.

I realized then that they are just like us. Most New Yorkers have never been to the Statue of Liberty either.

GETTING ACQUAINTED WITH THE MAASAI

During the first year of the Palliative Care Project, we met Rev. Msuya, a Lutheran pastor who wanted us to visit a Maasai tribe who were part of his congregation. Lutheran Maassi, I asked? They are

Lutherans?" I asked. He explained yes, and said they had just built a school for their kids with support from an international NGO and they wanted us to see it. So we drove to the village of Nadaruru for what turned out to be our first of many meetings with the Maasai.

The Maasai are nomadic, cattle herding people who reside in Kenya and northern Tanzania. For many years, they lived in what became the game parks of Ngorongoro Crater and Serengeti. However, the government's growing reliance on tourism resulted in the expulsion of the Maasai to other remote parts of the country where they had to settle, similar to the ways the US government treated the Native Americans. The Maasai have a strong culture which has been resistant to modernization or integration into the Tanzanian society. They are polygamous, which the Christian churches have overlooked.

We drove about 40 miles on the dirt road leading to the town of Maore. Lots of bouncing and swerving as our driver, Martin, tried to find the smooth spots and still maintain a decent speed. After about an hour, he slowed and turned off the road. Rev. Msuya pointed off into the bush and said "Nadaruru."

There was no sign or any indication that this was the place to turn, but Martin seemed to know somehow. We then went cross country, passing thorn bushes, going into dry creek beds, and crossing a desolate plain. Occasionally, we could see faint tire tracks or cattle droppings that indicated that there were people out here, somewhere.

After 20 minutes, I was hopelessly lost, but fortunately Martin wasn't. A small concrete building appeared and we pulled up and got out. After working the kinks out of our joints, we were ready to meet the Maasai who were waiting to greet us. Rev. Msuya introduced us to Chief Isaiah, giving me, as the oldest, precedence. The chief was short (maybe 5'6) and slender, but had an air of authority. He made eye contact as we shook hands. (Most Tanzanians give limp handshakes and don't like to make eye contact—it's too confrontational.) The rest of our five-member team of doctors and nurses was introduced and we went inside the building.

They sat us in a row on plastic lawn chairs in a bare concrete room. I think that Tanzania is the world's graveyard for plastic chairs. They are everywhere. Rev. Msuya translated their greetings to us from Maa (Maasai language) into Swahili which Rev. Joas, our Coordinator, translated into English since his English was better than Rev. Msuya's.

This translation chain reported that the school was built with funds from World Vision. "The Maasai did the construction and soon it would have desks for the children. The government would send a teacher and the children would go to school there.

Pam, one of our nurses, asked if the girls would go to school also. Chief Isaiah replied that yes, they would. This surprised us because traditionally the Maasai do not send their kids to school, especially the girls. He went on to say they knew that sending the children to school would lead to changes in their culture, but he thought it was best for them if they learned.

You have no idea how much, I thought to myself.

While the Chief was speaking, the women of the tribe came into the room. They were dressed in their best, with beads, necklaces, and earrings dangling from their drooping earlobes. They sat on the floor opposite us, without speaking. Opposite me was clearly the eldest woman in the tribe. The younger women made sure she was comfortable. I learned later that this was Mama Maria, the senior woman in Nadaruru and possessed of great authority and status. All I knew at the time was that she was staring directly at me with a skeptical expression on her face. I guessed she was thinking I was just another Wazungu from America.

While the Chief continued to describe the construction of the school, women began bringing in lunch. Rice and goat meat were in plastic buckets and were ladled into bowls for each of us. We were given tablespoons and we dug in. Accepting hospitality is critical in Tanzania, especially with the Maasai. The only people eating were the Americans and the Maasai men who were the elders. I learned later that women never eat with the men. Always separately and always with the less desirable parts of whatever meat was served. The women then brought in our beverages. All Coca Cola products. Coke has most of the market, at least in this part of Tanzania. They have been very successful in marketing its unhealthy beverages to the people of Tanzania. Soda breaks during training programs are common and attendees expect that they will have them twice daily.

So we sat on our plastic chairs, eating goat and rice with our big spoons and drinking warm Coke or Sprite. After lunch, the women took our bowls and began to clean up. We made a few comments congratulating them on their school and were getting ready to leave.

Then Pam asked, if they had any other problems or issues they wanted to tell us about.

This opened the floodgates. Several Maasai, both women and men, began speaking quickly and one man very passionately. I was getting nervous about all this emotion and looking at the long sharp knives the men carried. Our interpreters had a hard time keeping up with this emotional outburst. But the gist was that their women were dying in childbirth. They live over 16 miles from the nearest health facility and there were not even any traditional midwives in Nadaruru. If a woman had a problem with the delivery of her child, she started walking towards town and usually died along the way. We learned later that maternal mortality among the Maasai is twice as high as the rest of Tanzania - 578 deaths per 100,000 live births. The US is 27/100,000. We also learned that girls are married when they are as young as 12 years old and they have not fully matured physically. Traditionally women reduce their calorie intake during the third trimester hoping to have smaller babies which will be easier to deliver, not realizing that this malnutrition can negatively affect them and will definitely cause development problems for their babies.

We expressed our sympathy with the Maasai and our hope that they would find a solution to this problem. Then we returned to our hotel.

Later that afternoon, I went out to the hotel patio to have an informal debriefing with the team. This was a customary way for us to process the day's experiences and share any insights. As I sat in my plastic chair, Pam turned to me and asked "what I was going to do about it?" When I asked her what I was going to do about what, she said "The unacceptable mortality rate among the Maasai women." I explained our project deals with death at the other end of the spectrum, people dying from AIDS, and although the Maasai situation is very sad, it was outside of our project goals. She indicated that she and the rest of the team agreed that they didn't care about project goals. We have to do something, and we want you to do it, she explained.

Although Pam wasn't a Bishop, she was persuasive and I was unable to resist her heartfelt plea and agreed to try to do something about it. Thus began our long connection with the Maasai. And my first step to Maasai chief.

Maasai Church. Left to Right: Todd Byerly and Evangelist.

Because our first partner was the Pare Diocese of the ELCT, we usually attended services where the staff worshipped. About 40 percent of the Tanzanian population is Christian of various denominations, and 40 Percent are Muslim with the remainder belonging to various nativist religions. All of them seem to get along pretty well, except for the fanatics, of whom some are still at large.

We attended Lutheran services in several different rural communities, including the Maasai, where the service was recognizable even though it was done in Swahili. Since there were no local newspapers, a part of the service was devoted to a report on the latest local news, and a delegation from Iowa was always news. We were called upon to stand, identify ourselves, and deliver greetings from the Bishop in the US.

Because of all these extras, the service lasted at least two hours. The time flew by quickly with the help of the churches' outstanding choirs. Whenever they knew we would be attending, the church would take up a collection at least one additional time. Usually, there were at least three collections. We filed up row by row and dropped our contribution into the basket, being careful to use the right hand. Lefties are in trouble in Tanzania. The left hand is considered unclean because it is used for personal hygiene after urination or defecation. The right hand is used for eating and social interaction. Use of the left hand in these situations is considered an insult.

Many in the congregation were too poor to donate cash, but contributed produce, eggs, chickens, and occasionally a goat. After the service, there was an auction of these items with the proceeds going to the church. Once during a service, a chicken escaped its bonds and ran squawking down the aisle. It was easily captured, returned to the front of the church and tied a little better. If my colleague Sheri went with me, she would start a bidding war for some item being auctioned—a piece of sugar cane or some beans. It didn't matter. Her goal was to keep bidding until the competition (yours truly) got tired. She'd either bid again and pay or leave me with the winning bid. Whatever we bought, we would donate back to the church again. The congregation thought we were crazy and laughed as our bidding went on and on.

At a service at the Lutheran Cathedral in Same, we stayed for the auction and suddenly there was a lot more laughter than usual. A man's wife had donated all his clothes and he had to try to buy them all back. He kept recognizing his shirts and trousers. He couldn't decide whether to chastise his wife or keep buying his clothes.

CORRUPTION

Corruption is one of those words that is best defined within a cultural context. In Russia, what we call bribery, they believe is part of their compensation, just like tips for a waitress. In the US, we send bottles of scotch or Omaha steaks to our best customers and consider this a cost of doing business. We also have plenty of instances of outright theft or corruption. (The last three Governors of Illinois are still in jail and the Mayor of Charlotte, NC resigned because of taking bribes). So I will be careful about criticizing other countries for corruption.

A story I heard, probably true, illustrates Tanzanian attitudes about this. At a meeting of senior leaders of the ELCT, a Bishop says, "I do not understand these Western donors. They think that their money pours like wine from a metal chalice when it really flows from an earthen vessel and some of it is absorbed by the vessel."

This story reveals the common attitude by Tanzanians about receiving donated funds. Some should stick to you, just because of your position, and that is perfectly okay. When Westerners object, Tanzanians are puzzled. Why else would anyone want to seek those high positions and do all that extra work unless some extra funds were part of it? As in many cultures, these unofficial payments to "grease the wheels" are perfectly acceptable to them and are part of the cost of doing business there.

However, Tanzania is one of the few countries with an official government department devoted to exposing significant corruption and eliminating it. Like many developing countries, determining what an acceptable level of these unofficial payments is, is a major problem but the government takes this seriously. It is still necessary to understand and accept what the "earthen vessel absorption" concept is in relation to any specific culture. Including ours.

During the early days of the Palliative Care Project, I was in Tanzania with two nurses. Our Tanzanian Coordinator had another commitment one day, so he arranged for us to visit a health center to take a tour. We drove to a very dusty, desolate little village and arrived too late for tea. But our host, the CEO said we could do the tour, have some conversation and then join them for lunch.

It was a typical health center with capacity for some treatment, testing, minor surgery, and uncomplicated deliveries. When necessary, it made referrals to hospitals. It had some patients in the outpatient department and some waiting in the HIV testing and counseling center. The facility was getting rundown and some of the equipment wasn't working. But the CEO and the staff were optimistic and pleased with what they were able to do for the people in the large area they serviced.

We went to the courtyard and had lunch. I sat next to the CEO and we engaged in a conversation about Obama's chances for election. I was surprised at the degree of interest and understanding about the early stages of our Presidential electoral process. We tend to underestimate how important the United States is and people's interest in it. In this case, of course, the potential election of a black man with ties to Kenya increased their curiosity.

Then, without any preliminaries, the CEO turned to me and asked if there was a test for cancer. I wondered why he was asking me the question. I told him that there were many tests to identify many types of cancer, but we do not have one test for all of them.

His next questions was "Is there a cure for cancer?" I explained there is no cure, but there are treatments that can cause a remission which might last for five years or longer.

After these two extraordinary questions from a health professional, we finished lunch with more discussion about Obama. Then we completed our tour by going to the CEO's office. We entered and saw there were a dozen women sitting around the walls.

He turned to me and again asked if there was there a test for cancer. I gave him the same answer as before, no single test. And then he asked again if there was a cure for cancer. And again I said the same as earlier, no cure, but treatments that can prolong life.

I was really puzzled by this until he turned to me and explained that the woman sitting there in the office thought they had cancer. Some of them began walking at 2 AM to come because they heard that we were coming. They had never been to the facility and had never been examined. They thought we were there to give them the cure. He asked us to please tell the woman to register and be examined so they could find out if they really had cancer.

I repeated that there was no single test for cancer and no cure, but that they needed to be examined to find out if they had cancer and then the health center staff would prescribe the appropriate treatment. As all this was being translated, I could see their faces fall. The Wazungu did not bring them a cure. I wondered, were they thinking that we did have the cure, but didn't want to give it to them?

We left after getting a commitment from them to register and be examined. As we walked out, we felt about two inches tall. We dashed their hopes that the white people from America would solve their problem. This was one of the first times when we learned the limits of our resources and of the disconnect between what we could do and what many Tanzanians wanted. It was a good learning experience for us and confirmed our approach of focusing our energy and resources on activities where we could make a difference. We could not cure cancer, but we could convince these women to be examined to determine if they had cancer.

YOU HAVE WATCHES, WE HAVE TIME

One of the most difficult cultural differences between us Westerners and the Tanzanians relates to time. We think of time in discrete segments, each of which should be filled with something— preferably something determined to be useful. Even exercise or recreation is scheduled. Tanzanians think this is crazy but are too polite to tell us but just give us their best enigmatic smile.

In their traditional world, there is daylight and darkness. There are seasons and there are holidays (a lot of them). There is a workday schedule beginning to appear in urban areas, but for the most part, time as we understand it, is a literally, foreign concept.

Tanzanian attitudes towards schedules and appointments are best thought of as fluid in terms of what will happen and when. Arriving an hour late is not considered late, although as Westerners, we are hysterical by then. Tanzanians calmly tell us that we have watches, they have time. Even if you have an appointment with an official, you may show up at his office only to learn that he is in Moshi for a meeting. You ask when he will be back. His staff says they do not know. So, you reschedule and hope that something else doesn't happen. Sometimes, you show up for your appointment and he is present, but is in the middle of another meeting, usually with a higher official from Dar Es Salaam, and cannot meet with you. None of this is considered rude or unusual. If you are a Westerner reading this, you may feel your blood pressure beginning to rise. But in Tanzania, it is totally normal and acceptable.

If a Tanzanian is on his way to meet you and sees a friend, he thinks nothing of stopping to chat for 15 or 20 minutes. Relationships are all important in this society and every effort is made to strengthen them and keep them current.

At the ELCT Pare Diocese, each morning there are devotions which can last half an hour. Then a couple of hours later, the bell is rung to announce tea, which is mandatory and can last another half hour. To call these time wasting rituals evokes a benign smile from Tanzanians and a statement that they are important rituals that bind the staff together. It is much less expensive and much less risky than the team building exercises in US businesses that involve white water rafting and wall climbing excursions.

The best way to deal with the Tanzanian's response to time is to relax and recognize that being an hour or two late for an appointment is not unusual and does not count as tardy. The only exception is when we are told that a meeting will begin on "American time." Then we are sure if it says 9 AM, that's when it will be.

For Tanzanians, time is not discrete blocks, but rather a slowly flowing stream which allows opportunities to connect with friends and relatives and permits activities to occur at a pace that recognizes that there is plenty of time.

Perhaps they have a point. Because they've got nothing but time.

A HOSPITAL, HEALTH CENTER, CLINIC, OR SOMETHING

After the first visit with the Maasai, each time a team went to Tanzania for our Palliative Care Project, we went to Nadaruru. We spent about 18 months and four or five visits figuring out what to do. Part of this process was working through what the Maasai wanted.

At first, they wanted a hospital. When we said that was impossible, they then asked for a Health Center, similar to an urgent care center with some capability for surgery and overnight accommodations. We said that wouldn't work either—too expensive and no available clinical staff. So, our discussions continued.

Nadaruru Clinic.

Whenever we arrived at Nadaruru, we were always invited for lunch—and it always was with the men of the tribe. The women brought the food (usually goat and rice) and then left. Rev. Joas, who was doing much of the interpreting, decided that the women needed a greater voice in the planning. He told the men that we needed the views of the women because this project was for them. And that we wanted to invite them to meet with us. The men did not object—probably too shocked at this request. He then went to the women and explained that the clinic was for them so they must meet with us and they must speak up. They came and some of the brave ones asked to speak and made useful comments about what they wanted in terms of services and education. This began the process of developing the response to their needs.

Rev. Joas then explained that we needed a committee to manage this project and women must be members. And even the chair of the committee should also be a woman. It was clear that the Maasai men were shell shocked with all these cultural changes, but they recognized the importance of this project and they agreed.

So a Maasai committee, with a woman as chair, was created and worked with our Tanzanian staff liaison, Eli, and with us on our regular visits from the US to develop the plan for action. The plan had two parts. First, we would construct a small building in which services and education would be provided. Second, we would train six women to be birth attendants to provide the services required. We also added routine visits by physicians and nurses to assess the prenatal status of the pregnant women and to provide immunizations for the children.

A key component was direct participation in the activities by the Maasai. The men would provide sweat equity in the construction of the building and the women who were to be trained as birth attendants would have their daily duties performed by other women of the tribe.

The budget for the project was $10,000. We began fundraising from private donors and after several months, Dr. Jeff and I were in Tanzania and went to Nadaruru to meet with the committee and the entire tribe to give them a progress report. I announced that we had raised about $6,000 and that we would continue to seek funding within the next few months. The Maasai were very happy with this news. Then Dr. Jeff said that he and his wife, Ali, would provide the rest of the money and that we could begin immediately. The emotional response to this announcement was overpowering. Much singing and traditional Maasai dancing went on until we had to leave because dusk was falling. We needed to get back to the road and hopefully to town before darkness. Driving at night through the bush is very risky and even on the road back to Same it is almost as risky.

Within two months, the clinic building was done and plans were complete for the training of the women as birth attendants. We learned that a neighboring tribe of Pare people had approached the committee and asked if they could participate in the project and if some of their women could also be trained.

Training Birth Attendants.

The history of relations between the Maasai and the Pare is mixed and there had been conflict in the past. However, the Maasai committee agreed to allow Pare participation and added four of their women to the training.

When the training began, two Tanzanian health professionals, Nurse Nivo, an RN and certified Midwife, and Sister Agnes, an OB nurse, took the national curriculum and planned a two week training program for the birth attendants. We always used native speakers as principal faculty for our training programs. They selected a hotel about 8 miles from the Maasai village (or boma as they called it). They selected the Evangelist (a member of the clergy) who was bilingual to handle any necessary translation from the Swahili of the training into Maa, the Maasai language. The training was scheduled from 9 AM to 5 PM, five days a week for two weeks.

Each morning, the trainees walked from the boma to the hotel, some carrying their infants. Most mornings, Mama Maria, the senior woman of the tribe accompanied them. She was in her 70s and had arthritis, but knew that this was a critical opportunity to improve the health of her people. So, she walked with them. On the first day, I met with Nurse Nivo who asked me if I could find a manikin to help show the anatomy of the birth process. I sent an email to Dr. Yogi Shah (in Iowa at Des Moines University Medical School) who said he would donate one which would be brought by members of the team arriving a few days later. I was there when the manikin was unpacked and was surprised at how explicit it was in showing the female anatomy and the birth canal. The trainers were delighted. But they faced a quandary. The Evangelist doing the interpreting from Swahili into Maa was a man and Tanzanians, especially Maasai, are very conservative about these kinds of personal matters.

The trainers put it to a vote of the birth attendant trainees. Would they prefer to have the Evangelist present while the trainers provided detailed information about the biology of the birth process, using the explicit manikin, or would they excuse him and do the best they could without his translation. The vote was unanimous—he stayed. This was another breakthrough in the traditional culture of the Maasai, but the women were very practical in their decision. They told me later that the Evangelist was embarrassed at times, but that he stayed with it and did a good job of translation.

With construction and training completed, the clinic building was equipped with some office furniture, an examination table and birthing bed. The goal was for two of the birth attendants to staff the clinic every day. They would provide prenatal and well-baby care. They would also examine pregnant women to identify potential problems early and refer them to the hospital where they would receive the care they needed when they delivered their babies. To supplement these services, a physician and nurse from the Lutheran hospital and a public health nurse from the District Health Department would visit the site once or twice per month to conduct prenatal exams and immunize the children. In reality, however, everyone with any ailment from Nadaruru and the Pare village showed up on "clinic day." Dr. Amini from the Lutheran Hospital had to prioritize the patients. First, pregnant women, then postpartum women, then children. Then, everyone else. Clinic days saw over 250 people cared for each time. On the other days, the birth attendants saw eight to ten women daily for exams and prenatal education.

The clinic opened with an extravagant ceremony. There was a procession with traditional Maasai singing and dancing. Choirs from the nearby churches sang. They even prepared a drama

Nadaruru Clinic.

Drama and Dancing Open the Clinic.

mocking a traditional Maasai man who refused to let his wife go to the clinic and she died in childbirth. He then became an advocate for the clinic. The Lutheran Bishop and the District Commissioner made speeches and cut the ribbon. We then adjourned to the nearby school building for lunch where we saw another indicator of the importance attached to this ceremony. The Maasai butchered one of their cows to feed their guests. Cows are the measure of wealth in the Maasai communities and they are rarely used for food. This was a clear indication that what we had done was very important.

LET THERE BE LIGHT

Installing Solar Lighting.

Nadaruru was 8 miles from the road and 16 miles from the next closest town. It was also not on the electric grid. So, when darkness came, work ended at the clinic, except for emergencies. When we asked them what happened at night, we discovered that in emergencies flashlights were used. So we went to Moshi and found an electrical supply store that had solar lighting kits for $600. This kit had the old fashioned glass panels, car battery, cables, and light bulbs. The solar collector provided power for four lights for up to six hours. We bought four kits and planned to install one at different clinics.

The next clinic we visited was having "clinic day" when we were there, so our two nurses worked while Rev. Joas installed the solar lighting system. It was very crowded. One of our nurses, Monique, had advanced practice training and could work independently. So she was taking care of the many babies brought by their moms. Nurse Carlene was working with Dr. Amini from the hospital doing prenatal exams and, later, taking care of the men who arrived with other complaints. In the meantime, a public health nurse was injecting children with their immunizations. So, in a 10 by 20 foot room, there were 30 or 40 moms and babies and many other children being immunized.

Meanwhile Rev. Joas had completed the installation of the solar panels on the clinic roof and he snaked the cable inside to connect it to the storage battery. Then he stood on a rickety table stapling the cable to the ceiling for the lights. But the moms wanted their babies seen or immunized, so they didn't move. Instead, they crowded around his table, so closely that they inadvertently gave him support while he was stapling and fitting light bulbs into the ceiling.

Just as dusk was approaching, the doctor and nurses were finishing with the last of their patients. For safety's sake, I wanted to get our team out of there and back to the road before nightfall. But then Rev. Joas flipped the switch to test the solar lighting. The bulbs lit up the whole building and people took this as a sign that the clinic was still open. Another 40 patients showed up. In Tanzania, no clinical person leaves until all the patients are seen.

So, while they now had light, we drove back in total darkness.

IMPROVING WOMEN'S HEALTH

Health Improvement Meeting.

The most significant effort Empower Tanzania makes in empowering women is the Improving Women's Health Program (IWHP). This is the creation of Dr. Jeff and me. We knew that women were the key element in keeping the family together as well as a major economic force, so we developed a plan to provide basic health education to them with the expectation that they would adopt some of these health improvement behaviors for themselves and their families. We would be empowering them with knowledge. Another empowerment strategy was to use women to deliver the health education.

Dr. Jeff obtained a five year commitment to fund this project. IWHP hired a Program Manager who then proceeded to hire 26 Community Health Educators (CHEs), all women. There is one CHE in each Ward of the Same District. A redistricting added new Wards leading to an additional seven CHEs trained during the second year of the program for a total of 33 CHEs. The CHEs provide basic health education and coordinate their efforts with another of our projects (Palliative Care) in which we trained over 200 Community Health Workers (CHWs, virtually all women) to deliver basic health services.

To manage the program, we hired Efrancia Nzota, a young, recent university graduate. She later said she enjoyed working for Empower Tanzania and the Americans because it was so different from Tanzanian companies which were top-down organizations in which you had specific duties and you did them. With us, she had the freedom to define her position and its duties. We were unpredictable but interesting. She had primary responsibility for recruiting and supervising the women who would become the CHEs.

These CHE women were trained in methods for planning, marketing, and conducting education programs. They also learned how to do follow up observation to determine if the concepts taught were being used. They were given small, battery-powered projectors, and speakers. Educational content was created by Dr. Jeff and taught in Swahili and English by two Tanzanian women who lived in the US. Videos on such topics as Safe Water, Hand Washing, Malaria Prevention, and HIV/AIDS were produced and loaded into the projectors of each CHE. We had a small setback the day after they received their projectors. Dr. Jeff had told them to practice with them that evening and come back with questions and problems the next day. Some reported that they had no electricity in their homes to recharge the projector battery. One said she had never plugged in anything and didn't know how. By then, though, these women were a family and they helped each other find solutions to their problems.

The bulk of the training was done by Dr. Jeff and Sheri, an Empower Tanzania board member. Sheri used training techniques never seen before in Tanzania. She was enthusiastic, included the trainees in the discussion, and taught them the techniques for successful meeting planning. Dr. Jeff could have been an imposing figure but instead he exuded a fun loving persona. While he gave them a great deal of clinical information, he also related to each of them on a personal basis. He danced with them and did silly things like acting as though he were President Kikwete and President Obama congratulating them on their successful training. This unpretentious behavior was sincere and the trainees knew it. They loved him.

The District Commissioner, appointed by President Kikwete, was Herman Kapufa. He was a former schoolteacher and was very supportive of the project. He came to the training sessions to encourage the CHEs and to offer his direct assistance. He gave them his personal phone number and told them to call if they had any problems. Then he developed a letter to each of the Ward Executives (who report to him) which said that they should help the CHEs do their work.

After a year, it became clear that this program was empowering the CHEs and the women who attended their educational sessions, thus improving the lives of people in Tanzania. The CHEs are more confident and are proud of their knowledge and accomplishments. Some CHEs are holding more than 10 meetings per month with an average of 30 participants. Each month, over 13,000 people attend these meetings. Although the focus is on women, we were surprised to learn that about 30 percent of the attendees are men. These CHEs have become respected members of their communities as a result of their knowledge and their linkage with an international project. The women who attend are showing their empowerment, too. They are now purifying water, using mosquito nets, and washing their hands. The next step is to use government data to show that these new behaviors are leading to reduced levels of infections and fewer cases of malaria and diarrhea.

These women have proven that they can learn new information, master unknown electronic equipment, and make public presentations. They have empowered themselves—all we did was give them an opportunity.

SCHISTOSOMIASIS, OR JUST WHEN YOU THOUGHT IT WAS SAFE TO GO INTO THE WATER

At the training session for the CHEs, a member of the District Health Department attended and asked to receive copies of the training videos which he planned to use in waiting rooms at health centers. Dr. Jeff was very happy to respond to this request because it would bring his videos in front of many more people.

But (there is always a 'but'), the Health Department member asked

Dr. Jeff to produce another video on schistosomiasis, a disease from walking barefoot into standing water. Tiny snails in the water release a parasite that bores through the skin and travels to the liver and bladder. This causes increased risk of cancer, ulcers in the esophagus, and weakening of the immune system.

Dr. Jeff thought he was done producing videos for the year, but since he had planned to make such a video eventually, as this is a chronic problem in Tanzania, he agreed to do it sooner because it was an opportunity to develop a good relationship with the Health Department.

Our lead staff person, Eli, said he knew a place and we took off and soon were on a really bad "road" which was just a series of dry creek beds, eroded soil, and holes. We bumped along for a mile or two before turning off into the yard of a house and outbuildings. Eli got out and said it was time for some Community Development work. A few minutes later, he returned with an elderly man.

Eli introduced Mzee Thomas and we all shook hands. (Mzee [mm-ZAY]) is a Swahili word meaning wise, old man and is a term of respect). Eli explained that Mzee Thomas would take us to a water hole and he had called people to meet us there.

Another mile or two of very bad road and we could see a bowl about 30 yards across with a foot or two of dirty water in it. Across from us were some cattle and donkeys clustered in the shade of some trees. But the number of droppings around the water testified that the animals had been in it. As we arrived, we saw several young men and children with jugs and containers getting ready to enter the water. Dr. Jeff quickly went over and began filming. They went in and began filling their jugs and the kids were splashing around.

After a few minutes a young woman arrived, pushing a bicycle with three jugs tied on. She untied them, lifted up her skirt and waded in to begin filling her containers. The kids came over to help her and after about 10 minutes, she had all she needed to take care of her family. She lugged the containers out, tied them on to the bike and began pushing it through the dusty soil. She was doing her duty as mom—getting water for cooking and washing. Yet by collecting this water, she was putting them at risk of bacterial infections and herself at risk of schistosomiasis.

Just as Dr. Jeff was finishing his filming, a herd of goats trotted over and began drinking from the water. Of course, they had to walk into the water and some needed to urinate and defecate. This entire situation is typical of water collection all over Tanzania.

Dr. Jeff thanked the kids and Mzee Thomas for their help and told them about the risk they had been running by being in such dirty water. They understood but this was all there was for them. Dr. Jeff explained how to help protect themselves. This will be a video that will do a lot of good when it is shown all across the Same District and eventually all across the country. It should lead to behavior changes that will eliminate much needless illness and suffering.

But it was still a somber mood in our truck as we drove back to town realizing that these people had put themselves at risk for us. They would have done this anyway, but we still felt responsible. Sharing information with them meant they would be better equipped to protect themselves in the future.

The good news is that this village is in line for a major water project—a new well and piping to a communal tap. We hope that the funding comes through and that it is built soon. Then the kids will never have to go into that filthy water again.

EMPOWERING WOMEN

Maore Support Group

Support Group in Uniform.

We knew from the beginning that working with women in Tanzania would pay big dividends. This is because they do most of the work—fetching water, gathering firewood, cooking, taking care of the children, and often doing the farming. Despite knowing this about women, we had been sidetracked in our activities for the first few years here and did little directly related to women .While our Palliative Care project and wells projects had affected women and even employed them, we had not focused on their needs or explicitly empowered them.

Then I read the book "Half the Sky" by Nicholas Kristof and Sheryl WuDunn from the Chinese proverb that women hold up half the sky. The book was powerful and inspirational as it described women escaping the most terrible conditions and becoming successful. It convinced me to add a focus to projects directly affecting women. The IWHP efforts were making great strides and we had learned a few things from our work with the birth attendants in our Maasai project, but we needed a place to do more.

THE MAORE SUPPORT GROUP

We knew that in Tanzania, like everywhere else, there was a problem with gender based violence (GBV), but we needed more information, especially cultural information. I asked Rev. Joas, our Palliative Care Coordinator, to set up a meeting with someone who could tell us more about GBV in Tanzania.

We traveled to the same hotel where the birth attendants had been trained. But this time, Pastor Rose from the Lutheran Church in the nearby town of Maore met us. She brought eight women from her congregation. Pastor Rose knew that each had been victims of GBV but none of them knew about the others because of the culture that encouraged secrecy regarding family matters.

Our team consisted of Susan, a volunteer on the trip, Sheri, Dr. Jeff, and me. We greeted these women and tried to make them comfortable. We described our interest in learning more about GBV in Tanzania. There was no response. After a few uncomfortable minutes, Dr. Jeff told them that GBV was a big problem in America, too, and we hoped they could tell us about what happens here in Tanzania. The women looked shocked. Finally, one of them spoke up and said, "My husband beats me." Heads were nodding. Her bold first step opened the gates with each woman encouraging the others.

Yet another one said her husband tried to kill her with a knife. She escaped and went to the police and they did nothing. Now it was our turn to be shocked.

Even another one said this was her experience also in reporting her husband's actions. She said the police just sent her home.

The stories came tumbling out, each more terrible than the last. One widow was being evicted from her home and farm because her late husband's family was claiming that women could not own land. Another said that they wanted to take her children away.

Soon, the tears were flowing and they were hugging each other for comfort. We cried too and got hugs.

One of them spoke up and said how it had been good to discuss these things and to share the pain. All of the eight agreed. Sheri explained that in America we call this kind of thing a support group. Women with these problems meet, share, and help each other.

They all agreed that they should form such a group in Maore. Pastor Rose agreed to host the meetings at the church and that they would call it Bible Study.

Dr. Jeff told them he had some T shirts that he wanted to give them. They had been donated by a friend who lost an election. They were Kelly green and the eight women and Pastor Rose put them on and decided this would be their uniform for the support group. They left feeling that there was hope for each by sharing with the others.

Six months later, Sheri and I were in Maore and we met with the support group and Pastor Rose. The women explained they were meeting and it had helped them. They were planning to start a business soon in which they would buy rice just after harvest when it is cheap, keep it until it was in short supply, and sell it at a higher price. The profits would be shared among all of them. Sheri was impressed and she encouraged them to move ahead with this idea.

After another four months, Sheri, Jodi (another Empower Tanzania board member), and I were back in Maore. We met again with several of the women at the church. This time, we wanted to know if they had made any progress with their business idea. So, we asked them several questions about when they would buy the rice, what the price would be, how much they would buy, where they would store it, and when would they sell it.

They were well prepared and answered the questions quickly and with information that showed they had studied the business opportunity and had planned well. They wanted to buy 100 kilos (About 220 pounds) and would store them at Pastor Rose's house so they would be secure and dry until they sold them. They explained they had saved nearly 70,000 shillings (about $40) and we need about 640,000 shilling to buy the 100 kilos.

At this rate, it would take them five years to accumulate the money necessary, I thought. I looked at Sheri and Jodi who said they had a donation from a friend and they could provide enough to get them to the $400 they needed.

Sheri explained they were giving them the rest of the money so they could begin right away. She went on to explain this was not charity and it was not a loan, but that they wanted to be partners in this business project. She wanted them to write down everything they did and keep records of all the expenses and profits. They would use this experience and become consultants to other support groups that we would establish and they could help other women to get started.

They were stunned. The secretary of the group proclaimed this a miracle. We handed over the cash and there was more hugging and tears of gratitude.

As I was walking out to the car feeling overcome with the knowledge that we had changed the lives of these women, I looked up to the sky and said, "People ask me why I do this. This is why."

INFRASTRUCTURE...WHAT INFRASTRUCTURE?

One of the hardest things for us to adjust to is the limited infrastructure in rural Tanzania. Even though Same has a population of over 25,000, it does not have safe water. In fact, even in Dar Es Salaam, population almost 5 million, bottled water is a necessity. That means boiling or treating all the water you will drink or cook with. It also means remembering to use bottled water for brushing your teeth.

Electricity is also a critical part of infrastructure and, while many parts of the country are connected to the grid, power often goes off. Some power outages are amusing, such as when power is cut off during dinner. Suddenly in pitch blackness, you cannot see your mashed potatoes, everyone struggles to find their flashlight, and the biggest concern is that you might spill your beer. Usually, the hotel generator kicks on after a few minutes and everyone is relieved to see again.

Some communities have very limited connection to the electrical grid which makes it difficult to fully participate in Empower Tanzania's projects. During the CHE project training session, the students were given LED projectors to show educational videos. They were told to take them home to practice. The next day, Dr. Jeff reminded them that these battery-powered projectors must be recharged after 60 minutes of use. He asked them how many had electricity at home. Only one of the 33 trainees raised her hand. The others all did find a place in their village where they could recharge the batteries.

At one of our program sites, Kanza, the health clinic did not have electricity. I met the CEO and asked about patients coming in the middle of the night. Women in labor come from the village at all times of day and night. The CEO explained that if there is time, they get the mother to the hospital. Gonja Lutheran Hospital is about an hour away. If there is no time, they deliver the baby at the dispensary, using flashlight if necessary.

Empower Tanzania installed one of the $600 solar lighting systems at this dispensary. The mayor came and thanked us and told us that this was the only place in the village that had power. He said that they would use the clinic for meetings and evening education whenever it was not in use for medical needs or the training programs we were offering.

One area in which Tanzania does have modern technology is its mobile phone system. Traditional land lines with copper wire systems were too expensive to install, but cell towers are easy to put up and offer very good quality service. Phones are relatively inexpensive and many people have them. It was surprising when we were meeting with Maasai elders to have a cellphone ring and stop the meeting while, they all dug into their robes to see whose phone it was. In the photo section, you can see Maasai Chief Isaiah listening to his phone, squatting next to a fire near a warrior who is cooking a goat loin for the guests.

A COMEUPPANCE

As the oldest member of the delegation and President of the Empower Tanzania Board of Directors, I was treated with great respect by Tanzanians. They called me Mzee, meaning wise old man, though my wife might have translated it as wise ass man. So I got used to going first and sitting in the front seat and being waited on.

When I flew from Mbeya to Njombe, in the south central part of Tanzania, with an ETI board member, Singo and Carlene, a nurse, who had been to Njombe before, the pilot buzzed the airfield and circled before landing. I had been feeling pretty brave on the flight over, which was new for me, so I asked him why he did that.

He explained there was two reasons. First, he wanted to be sure that they cut the grass and second, he wanted to be sure that there were no cows on the runway. I blanched and tightened my sphincters, brave no more.

As we taxied to a stop beside the terminal building, I could see a large crowd gathered there, some holding flowers and, as I opened the door, I could hear a brass band playing. Wow, all this for me, I thought.

Did you ever get the feeling that people were looking right past you? Well that happened to me as I stood on the steps leading to the ground. It was suddenly pretty quiet. As soon as Carlene appeared, the shouting and noise and band playing began again. I did the best I could by holding her hand and presenting her to The Honorable Ann Makinda, Member of Parliament for Njombe and Deputy Speaker of Parliament, also, an old friend of Carlene's. I stood in her reflected glory and took my dose of humility with good grace.

Fame is fickle, I thought. Especially in Njombe.

DRIVING MISS MAKINDA

The next morning, Carlene and I were met again by the Honorable Ann Makinda (Hon. Ann) in her Toyota with the Tanzanian flag flying from the left front fender. We drove into a rural part of the Hon. Ann's constituency where we were to meet some people dealing with the AIDS crisis. This part of Tanzania is especially hard hit by HIV. We stopped at a run-down building in a small town. Inside were about 20 people, mostly women, who help their neighbors suffering from AIDS and its complications.

We heard several sad stories about people who died and it was obvious that they love the Hon. Ann because she shared in their suffering and helped them with funds from the Ministry of Health. One woman spoke about her husband who was infected when he was working in Dar Es Salaam and returned home to infect her. The Hon. Ann helped her get the anti-retroviral drugs that were saving her life.

Hon. Ann told Carlene and me that the woman lived far from where we were. With tears in her eyes she explained that the woman began walking at 1 AM to be there to thank her. I thought about how dangerous walking in Tanzania is in the middle of the night and how much this woman risked to come say thank you to Hon. Ann. Carlene looked at me and I knew we were both thinking how different it was from the US where we feel so entitled that we wouldn't even cross the street to say thank you.

The meeting and the stories continued for about an hour. Then Hon. Ann's phone rang and after taking the call she explained that we must leave and hurry back to Njombe. President Jakaya Kikwete was soon to arrive for the opening of a new yogurt plant and she must greet him.

We got into the Toyota and she told the driver the Tanzanian equivalent of, "Don't spare the horses." I am certain this is what she said because we are soon speeding down two lane roads at what seemed to be 80 mph. I was too nervous to try to read the speedometer and convert kph to mph. I just knew we were going really fast. Somehow, people knew it was an official vehicle and they got out of the way. China had a red card in the window. Maybe Tanzania used a flag on the fender. I have no idea. I was just thankful when the ride was over.

We zoomed up to a parking lot where security saw us and waved us in. Hon. Ann put Carlene and me in a line of people and told us to wait there and she would come back for us.

A well-dressed white woman came up and asked us if we were Italian. While I was struggling to remember when my paternal grandparents left Naples, she looked me over and sniffed, "American."

I asked Carlene what that was all about. She explained that this new plant was a joint venture between Italy and Tanzania and today was the grand opening. People were there from the Embassy of Italy and were waiting to see President Kikwete.

Okay, I thought, but how did she know I was American? Perhaps it was my casual clothes or my uninteresting haircut. Or maybe she saw my class ring when I was digging out dust from my right ear with my pinky. No one ever said for sure.

Just then, a black SUV pulled in and security popped out followed by President Kikwete. Like all politicians, he couldn't resist a line of people, so he started shaking hands. He looked surprised when he reached Carlene and me, but we got a handshake anyway.

He made a speech about the opening of the yogurt factory and a nice person behind Carlene and me provided a running translation.

He closed by saying in English, that soon, the yogurt and cheese from this factory will be in the fanciest hotels in Dar Es Salaam. Even the Kempinski. He was looking right at Carlene and me as if he knew we had stayed there the previous night.

For a moment I thought he must have a great source of intelligence. But then I looked around and realized that Carlene and I really do stand out in a crowd here. Plus the Kempinski was the classiest, and most expensive hotel in the city and suitable for foreigners.

About a month later, Todd and I wangled an invitation to meet President Kikwete. We got through security at the Tanzanian White House and were interviewed by a very astute woman to learn what we were doing there and what we wanted to discuss with the President. When Todd and I walked into his office, the President looked up and I thought I detected a shocked look of recognition from the handshake at Njombe. But then he waved away the fly that was bothering him. I understood then that he didn't remember me and really, all Wazungu look alike to him.

WHY CAN'T THEY SPEAK ENGLISH?

Tanzania was a British colony for about 40 years before gaining independence and was an English speaking country. But for most people, English is a distant memory. Their first language is their tribal language and the second is Swahili, which is the national language. English is their third language and is used in business. While it is required in Secondary School and University, most people forget what they have learned or never learned it in the first place. Their Secondary School English teachers are usually not very good, so the students don't learn what they should to succeed at University or in the business world.

We have to use interpreters for our training and communication with the local people. They do a great job explaining what we are saying and putting it into a context that is meaningful to the audience. Some Empower Tanzania volunteers have made the effort to learn Swahili to be able to confirm our education is getting across and to show we are truly interested in the Tanzanian culture and in our partnership.

However, in the real world, confusion is not so easily avoided. One evening, Dr. Jeff ordered dinner and wanted to substitute vegetables for the mashed potatoes. The waitress understood "carroti", but had no idea what peas were. So, he made the classic mistake of repeating what he said only slower and louder and with a rolling gesture with his thumb and index finger. She still looked puzzled, so he tried again only slower. Still no result, so he gave up.

I imagine the Swahili conversation in the kitchen went something like this. "The Wazungu wants vegetables, not potatoes," says the waitress," but I cannot understand what else he is saying about the vegetables he wants."

"Which Wazungu?" asks the chef.

"The younger one with the beard", she replies, "The older one eats everything."

"Let me see what I have for vegetables," the chef concludes.

Dr. Jeff's dinner appeared an hour later—with carrots and peas. He showed one to the waitress and said "pea" very slowly. Perhaps she understood. Or perhaps she decided to humor the Wazungu honky.

POLITICIANS ON PARADE

When we established Empower Tanzania, one of our initial board members was Singo, a native Tanzanian who was now, like me, a captive Iowan. He arranged a meeting with the Honorable Anna Kilango Malecela (Hon. Anna), Member of Parliament (MP) for Same East. She was impressed with our work and arranged for a meeting with Prime Minister (PM) Mizengo Pinda. Hon. Anna had a lot of clout, having been primarily responsible for the ouster of the previous PM for corruption. She wanted to know why we were only working in Kilimanjaro Region. We explained the reasons for our linkages in Pare Diocese but said Empower Tanzania was interested in finding projects and funding anywhere in the rural parts of the country.

In planning the next visit, the Hon. Anna told us to add a couple of days at the beginning of the visit and to travel to Dar Es Salaam where she would meet us. Carlene and I arrived where the Hon. Anna was waiting in a restricted zone. She instructed us to give her our passports and luggage tags and one of her staff would handle the passport control and get your bags. We went to the VIP lounge for tea while we waited.

After 20 minutes, we were in a van going to the Kempinski Hotel. It was about midnight by then but the hotel manager was there to greet us and to take us to the executive level where we each had a suite. He told us the PM would send a car for us the next morning to take us to the airport. You were going to visit Mbeya region, his constituency, to see some of the country besides Kilimanjaro Region.

The next morning we asked the staff if we should check out so they could rent those suites and were informed there was no need and that they would be kept for us until we returned.

At the airport, we met Singo. He splits his time between Iowa and Tanzania and joined us on this journey. The Hon. Anna introduced us to the Regional Commissioner (RC) for Mbeya who would be our host for the visit. An RC is the equivalent of a Governor, except he is appointed by the President and doesn't face election.

We boarded the twin-engine plane and took off for the two-hour journey to Mbeya. By now you know how much I hate flying. Part of it is that I cannot understand how those heavy things stay up in the air. My ignorance of aerodynamics and some negative and disheartening experiences (mostly with Aeroflot in Russia), gives me a reasonable fear of getting on a plane.

Even on short hops in small planes in Tanzania, unsettling things have happened. For this flight, our pilot held the wing and prayed before flying. This live illustration of "a wing and a prayer" was not comforting to me. On another occasion, the pilot of the 12-passenger plane that would fly over Lake Victoria told us about safety features, including life vests. Of course, we were so packed in the plane it would have been impossible to put the things on. Even if that could be done, we could never have duck walked to the back of the plane to get out the small door. The reality was, we were going to the bottom of Lake Victoria if anything went wrong. I really hate flying.

This time, after the pilot's prayer, our trip was uneventful. We landed and were met by three Toyota sedans flying the flag of Tanzania. We visited the nearby referral hospital where we were met by the Chief Physician who took us on a tour. It was a busy place with a full OB/newborn department in which the moms and babies were sharing a bed. This is customary in Tanzania and when some Americans donated bassinets, no one at the hospital knew what to do with them. Mothers are never separated from their babies—so the bassinettes are used to deliver clean laundry to the hospital wards.

We noticed that the pediatric ward was not that busy. The Chief Physician explained that was because of the mosquito nets. He went on to say they had been a godsend as they cut the admissions for malaria in children by half..

When we left to visit the next place, we noticed that three more Toyotas filled with local politicians had joined us. We went to the nearby river, where at a shallow spot women were washing clothes or collecting water for home use. The politicians sensed a photo op and lined up behind the women who were collecting water. They put us in the middle and pretended to be collecting water for their families. Photo taken, it was back to the Toyotas where three more vehicles had joined the caravan.

The next stop was a field in which the harvest of a grain was underway. Women were using wooden pitchforks to lift and toss the grain. Another photo op for politicians to show how they were tied to the people by tossing some grain and pretending to be interested in this process. Fortunately the photo was done before they looked like foolish amateurs tossing grain.

The RC explained that the stop we made at the river was the site of a proposed hot spring for tourists and the grain was part of an agricultural test to increase yields. He told us these were potential projects for ETI to do in this area.

Finally, the photo ops with the visiting white people were done and the local politicians left us. It was a reminder that politicians are the same everywhere, kissing babies, posing for staged photo ops, or eating those dreadful loose meat sandwiches at the state fair.

RAMPAGING ELEPHANTS

After escaping the politicians, we drove to a nearby small game park lodge where we spent the night. It was a small place with about a dozen tents in a semicircle adjacent to a lodge. The South African couple managing the place met us, helped us with our bags and got us settled in our tents.

These were luxury tents—nothing like the pup tents of my Boy Scout days. They were on platforms, had bunks with mattresses, a chemical toilet, solar lighting and hot water for the shower. They even had deck furniture.

Our hosts treated us to drinks as the sun went down and the barbeque dinner was cooking on an open fire. It was a beautiful setting and when darkness fell, the spray of stars overhead was spectacular. Solar powered lamps came on to light the way to our tents.

There will be no need for you to leave your tent until morning, our hostess told us. The lamps would go out in about an hour, but your tent lights would last until morning.

Her husband went on to tell us they had a lion around the past couple of nights, but there wasn't anything to worry about from him. It was the elephants that were a concern. They just go wherever they please, and it isn't wise to get in their way. "Ha ha," he concluded with a jaunty laugh.

I read for a while, but the absolute quiet made sleep come easily and soon bright sunlight was spilling into the room. The solar heater for the shower worked great and I was refreshed when I walked to the lodge for breakfast.

Singo was sitting there nursing a cup of coffee. I greeted him with a cheery comment about it being a great day.

Looking at me with bloodshot eyes, he said the day was OK, but the night was definitely not. He couldn't get any sleep as there was an elephant outside his tent and all night long it rubbed against a tree trying to knock down the coconuts.

I was optimistic after a good night sleep, encouraging him to look on the bright side, as at least the tree he was after was beside your tent and not in front of it. He'd be squashed! I am not sure he appreciated this.

Rampaging Elephant.

In the park, we stopped to look at and photograph a herd of elephants about 50 yards away. The old bull elephant guarding the herd didn't like the looks of us standing outside the Toyota. He swung around, raised his trunk and spread his ears. Then he started charging at us, trumpeting angrily.

Nervously I asked if we shouldn't leave. The RC, commented that the elephant was only bluffing. As a politician, he should know a thing or two about bluffing. But the elephant kept coming. I was starting to move toward the Toyota, foolishly expecting that it would protect me if the elephant decided to attack us. The elephant was moving faster and my palms were sweaty. Could they smell fear? I wondered.

Barely ten yards away from us, he stopped, having successfully terrified me. Add rampaging elephants to my list of phobias. At least there weren't any boats in Tanzania.

INDY 'N ME

We set out for our last stop in Mbeya in our three-Toyota caravan. We drove through some tropical scenery and passed a river with crocodiles in it. They haven't changed in thousands of years and they look like it. We also passed the carcass of a hippo partially eaten by scavengers. Even partially gone it was still huge.

The RC said the hippos leave the river at night and walk on the roads, and it was best not to run into one because they are ill-tempered.

This is not a place for nightlife, I thought to myself. Hippos walking, elephants looking for coconuts, and lions that may or may not be a problem. No staggering home from a bar at 2 AM. around here.

After an hour, we pulled up at a river bank. Greeting us were more politicians and cameramen. We walked to the bank overlooking a slowly moving river, brown with silt. It was about 10 yards across and there was a plank bridge across it.

The RC instructed us to come with him and he stepped on the bridge which looked about two feet wide, but had no rails, or even ropes. Even Indiana Jones would skip this one, I thought. But what could I do except follow him? So, I did. Actually, in retrospect, I could have run screaming for the safety of the Toyota. But I didn't want to be a chicken. That was what got me in trouble so many times when I was growing up. I hope my luck held.

The bridge was remarkably stable, at least until eight or ten more people joined us. Their steps as we moved toward the center led to a scary up and down motion. When we got to the center, the RC told us to look upstream. To do this, we all had to pivot on our left foot and face up the river. He explained up ahead was where they wanted to build a dam which will irrigate farmland and also be a reliable source of water for the people in the next village. This was another project in which we might be interested.

But the only thing I could think about was that in just a few more minutes on that swaying bridge, I'd fall into that river and probably be eaten by a crocodile or hippo or squashed by a passing elephant. Somehow, we made it back to the bank and I asked him why he couldn't just tell us about the dam from here on the bank as the view was perfectly fine?

"I wanted you to get the full experience of seeing the river," he said smiling innocently at the Wazungu who was barely controlling his sphincters.

WATER

Mpinda at water source for Pangaro Village.

Water source.

Rainwater collection system and storage tank.

Water is essential to life. You can live without food for weeks, but your body starts breaking down after a couple of days without water. Water is especially precious in Tanzania because there is so little of it. Tanzania has two rainy seasons—the "short rains" in October/November and the "long rains" in March/April. Otherwise, it is very dry. Climate change has affected both rainy seasons and sometimes there is no rain at all. Tanzania's rain comes from the east—the Indian Ocean monsoon. The monsoon is projected to end in the foreseeable future at which point Tanzania will become a desert.

Water in Tanzania comes from three sources: rain, ground wells, and rivers. Each has its problems. Rain is scattered in 2 clusters each year and is unpredictable. Wells are expensive to dig. Rivers in Tanzania are usually full of sediment. Water from them must be filtered to trap the silt and then boiled or treated to make it potable. This can be a complex and lengthy project. Rivers can be dangerous places as ill-tempered hippos, water buffalo, or crocodiles can be there to attack unsuspecting women seeking water for their families.

Getting water from any source is a daily task for women and children. A cubic foot of water weighs 62.4 pounds and carrying this on your head is difficult and results in lifelong injuries. But carrying water is often necessary for women for their families to survive.

Empower Tanzania has been involved in water projects using all three sources and each of them suffers from the same types of problems: technical, financial, and managerial. Despite good engineering studies, there is still uncertainty if water will be found if a well is dug. Piping water from a source to a village can be expensive and the pipe can be broken by people who steal the water. Finding honest contractors who will do the work properly is often a challenge. Many wells fail after a few years because the contractor did not encase the entire well in cement. And when the well fails, they do not know how to fix it.

If the technical problems are solved, then raising money to fund the projects is the next issue. Water projects are expensive. Wells cost up to $30,000, river diversions may be over $50,000, and rainwater collection can be $20,000.

Both technical and financial problems can be overcome from abroad, but management and governance problems are local and very difficult to solve. In one case, a local church was the leader in a project that captured mountain stream runoff and piped it to a nearby village. A local governance committee was formed to manage the water and because of personal grievances with church elders, the tap at the church was shut off. This continued for over two years with residents in that area having to walk a considerable distance to another tap for their daily water until the US partner was able to prevail upon the district government to intervene. This was an extreme case of management problems, but inability to set a price for water, collect the funds, and retain them for maintenance or future expansion happens with regularity.

Securing a water supply is just the first step. Next, you have to make it safe. There are many methods of purifying water from simply boiling it or filtering it or treating it with chemicals. There are hundreds of solutions and all of them work to some extent and virtually all of them fail for one reason or another. Some are too complicated, some are too expensive, some produce water with a chemical taste. All of them require some degree of commitment and often this is too much work because it may not be understood that untreated water can make you sick. Because of this, people are afflicted with many diseases which come from untreated water, such as typhoid, cholera, and diarrhea. Until clean, safe water is widely available, as well as the education regarding its importance, these diseases will continue to ravage the country.

When Rev. Joas visited Iowa, I asked him what the most significant thing he had seen was. Getting safe water from the tap, was his reply.

IT'S NOT FAR

As the Tanzanian Coordinator for the Palliative Care project, Rev. Joas made regular visits to each of the project communities to pay the stipends for the Community Health Workers (CHWs), collect data, and solve problems. He also made house calls. Rev. Joas is a gifted man with great empathy for people and they can tell that he cares about them. Even though he is a Lutheran pastor, he calls on people of many faiths and they are glad to see him and to receive spiritual comfort from his visit.

At times when I visited Tanzania, I would go with Rev. Joas to the program sites and make house calls with him and the CHWs. It was a remarkable experience. Virtually all the patients that I visited were very poor and living in difficult conditions. Their homes were mud brick, with dirt floors, no electricity, no plumbing, and had very little ventilation. They were terminally ill and their family members were providing most of the care that was possible. There wasn't much anyone could do, other than to make them comfortable. But they did this very well.

The patients and their families were always happy to see us—we were considered to be a blessing. One such visit was in Mbaga, a beautiful town high in the Pare Mountains. After a long bumpy ride we arrived and met with the nurse supervisor, the CHWs, and Rev. Timothy, the pastor at the Lutheran and an active supporter of the work of the CHWs. After lunch, we agreed to make a house call.

I asked Rev.Timothy if we should drive there, but he assured me it was "not far." So, we set out walking along the road. But only for about 20 yards. Then we went cross country, up and down hills, over streams, along goat paths. Our Tanzanian friends nimbly

Hilly Mbaga.
Photo Credit Judy Trumpy.

trotted along in their flip flops while I struggled along trying to keep up. After about two miles, Rev Timothy said we were there.

I asked where as it was clear we were nowhere. He told me we were at the home of the patient and when I still looked blank he pointed up the steep bank next to where we were standing and told me "up there."

After all that rough walking, it looked like Mt. Everest to. But we made it up, squeezed into the small house made of mud bricks, a metal roof, and a dirt floor. We then prayed, sang together, and had a good visit with the patient and his family.

Two months later, Rev. Joas and I were back in Mbaga with Rev. Timothy and were preparing to make another house call. "It's not far," said Rev Timothy. I gave him a disbelieving look. He assured me we could drive there. After a five minute drive, we stopped and got out of the truck. Again I didn't see a house but Rev. Timothy pointed up an embankment again. This time the climb was nearly vertical and took 20 hyperventilating minutes. But the greeting by the patient and his family was the same – warm and friendly.

Tanzanian perceptions of distance are quite different from ours. Because they walk everywhere in rough country, they really don't consider these to be great distances. These views are also affected by their understanding of time—they have plenty of it. Taking a 40 minute walk to see a patient is routine for them.

Mbaga was one of my favorite sites, partly because it was in beautiful country and partly because the CHWs were outstanding and very enthusiastic. It was also a convenient place to visit since, as Rev. Timothy noted, nothing was very far from anything else. But we still drove.

FGM

During the training of the Birth Attendants for the Maasai clinic at Nadaruru, Nurse Nivo explained the long term consequences of Female Genital Mutilation (FGM), sometimes called Female Genital Cutting.

FGM removes the external genitalia of women and is usually done prior to puberty by a woman in the tribe who does these procedures. This is common practice within some Middle Eastern and African Countries. Aside from the risks of hemorrhage, infection, and reduction of sexual pleasure, scar tissue from FGM makes normal deliveries difficult and increases the risk of maternal and infant mortality.

Maasai are one of the tribes that still do this horrific procedure. Many men refuse to marry women who have not had this done. Mama Maria was attending the training that day and she said, "Stop." She left and returned 10 minutes later with Chief Isaiah. She asked Nurse Nivo to please explain the consequences again.

So, she explained the list of symptoms and problems again and Chief Isaiah interrupted telling us they would not do any more of the procedures. Three girls were scheduled to undergo that procedure that week and were spared.

After we learned about this, we asked Mama Maria and Chief Isaiah to visit other Maasai villages to tell them about the dangers of FGM and to urge people to stop doing them. They visited five villages and were well received. This was the first step of what will be a long term effort to end the practice. Chief Isaiah and Mama Maria made a second visit to these villages to discuss Family Planning and inserted information about FGM as well. They identified two people from each village who will come to Nadaruru for additional discussion and training regarding Family Planning and FGM.

But the women who make money doing these procedures will resist ending FGM. It may be necessary to subsidize them in lieu of the income they would earn performing FGM. This will eliminate the financial incentive to perform this procedure. Additional efforts will be required to convince men that women who have not had FGM are suitable as wives.

Giving women control over their bodies is a key tenet of Empower Tanzania's efforts to empower women.

MAKING POLITICAL FRIENDS

The World Food Prize (WFP) is a major international event, held in Des Moines, Iowa, which each year honors someone who makes a significant contribution to the production or distribution of food.

Over 1,000 people attend the three-day program. In 2009, during one of the presentations, Ambassador Ken Quinn, WFP President, said that there should be an annual program about Tanzania and that Empower Tanzania should manage it. To open the first year's program, he wrote a letter to President Kikwete of the United Republic of Tanzania inviting him to attend the Tanzania Summit. Ambassador Quinn asked me to deliver the invitation personally.

On a subsequent visit to Dar Es Salaam, I learned that the President was out of town, but that Prime Minister Pinda would meet with me to receive the letter. Two of my colleagues joined me at his office. We were expecting a very brief meeting with me handing him the letter of invitation, him thanking me and all of us posing for a picture. Instead, he asked us to sit down and give him a report on Empower Tanzania's activities and a description of the World Food Prize. He kept asking questions and after 30 minutes, it was finally time for a photo. Two of us went outside to wait for Singo, who stopped to explain to the photographer who we were for the caption.

While we were waiting, I noticed a line of large, tan Toyota Land Cruisers with their engines running. When Singo appeared, I asked him who these people were. He explained that was the cabinet. They were scheduled to meet with the PM half an hour before.

I was incredulous. Did he mean that we kept the Tanzanian government waiting while I made small talk with the Prime Minister? Singo confirmed this also indicating the PM knew they were waiting and decided to talk to us instead.

Wow, I thought, it's never a good idea to irritate powerful people. Fortunately for us, all Wazungu look alike to them. So we shouldn't be recognized in the future. Probably for the best.

ROADS AND DRIVING

The major north-south and east-west roads in Tanzania are paved. The rest are dirt. Not the smooth graded dirt of Iowa, but narrow, rutted, potholed, dusty nightmares. Riding on one that is as bad as a washboard is a treat because most are much worse. It's not that they don't maintain these roads. They do, even though Tanzania is a poor country. The problem is when it rains, it pours, and then the smooth graded road becomes full of holes and ruts. It is even worse in the mountainous part of Tanzania where we work.

The roads are not only rutted, they are also narrow, winding and dangerous. Guardrails are very rare.

On such roads, the only practical passenger vehicle is the Toyota Land Cruiser. Toyota builds these especially for East Africa. They have extra strong transmissions (4-wheel drive is standard), shock absorbers, springs, and tires. Of course, these vehicles are expensive ($40,000-$50,000) and they only get about 8 miles to the gallon of diesel. Buses that travel between cities are generally available. The best one advertises, "Only one passenger per seat." You can imagine what the others are like. For short distances, there are the unscheduled "dalla-dallas" which are minivans that travel a specific route. Usually they will contain 15-20 people and one of them is hanging out a window, acting as lookout. Many people travel on motorbikes which are relatively inexpensive. Often they break the law and carry a passenger. I have seen as many as four children as passengers on one motorbike. Then there are more informal modes such as pickup trucks with 12-14 people in the truck bed, bicycles, carts drawn by oxen, carts pushed by people, and the occasional skateboard. In the congested urban centers, all of these vehicles are jockeying for the right of way and pedestrians cross wherever they dare. It makes Boston traffic look tame.

Dar Es Salaam, the historic capital, has almost 5 million people but its infrastructure supports about 1 million. This crowding and congestion is most apparent on the streets of the city. Reliable sources state that five pedestrians are killed every day in traffic. Traffic jams are common and in the hot, humid climate, drivers get stressed quickly. The next largest city, Arusha, has many of the same problems, but on a smaller scale. However, it only has one traffic light which does little to control the uninhibited driving of the locals.

On the paved highways near the cities, traffic is increasingly congested, although Tanzania is widening the major roads from two lanes to four. In the meantime, the many overloaded, slow moving trucks are a major hindrance to travelers.

Paved roads are narrow and go through villages which requires a drastic reduction in speed. This is enforced via speed bumps which are effective at slowing Tanzanian drivers, who go too fast and take great risks on the highways in vehicles that are usually overloaded.

Despite the congested, speeding, overloaded traffic, the paved roads are much better than the unpaved ones. In the mountainous areas, dirt roads are terrifying as they cling to the side of the slopes, climbing steeply and featuring hairpin turns overlooking the void below. I became adept at not looking down as we drove to villages at the top. On the way back down, I looked at the hillside out the other window. This strategy worked well until the time we visited Chome, a village Empower Tanzania had taken over from another palliative care program. Most of the road to Chome goes along the crest of the mountains with steep declines on both sides. During this ride I was frozen into immobility and stared at the floor until we arrived at the village. Coming back down, I focused on controlling my sphincters while looking at my feet the whole time. That was my first and only trip to Chome.

On one occasion, I was going to be in Tanzania for two delegations arriving only two weeks apart. I decided to stay the six weeks and avoid two air trips. A friend suggested I rent a car and drive around the country. I ignored his advice and when he later made a visit, he understood why. He commented Tanzanian drivers could successfully drive in Boston. He understated the case. They would rule the roads in Boston.

TEARS OVER A SINK

Paulina at her old residence.
Photo Credit Judy Trumpy.

The author at Paulina's new house.
Photo Credit Judy Trumpy.

During one of our visits we met Paulina, a poor widow who works for the Pare Diocese making communion wafers and serving tea during the midmorning break. Todd had developed a relationship with her family and was paying school costs for her oldest son. He introduced us and we visited her home - a 9 by 12 room in which she lived with her three children and a grandchild. About 80 percent of the space was taken up by the bed she shared with her children. She insisted on feeding us omelets and bottled water. We were overwhelmed by her generosity in the context of great poverty.

Even though she was very poor, she did have a lease on some land at the edge of town. Under Todd's leadership, we participated in a fundraising effort to build a house on this land for her and her family. My wife, Judy, worked with Todd to raise the $9,000 it would take to build a good house. Judy hosted fundraising events and collected many small donations from friends. Todd supervised the construction of the three-bedroom house with an indoor kitchen and dining room. It also had a rear patio with a sink and three small attached rooms for a toilet, a shower, and one for storage. It had a water tank to feed water to the house and a solar collector to provide light at night.

Paulina's first sink.
Photo Credit Judy Trumpy.

Judy was part of a delegation to Tanzania just as the house was being completed. As usual, Paulina invited us to her old place for omelets and water. When we were getting ready to go to see the new place, Todd told Paulina that Judy had helped raise the money for the new place. They clutched each other, sobbing, and Paulina never let go of Judy's hand. At the new place, they took a tour and when they went out on the rear patio, Paulina said, "I have never had a sink before." There was more hugging and crying. It was a powerful day.

TANZANIAN WORLDVIEW: POVERTY AND FAMILY

Tanzanians have a unique culture as well as unique attitudes and beliefs about money and personal property. Most of their views stand in stark contrast to the beliefs of the donor countries, especially the US. The two biggest elements that have shaped the Tanzanian way of thinking are extreme poverty and close family ties. The latter likely growing out of the former.

Extreme poverty influences everything about daily living. People do not have cash and thus much of the economy is barter. This also means they don't have bank accounts and savings which makes ordinary transactions very difficult and collecting taxes to run the government impossible.

The second largest factor affecting attitudes about money is the strong family ties that grow out of poverty. When you have no money, family members must rely on one another to survive. These ties result in the attitude that resources in a family are collectively owned. As a result, if one member works for an NGO and gets paid in cash, other members have a perfect right to ask—and get—some of that income for their own use. This attitude also applies to any other assets: cows, chickens, water, food, and anything portable.

These two factors alone—lack of income/ownership and close family ties—lead to many misunderstandings and problems with sustainability of projects.

For example, a man was walking through the village going past the community well that a charity group had built. He saw a bolt on the pump that was exactly like the one he needed. So he took it, which disabled the pump affecting the entire village. Since everyone owns everything, there was no reason why he felt he should not take the bolt.

TANZANIAN WOMEN

The 33 women trained as CHEs came from all over the District and, prior to their training, they did not know each other. They are from different tribes, speak different languages, one-third of them are Muslim, and the rest Christian from several denominations. They became friends during the initial training and helped each other learn this new information and technology.

Monika was one of the initial group of 26 women from the Wards in Same District who were trained during a week-long session in October 2012. Dr. Jeff and I were there again in March 2013 to conduct a three-day refresher training. These women come from across the District, traveling some very difficult roads with limited public transportation. Monika had to leave home very early in the morning to get to Same by the 8:30 starting time.

She was riding in a small van and had turned onto the road from the town of Maore towards Same. The road goes through some remote areas with a game park on one side. At about 5 AM, the road ahead of their vehicle was blocked by a downed tree. When the van was forced to stop, bandits appeared and robbed everyone. The driver was so shaken by this, that soon after they resumed their journey, he crashed the vehicle into another tree. Monika received serious head injuries and was taken to the Same Government Hospital. Because she was still unconscious, she was transferred to the Kilimanjaro Christian Medical Center in Moshi where she was admitted to the ICU. A few days later, she had recovered enough to be discharged to the home of her sister in Same. Dr. Jeff and I visited her and he tested her responses to be sure that her concussion had not resulted in any permanent brain damage. He also examined her lacerations and the stiches used to close the four-inch wound. He provided her with more antibiotics and changed her dressing. She had much improved, but was still pretty groggy. Dr. Jeff returned to see her once more before we left for America.

We learned later that Monika returned home a few days later and that she went right back to work. She conducted six training sessions that month and has continued a full schedule ever since. She is a remarkable and determined woman. She personifies what an empowered woman in Tanzania is able to do. She is our hope for the future.

During the re-training session in November 2013, Monika spoke to the group and thanked them for their kind words and visits while she was recovering at her sister's house and when she returned home. She also thanked them for their help in providing the training that she missed because of her injuries. Her colleagues had met with her and provided the updated information about the new training materials she had missed.

When people say that relationships in Tanzania are important, they understate the situation. In the case of these women, relationships are crucial. They bonded during our training and they supported Monika when she was injured. These women are remarkable and the bonds they have forged will continue to make a difference in their lives and the lives of others in their community for years to come.

BECOMING A CHIEF

Maasai Boma (village).
Photo Credit Rob Craig.

Dr. Jeff and I were invited to become Chiefs of the Maasai of Nadaruru. This was a great honor bestowed on us because of our work in getting the clinic established. At dusk, we drove from the nearby hotel to the "turnoff" for the way to the Maasai clinic. It was dark when we reached the clinic and I assumed that the Maasai boma (village), which was our destination, was nearby. I was

Maasai Boma (village).
Photo Credit Rob Craig.

Preparing the Goat.
Photo Credit Jeff Carithers.

Chiefs Latessa and Isaya and Rev.
Mpinda. Photo Credit Jeff Carithers.

mistaken. Our driver continued on, going through dry creek beds, past thorn bushes, and around trees until I was certain we were hopelessly lost. Then in the headlights was a woman, opening the thorn hedge which surrounded the boma. We drove in and got out to be greeted by Chief Isaiah and the men of the tribe. Dr. Jeff and I followed them into the bush with a few flashlights to show the way. While some of the men started a fire, others brought in a baby goat for inspection and then began butchering it. Dr. Jeff is a surgeon and he watched this process with considerable attention. I looked away into the fire or the darkness, trying to ignore Dr. Jeff's running commentary. "They are doing a very neat job. At least as good as meat lockers in Iowa that dress deer and sell sides of beef. Now, they are removing the entrails…" One of the men took the less desirable parts of the goat to the women for their dinner. The loin was roasted over the wood fire for the men.

While it was roasting, I noticed that there was some blood pooling in the chest cavity. We were offered the chance to go first, but said no thanks. The men then began dipping their hands in the blood and drinking it. Then, Dr. Jeff said "Why not? I'll try it." He bent over the remains of the goat scooped up a little of the blood and drank it. The men were pleased that he had done this. (Six weeks later, Dr. Jeff was diagnosed with two parasites which he claimed came from drinking the blood after all the Maasai had put their hands in it and contaminated it).

By now the goat roast was done and the Chief and another man walked around our circle, cutting off small pieces of the goat and

Where Jeff and the Author Overnighted.
Photo Credit Jeff Carithers.

Jeff's Roommates.
Photo Credit Jeff Carithers.

Goat Roast Interrupted by Cell Call. *Photo Credit Jeff Carithers.*

giving them to us in turn. His knife was razor sharp and with a smooth stroke, he cut these little pieces off the roast. Dr. Jeff was busy taking pictures and twice refused the goat meat. I told him to please accept their hospitality. I had no idea if they were getting offended, but I don't want to risk it since they are so adept with those knives.

So Dr. Jeff accepted the pieces of meat as the Chief made the rounds until we had consumed the loin. In the darkness, I didn't notice that Dr. Jeff was stashing pieces of meat in his shirt pocket. The Chief was coming around too fast for me to keep up, explained Dr. Jeff later. He didn't want to discard the meat in the bushes where the men might find it in the morning. So he figured using his shirt pocket seemed like a good idea.

We then walked back to the boma and learned that the women had prepared dinner for us. This was a traditional part of the ceremony of installing Chiefs. It was about 11 PM and we were tired, but we accepted hospitality and ate a bowlful of goat and rice mixed together. Chief Isaiah asked if we wanted to sleep on skins or mattress. Dr. Jeff took the skins and the Chief led us to one of the houses made of stick and mud construction with a thatch roof. Dr. Jeff was taken to a room on the right and I went into the room on the left.

I commented to Jeff that there was a chicken in my room. He replied that there were baby goats in between the rooms. He handed me a pill, instructing me to take it. It was half a tablet of Ambien, so I could sleep. I never have problems sleeping, but I swallowed it anyway.

I walked past the chicken and climbed onto my mattress, which was about two inches thick on a wooden frame. I rolled up my jacket as a pillow and the next thing I remember was a beam of sunlight hitting me on the face after it passed through the two inch wide "window" in the wall. I got up, greeted the chicken which was still roosting in the same spot, and went outside where everyone else was already up and busy.

Rested and feeling good, I asked Dr. Jeff how his night on the skins was. His less rested look was confirmed that it wasn't as good as mine. He said whenever he tried to sleep, he heard this scratching sound, but when he turned on his flashlight, he couldn't see anything. After the third time, he saw a rat's tail and decided it was in a hole under the bed. Just as the Ambien was kicking in and he was dropping off, he realized that he had a pocketful of meat pieces and his last thought was that he would awaken with his left nipple missing. Fortunately, he awoke with his breasts still intact.

The Chief took us to the corral surrounded with a thorn bush fence to see his wealth. He had about 40 head of cattle and we congratulated him on being a rich man. The rest of the ceremony took place in the corral after the cattle had been taken out to graze. We stepped gingerly around cow patties and found stools about 18 inches high. If I sit on this, I'll never get up, I thought. But I hunkered down and the Chief wrapped a traditional Maasai robe around me and said some words in Maa. Then he handed me an ebony stick about an inch in diameter and 12 inches long. It was wrapped in complex beadwork.

Chief Latessa back in Iowa.
Photo Credit Rob Craig.

This shows that you are a member of this tribe and a Chief, said Rev. Joas, who was interpreting. He also told me if there were people fighting or arguing, just point the stick at them and say 'Stop', and they would stop"

A few minutes later, I had a chance to put this into practice when one of our team was arguing with the driver about where she would sit in the vehicle. I walked over, pointed my stick and said "Stop." And they did. Wow, I thought, this stick is powerful.

We thanked the Chief and returned to town. The next day, we started back to Iowa. After arriving home I tried the power of my Chief's status when my wife and her sister were in a heated discussion. I pointed the stick at them and said, "Stop". They looked at me as though I was crazy. I know Judy was thinking about inserting the stick into a particular orifice on me, but instead they continued on with their discussion.

Clearly the stick's powers do not work outside the Nadaruru Maasai boma.

NO FREE LUNCHES

The Maasai made Dr. Yogi a Chief because of his major role in planning for the clinic and providing the manikin for the training of the birth attendants. Rev. Mrutu explained that this required an overnight stay at the Maasai boma and that he would take Dr. Yogi there on his motorbike. I was nervous about that, having seen the motorbike, but Dr. Yogi was eager to receive this honor. After Rev. Mrutu fixed a flat tire, an ominous foreshadowing, they set off. What follows is reconstructed from both Dr. Yogi's and Rev. Mrutu's recollections.

They arrived at dusk at Nadaruru and the young men did the Maasai jumping dance, leaping straight up into the air and continuing to do this until all were too tired to continue. Dr. Yogi decided to join them and thought he finished pretty well until he learned later that Mama Maria told the boys to go easy on him. By then darkness had fallen and Dr. Yogi was a hit because he used his iPhone to take pictures of the kids and showed them to them. He was inducted with the same goat roast, although I never heard whether there was a chicken in his room that night or not.

The next morning, Dr. Yogi was officially installed as a Maasai Chief and he began his return trip to Same on the back of Rev. Mrutu's motorbike again. Halfway there, they had another flat tire in a very small village. Nowhere to fix it there, Rev. Mrutu left Dr. Yogi and pushed the motorbike to the nearest place to get the flat repaired. He was gone for several hours, partly because he met people from his congregation and stopped to chat, as Tanzanians do.

Meanwhile, Dr. Yogi was standing in front of a house and after a while, a woman came out, started a fire and began roasting some ears of corn. Dr. Yogi was very hungry and began using gestures to indicate that he would like some of the corn. The woman shrugged and gave him some.

Later, Rev. Mrutu returned and Dr. Yogi asked him to translate a request for how much Yogi owed the woman for the food. He thought that this was a business that she operated to feed passersby. After a few sentences in Swahili, Rev. Mrutu started chuckling. Explaining that the woman said there was no charge. That was food for her children's lunch but he seemed so hungry that she gave it to you. Terminally embarrassed, Dr. Yogi insisted on giving her money, despite her wish just to be hospitable.

People who love Dr. Yogi and think that he is all about doing good and saving children should know that once he became Chief, he took the food right out of children's mouths. I guess he is human after all.

BLAME IT ON CHRISTOPHER COLUMBUS

Tanzania is a multi-ethnic society, with traditional African, Arabic, British, Indian, and other influences that are evident in their cuisine. However, like many developing countries, most of the sophisticated cuisine is in the large cities, such as Dar Es Salaam or tourist places like Arusha. The rest of the country, especially the rural areas, has simple plain cooking. In a way, it is similar to rural parts of Iowa where the local cafés have plain cooking, but the big cities like Des Moines have haute cuisine. In rural Tanzania, starches predominate in the diet: potatoes, rice, pasta, yams, plantains, and corn flour porridge (called Ugali). As guests, we would be served all of those starches plus chicken that would be called "free range" in Iowa. It was very tough and requiring plenty of chewing to get it down. Beef or pork were pretty rare and pretty tough, too. In the hotels where we stay in rural Tanzania, the food is usually good, though pretty bland. Everything is cooked to order, which means, you must order early to allow at least an hour for preparation. So, we would order, then take a shower or do some work or have a beer or two discussing the day's events. This was a good reminder about the relaxed pace of things in Tanzania where there is no such thing as fast food.

On one occasion, I was in Dar Es Salaam with my colleague, Todd. We went to our favorite Thai restaurant atop a hotel overlooking the harbor, anticipating our favorite dishes. The maître d' told us that instead of the usual menu, they were serving a seafood buffet. Todd and I tried several different dishes, all wonderful with a perfect balance of heat and sweetness. Suddenly, Todd started gasping. I immediately checked to see if he was choking, prepared to do a Heimlich maneuver. He wasn't choking, but had bitten down on a small, lethally hot chili. He just couldn't talk. I scanned his plate before I went back to the buffet and carefully avoided the items on his plate. He eventually recovered and also returned to the buffet, but he meticulously separated all the items on his plate to be sure there were no little chilies hiding there.

Before Columbus, the chili pepper was confined to the New World. After his arrival, the chili advanced rapidly across the planet affecting cooking everywhere—and one of the chilies made its way to Todd's plate. Todd blames Columbus for that.

THE REALLY REMOTE MAASAI

Maasai Meeting Room.
Photo Credit Rob Craig.

Planning Meeting.
Photo Credit Rob Craig.

We received funding for another Maasai project that would provide basic health care services and some health education to 21 remote Maasai villages that were essentially cut off from the Tanzanian health system. Our original CHW training with the Nadaruru and Pare tribes had expanded at the Maasai's request. For this next project, we planned to train Maasai women from each of the villages as CHWs. This training would provide basic first aid and health knowledge for the woman to serve as the initial contact point into the health system. She would be trained to determine if symptoms required admission to a hospital and she would be part of a network of other CHWs which would also provide basic health education to the people in her boma—such topics as hand washing, making safe water, and improved nutrition.

Rev. Joas made time to visit some of these villages to describe the project and to obtain an expression of interest from the Maasai leaders in each village.

The US team arrived a few weeks later with the goal of visiting the villages, obtaining a commitment from the village leaders to participate in the project, and having them each identify a woman who would attend the Community Health Worker training. We had to explain the project in some detail and ask for their participation. Chief Isaiah of the Nadaruru village was influential among the Maasai in this area and supported our program. He endorsed it and recommended that those present should participate in the program.

Our plan one day was to visit Kambimbi and Makokane. We took the gravel road toward Maore to the Kambimbi boma where the representatives of the other bomas had already arrived and were seated under a tree. We began the discussion as the tribe's women began bringing lunch. They set plastic bowls with covers on a table. This brought the usual thousands of flies who had previously been swarming the cows and goats nearby. While we were talking to the Maasai leaders, we did a lot of shooing and as they served the roast goat and rice, the shooing increased geometrically.

As we finished lunch, the Maasai agreed to participate in the program and identified the three women who would be trained to serve the villages. Two of them were present and our team and interpreters interviewed them and obtained their basic information.

Stuck.
Photo Credit Jeff Carithers.

We left and, after a brief stop at Chief Isaiah's village of Nadaruru, we continued on the road through Ndungu and down to the edge of a large lake. To continue to Makokane, we had to ford the stream that fed the lake and clamber up an embankment. The Land Cruiser was up to the task. After driving alongside the lake for a few miles, we had to pull over to allow a small vehicle (seemingly powered by a sewing machine engine) towing a wagon piled high with logs to get by us. Several people were pushing the vehicle as it traversed a narrow ravine in the road that was about four feet deep and five feet wide. Once they got through, Martin gunned then engine and the Land Cruiser promptly got stuck in the ravine. It was perched diagonally with one wheel barely touching the ground and the right rear wheel jammed against the side of the ravine. After trying to get free, that wheel dug itself deeper.

We got out and took turns looking at the scene and offering useless advice. Two Maasai from Makokane arrived with intention of directing us to the boma where we would have our meeting. They helped to dig out the wheels and we spent a few nervous moments while Martin was under the car, jacking up the rear wheel and sliding a rock under the wheel. We pretended to help by pushing as Martin drove it out.

Then we faced the decision—go on or turn back. It had started sprinkling and it was after 2 PM and we had planned to be back in Same before dark. The Maasai told us that everyone was waiting for us, that they had prepared food and it was "not far." I shuddered when I heard this last statement. But Dr. Jeff thought we should go for it. So we did.

We climbed back into the Land Cruiser, and one of the Maasai behind my seat began giving directions to Martin, although he used hand gestures which Martin mostly couldn't see.

We kept driving for half an hour to this "not far" place, alongside the lake, through the bush, over gullies and through people's yards. We finally pulled up to a clearing where a group of Maasai were waiting for us. We were warmly greeted and we told them that our visit had to be brief because of our need to get back to Same before dark. They told us that Rev. Joas had called to let them know that we might cancel the visit and several of the people had left.

Chief Isaiah gave a brief presentation in Maa, which saved a great deal of time, although we didn't know exactly what he promised them. They quickly agreed to identify the three women who would serve as Community Health Workers.

Dr. Jeff told them we we need to leave soon, so he hoped it will be OK if we te the food you have prepared for us right then. When translated, this statement was greeted with laughter.

The village leader told us that when Rev. Joas called us, they thought we were not coming and they ate the lunch.

MEETINGS AND LUNCH

During one planning visit with the Maasai of Emuguri, a very old man slowly walked toward us. He was thin, had very enlarged earlobes, and his eyes were covered by cataracts. His name was

Mzee William. Rev. Joas translated his message which was that he wanted a drug to fix his eyes, referring to his cataracts. Dr. Jeff explained that there was no such drug and that he would need surgery in a hospital. This seemed to satisfy the Mzee and one of the women led him to a seat on one of the benches.

By now, we were ready to begin. We were greeted briefly by the village spokesman and then Dr. Jeff and I described the CHW project. Our English explanations were translated into Swahili by Rev. Joas and then into Maa by a local political official. I hoped that all this translation resulted in something close to what we proposed.

The village chief then spoke. He was old and clearly had arthritis. But he spoke clearly and he said that we were welcome and that the village would participate in the project.

The spokesman then rose again. A slender middle aged man, he spoke eloquently for 10 minutes and our interpreters struggled to keep up. He expressed the thanks of the village for being offered this health service and he called us "angels from America." He said they were proud to be associated with us and he identified the woman who would be sent for CHW training.

While he was speaking, I looked around at the setting of our meeting. We were out in the open, under the biggest baobab tree I've ever seen. It was easily 25 feet in diameter. We were surrounded by a dry landscape leading off into the distance where the horizon was pierced by purple mountais. Overhead, clouds were developing into thunderheads moving swiftly away from us. This was no boardroom or office cubicle.

We concluded the meeting with a promise to proceed with the project and stated that the CHW training would begin in three weeks. For the Maasai, this sort of commitment is crucial. For them, there are no gray areas and no excuses. While it is wonderful to deal with such straightforward people, we were always careful to be prepared to deliver on a commitment. Because of this, we had developed a reputation among other Maasai villages and we had credibility in Emuguri.

I then apologized that we did not mean to be rude, but we had a meeting in Same with Bishop Mjema and we must leave soon, so to please not prepare food for us. But it was too late. They were already barbequing the goat.

So we adjourned to a nearby, partially completed building—walls, but no roof and a dirt floor. The women brought hot milk and we interviewed the woman who would become the CHW. She was literate in Swahili, married with three children, and honored to be selected by the village for this training. She was however, nervous about going to Maore, a town of about 5,000 people some 20 miles away. She had never traveled that far from her village.

Claire, one of our team, reassured her that there would be 30 Maasai women also attending this training, and explained that she would stay in a guest house in Maore, and be taught by a nurse/midwife from the hospital. The training would last 15 days and we would pay for everything. She seemed relieved at Claire's explanations, but there was an undercurrent of anxiety that continued until she completed her training.

We then walked over to where the men were cooking the ribs and loin of the goat over an open wood fire. Like men everywhere, I suppose, there was some quiet chatting among them and they kept shifting the wooden skewers on which the goat was roasting. We watched and again I gazed at the incredible landscape.

A few minutes later, several of the Maasai indicated that we should follow them to the place where we would eat the lunch that they prepared. We went to another big baobab tree, perhaps 40 yards from the initial tree. This one was smaller, about 15 feet in diameter. Our host sat on a tree root and began carving pieces of the goat's liver. However, they had rushed the cooking of the goat and the liver was not completely done. Some of the team were pretty squeamish and while pretending to eat, they stashed their pieces of the liver in a plastic bag. One of the elders was looking at us when the several of the team continued to place gristle, undercooked meat, and liver in the bag. Fortunately, he had cataracts too, and couldn't see what they were doing. I took one for the team and ate the still rare liver which put a couple of drops of blood on my shirt.

Soon the ribs and loin arrived and were fully cooked. The spokesperson cut small pieces from the loin and gave them to each of us in turn until he had served all of it. Then he carved the ribs and handed those to us. After lunch, we met again with the elders and thanked them for their hospitality and for agreeing to participate in the project.

These projects deliver greatly improved health services to the Maasai villages. It also affects the balance of power between men and women as these CHWs gain knowledge, earn money, and associate with white people. Despite the colonialism of the past, working with white people boosts your status. Some of the elders are aware that these activities will create significant changes in the Maasai way of life. Some are looking the other way and others, like Chief Isaiah, take a more progressive view. He believes that by enabling their children to take on these new responsibilities and rewarding them when they succeed, these children will be better prepared to succeed in the new world. I believe he is right.

IGNORING RISK

Tanzanian drivers appear to believe in fate. That is, if you were meant to be able to pass two trucks and a dalla-dalla before the oncoming bus hits you, then you will make it. If not fated, then you become road kill.

Traffic police are common, standing beside the road in their crisp white uniforms. How they keep them clean with all the dust is beyond me. They flag down truckers and motorists according to a protocol that I do not understand. When you are stopped, you must produce your driving license, insurance card, and other documents. Sometimes using influence ("The Bishop sent us") or 500 shillings (about 30 cents) will work instead.

Breakdowns are also common, especially for the semis which seem to be maintained only on Blue Moon days. You will see a bunch of branches in the road and as you round a curve, and there is the disabled semi with the hood opened and a man with a wrench working on it. There is no auto club in Tanzania so maintenance of your vehicle is critical.

During one visit to Tanzania, we received the terrible news that 15 women from the town of Hedaru had been killed in a car accident. We had been working in Hedaru for six years and we knew some of these women.

They were returning from the funeral of an infant that drowned in a flood in a nearby village. All 15 of them crowded into the bed of a pickup truck for a ride back home. Their vehicle was struck head-on by a large truck traveling on the wrong side of the road. Their vehicle was then rear-ended by another large truck which had been following them too closely. All 15 women were thrown from the pickup truck and all died.

Poverty and lack of transport services lead people here to take the chances they do with transportation. Both travelers and drivers recognize the risks of traveling this way, but ignore them because of the limited options. To be fair, Iowa still does not have a law requiring motorcyclists to wear a helmet and many choose to ride without one. They ignore the risk of permanent brain damage or death in order to feel the wind in their hair. We are not so different after all.

I have learned that the most dangerous part of a visit to Tanzania is not infections, or malaria, or animal or bug bites. It is traveling on the highway. But this still doesn't make me any more at ease in an airplane or on a boat.

WHEN IT RAINS...

The northeastern part of Tanzania, where Empower Tanzania does most of our work, is very dry—almost desert-like with scattered bushes and stretches of sand. If the two rainy seasons arrive on time, farmers can often manage two crops on their land. Recently, the rainy seasons have become more variable and sometimes just don't come at all. This is devastating for crops.

On one occasion, a group of five Empower Tanzania representatives had arrived and we were greeted by Todd driving an aging minibus. The next day, we did quite a few errands in Moshi before leaving for Same in the late afternoon. Soon it had started raining and we expected it would stop soon. We were going along the highway toward Same, about 100 miles away, in the old van with barely functioning windshield wipers. Todd was doing a masterful job of keeping us on the road and maintaining a good clip.

At nightfall, we drove into Same and I was able to see the sign for the Elephant Motel, our destination. On closer inspection though, there was a string of taillights several blocks long that were stopped. Todd got out in the rain to find out what was happening. A few minutes later, a dripping Todd returned to report that rushing water had over flowed the culvert and left about six inches of mud in the road. Trucks could not navigate this and traffic had stalled. We could see the sign for the Elephant Motel but could not get to it.

Todd took us to the nearby Safari Bar to wait until the road was passable. After we sat down, the proprietor kept moving us from one table to another to avoid the roof leaks. Todd asked if he would make four chicken dinners for us as we waited with some beers. After half an hour, the proprietor returned and said he only had portions for two chicken dinners. We had another beer. Twenty minutes later, one chicken dinner arrived and that was all there was going to be. We split it between the 6 of us and had another beer.

Drs. Tim and Yogi, and Todd went to explore the situation. They returned with some news. The rain had finally stopped, but trucks still blocked the road. However, cars were able to get past the trucks on the shoulder of the road. We piled back into the van and Todd slowly drove past the stalled trucks and over the flooded culvert, making it to the gravel driveway of the Elephant Motel.

We were greeted at the front desk with the news that a wedding party was underway. It had been planned for the outside garden, but the continuous rain had forced it inside. They had saved our rooms but told us the kitchen was closed to all except the wedding guests. Exhausted, we gratefully took our keys and unpacked our soggy luggage which had been on the roof of the van since we left Moshi. Soon, Drs. Yogi and Tim showed up at my door and said that we had been invited to the wedding. I declined from being too tired from the journey. But they accepted the invitation, made many new friends, and enjoyed the few remaining appetizers from the reception.

The next morning, a volunteer with our group, Mary, and I walked down to see the damage wrought by the storm. The road was clear and men were working to clear debris from the culvert. Mary was 77 and I had been concerned about having a person that age on this trip. But she proved to be very athletic and part mountain goat. She nearly always took up the first position when we were hiking around. She said she had the most fun in years last night.

I asked if that meant that hanging around the bar for two hours while we moved around to avoid leaks was fun. She smiled and confirmed this commenting that she really enjoyed herself and perhaps we could do it again sometime. So Dr. Tim agreed to take her bar hopping back in Ames, Iowa sometime.

GOING ON SAFARI

Of course, no one should go to Tanzania without going on a safari. Safari means "journey" in Swahili. Where Empower Tanzania

Siesta.

Twinsies.

Wildebeests.

works in Northern Tanzania, they are just a few hours away from some of the most famous big game parks in Tanzania—Tarangire, Ngorongoro, and Serengeti. These safaris are designed for tourists; very few Tanzanians have ever been there.

The wildlife is amazing and the drivers are really good at finding them and getting close. The animals are not tame, but they are used to the vehicles - mostly Toyota Land cruisers- and ignore them. In the Ngorongoro Game Park, we came upon a pride of lions. They had dined recently and all of them were fast asleep in the shade. We were able to get as close as ten feet from them. After a few minutes, the male lion woke up, shook himself off and went over to one of the females. He nuzzled her and she got up letting him mount her. We got ready for an amazing display. Two pumps and that was it. What a disappointment. The female thought so too. She looked a bit disgusted and went back to sleep. The male yawned and fell asleep too. Clearly there is no foreplay or post coitus hugging in the lion kingdom. If artificial insemination ever arrives for lions, the males will be extinct since they serve no useful function, not even satisfying the females.

PROTECTION

The Serengeti is an enormous park spanning the Tanzania-Kenya border. It is the size of Connecticut, but without the toll roads. Some of my colleagues went on a Serengeti Game Park safari and after several close encounters with lions and the other big cats, we spoke with their guide, Joseph. They were curious about how safe we were, riding around in this open Land Cruiser. Couldn't a lion just reach in here and hurt someone?

Joseph replied that of course, it's possible but it had never happened during the 20 years he had been doing this. He was trained in how to recognize aggressive behavior in these animals as well as years of experience in knowing what to do and what not to do. For example, he never drives between a mother elephant and her baby elephant and he only goes close to lions after they have eaten and are napping.

They were reassured by his explanations, but as always, there was one person needing more information. Amy, a nurse educator asked if there couldn't be a time when something unexpected happened and your guests were in danger.

Joseph looked uncomfortable for a minute and then, he admitted, it was against policy for him to tell them, but guides do carry a weapon in case of an emergency. It's a rifle wrapped in canvas at the front of the Land Cruiser. Amy and all the colleagues were relieved.

Several days later, the safari was ending with some final photos and a generous tip for Joseph. Before they parted, Amy asked Joseph to see the gun. He was a little reluctant but then began unwrapping the canvas bundle at the front of the Land Cruiser. It was a jack, not an elephant gun.

He apologized for the deception, but said no one carries guns in the game parks. Not even the Rangers. The policy is that it is better to lose a few tourists than a park lion. Besides, the risk of a flat tire is much greater than an angry lion. Amy left the park humbled by her relative value to the Tanzania Tourism Ministry.

WOULD YOU PREFER BLACK OR WHITE, MADAM?

One of the most important topics that the CHEs presented in their training classes was family planning. This is a critical issue in developing countries, but Tanzanians had been exposed to poorly presented information and outright misinformation. Dr. Jeff wanted to develop a method for presenting this material in an interesting way that would assure that people would retain the information. Dr. Jeff reached out and sought the advice of Penny Dickey, an executive with Planned Parenthood. She explained that using a penis model to demonstrate proper condom usage was very effective.

A few days later, Dr. Jeff called again to say they needed 40 models and they were too expensive to purchase. Would it be OK for him to make some out of wood on his lathe? Penny confirmed that should work.

Dr. Jeff, who is also an accomplished woodworker, produced his 40 penis models, but in the process ran out of walnut for them and completed the rest using pine. As we traveled from Amsterdam to Tanzania, he told me about this. I asked where these 40 models were and he told me they were in his checked luggage.

I commented that I hoped we didn't run into problems at Tanzania Customs, already wondering how I would explain what these wooden things were for since it was obvious what they resembled. Fortunately, we were not stopped at Customs.

On the day of training devoted to family planning, Dr. Jeff lined up the 40 penis models on the table at the front of the room, with the black walnut ones on the right and the white pine ones on the left. He explained that these penis models would be for them to use in teaching proper condom use. There was some giggling among the CHEs. When he invited them to come up and pick one, this evoked widespread laughter. A few of the women in traditional dress covered their faces, but we could see their shoulders shaking.

Dr. Jeff watched as the CHEs came up to make their choices and was puzzled when the pine colored models were the most popular. He asked one of the women why she chose a white penis model.

She hesitated only a moment and then she loudly responded, "Because I already have a black one at home."

The room erupted in laughter.

WHY?
A FINAL WORD FROM THE AUTHOR

When my kids were small and in school, every year the school would host "Bring Your Dad Day" in which fathers of the students would come to talk about what they did. My daughter Michelle said that fireman, policeman, and truck drivers had visited the school. I asked my daughter Michelle why she never invited me. She replied, "Oh, dad, all you do is go to meetings and eat lunch. No one wants to hear about that."

For a minute, I was hurt. But the more I thought about it, the more I agreed with her. All I seemed to do was meet with people, have lunch (sometimes with the same people) and move paper around on my desk. I attended meetings in board rooms, offices with a view, and cubicles—and lunched at the top of buildings and standing by food trucks. Maybe the meetings, lunches, and paper shuffling were telling me something---work was interesting and remunerative, but it didn't really make a difference. I needed to feel the satisfaction of making a difference.

I searched for a way for a long time, doing my job, but not making any headway until I began managing medical exchanges between Iowa and Russia. These were stimulating and I had the opportunity to work with some outstanding physicians, nurses, and administrators. Still, Russia was a Second World country (despite their claims to be in the First World) and there was resistance to the reforms we were proposing. There was also the undercurrent of rivalry and cold war mentality.

Finally in 2006, I began working in Tanzania, one of the poorest countries in the world. Again, I had the opportunity to work with outstanding physicians, nurses, engineers, artists, and educators. But this place was different. We worked closely with individuals who knew that we could provide resources that would directly benefit the people. We could change lives—and save lives. I had found my purpose. I still had to attend meetings and eat lunches—but they were the kind that Michelle would have been proud to have her dad explain at school. They were with a remarkable people—the Pare and Maasai of Tanzania, far removed from board rooms or food trucks. We ate lunch in bare school rooms, in churches with dirt floors, and under baobab trees—and we planned programs that would empower them and help them live better lives.

Michelle and my son, Michael, have long since finished school. But perhaps my grandchildren, Liam and Henry, will find me interesting enough to invite to Bring Your Dad to School Day.

Even at age 70 with, it seems, a billion airline miles under my belt, I hate flying. So, many people ask me why I do this. Why do I go to Tanzania about four times a year, taking three flights each way totaling 20 hours, traveling on dangerous roads, staying in a hot climate with many serious endemic diseases? On most trips, while flying, I start asking myself the same questions. I could still make a contribution to the work of Empower Tanzania from home on my computer.

But then we land at Kilimanjaro International Airport and I walk outside to meet my colleagues. I smell the distinctive odors of Tanzania—wood smoke, flowers, herbs, and animals. We travel to the sites of our programs and meet people whose lives we are changing and children whose lives we are saving. We meet women who now are empowered to make a tremendous contribution to society, who can earn money and feel independent. We see our friends, the Maasai, who now have primary health care services and whose women are training to become health providers and health educators.

Usually when people make their first visit to Tanzania, they are overwhelmed with the poverty, lack of infrastructure and problems of daily living. It's easy to lose hope and feel that nothing we do can make a difference. Being there is vastly different than seeing it on television or reading about it. Engaging all your senses makes for a powerful experience. Even though Empower Tanzania is a small organization with limited resources, we are able to make a difference in the lives of people by working together with them to solve problems. We can make a difference in the lives of thousands of people. Most of the time, our volunteers understand this vision and are energized after experiencing it in person.

It's more than that, though. We all need a purpose in our lives. For me, Tanzania is the purpose that gives focus for my energy. What keeps me going is the people I work with. In the US, they are some of the finest, most generous people I have ever met. Sure they give their money, but more important, they give their time. In Tanzania, I get to work with honest, energetic people who work very hard to improve their lives and those of the people in their country.

It took over 20 years of this international work to find my purpose. The trips I made to Russia, China, Ukraine and Italy were interesting and rewarding. But it was in Tanzania that I found out why I am here. My epiphany came when I made my first house call to a terminally ill AIDS patient. Rev. Joas and the CHW were with me and we talked to this very sick person who welcomed our visit as a blessing. He praised the CHW and the help she had given him and his family. He thanked me for helping him die a good death. When the tears came, I knew that I would devote myself to helping these people.

Thank you, too, for helping these people as part of the proceeds of this book will go to Empower Tanzania. If you would like to make a donation, see current projects underway, or continue to follow the progress of the projects you've just read about, visit our website **www.empowertz.org**.

EPILOGUE
ONGOING PROJECTS

As of August of 2015, the women in the Maore Support Group have continued meeting and they are now engaged in several enterprises—making bleach, sewing clothes, making soap. They have bonded with each other and with Pastor Rose. They are stronger. Empower Tanzania has established 10 additional women's support groups across the Same District and Nardi, our program director, visits each site twice a month and does group and individual counseling.

We learned from the women who make up the support group in Maore that Gender Based Violence is common in Tanzania, just as it is in many countries—even the US. As is often the case, there is widespread denial that this occurs and efforts are made to minimize or trivialize the problem.

Tanzania has passed laws outlawing GBV, but these are not enforced uniformly. Two of the women whose husbands had tried to kill them went to the police. The police refused to act. In cases of rape, the victim must obtain a form from the police, which she must take to the doctor who is treating her and he must complete the form which she then returns to the police for action. This cumbersome, humiliating process is obviously discouraging to victims and all too often, the police refuse to act anyway. Resolving this problem will take a long term multi-pronged effort.

We began by getting funding from a private donor for a five-year project to develop and assist support groups in Same District. We received over 30 responses to our advertisement for a Program Manager for this project. We preferred to hire a women and it was not a problem because no men applied. We screened the applications down to six finalists and brought them to Same for interviews. We used a group interview process and included both Tanzanians and Americans as the interviewers. Three of the candidates were impressive, but one, Nardi, was clearly superior. However, none of them had any significant counseling experience. This would be a crucial skill for the Program Manager to have so that the support groups would receive the kind of assistance that she could provide. We arranged for Nardi her to take a six-month course in counseling at a university in Arusha. She is now setting up support groups in 10 different communities.

Meanwhile, we are working on a better understanding of the system related to women's rights and how to get them recognized and accepted. We will learn workable methods for dealing with these social and political problems - methods that are feasible in Tanzania. For example, in small villages a woman's shelter is probably not feasible. But perhaps women in very bad situations can go to a relative. Still, it should be the men who are causing this problem who should be inconvenienced. An attitude change is possible over time and we are working to develop methods to effect this change.

Perhaps more men will realize just how important women are in their lives here. They get water, get firewood, cook the meals, raise the children, and tend the garden. An understanding of their critical importance merely as economic contributors should help gain more respect for women.

Maybe we can't change the attitudes of all men, but we can make them understand that the society won't tolerate this behavior and will punish them socially if not legally. Eventually, this can be shown to be a shameful way of treating your wife.

This will take time and there will be resistance. But we are determined.

Our Improving Women's Health Program is continuing and the Community Health Educators, like Monika, are delivering messages to adopt healthy behaviors. Now, 15,000 people each month attend these educational programs—and one-third are men which was totally unexpected. Preliminary data show that there are fewer infections and fewer instances of diarrhea in children.

Our work to eliminate Female Genital Mutilation continues through education. We know that this major cultural change will take time, but we are determined to keep working on it.

We just completed the second training of the 30 Community Health Workers from the 21 remote Maasai villages. They received enhanced training in family planning, prevention of malaria and prenatal care. But we also introduced them to the 21st century by giving each of them an Apple iPad preloaded with 48 educational videos. None of these women had ever seen anything like this—in fact none of their villages have electricity—so we provided solar collectors to charge the iPads. Within 10 minutes they had mastered the equipment and were looking at the videos. These will be extremely interesting in their home villages and everyone will want to see them—and they will be learning healthy behaviors while they watch. At the request of the women last year, we added a two-day educational program for men. We covered topics that included building and using latrines, family planning and gender based violence. This education was important, but even more important was this opportunity to have the men recognize the value of this program and to gain their support, their "buy-in", so that the women could do their work. When we were done, we had the enthusiastic support of the men. A longer story of how these amazing Maasai woman embraced a foreign technology is available on my blog/website **www.philipflatessa.com**

WHY PROJECTS FAIL

When US churches partner with congregations in Tanzania, it doesn't take long for the Americans to start thinking of projects to improve the lives of the Tanzanians. However, it also doesn't take long to encounter many problems while trying to conduct projects in Tanzania. Cultural and economic conditions created unforeseen barriers to improve conditions there.

It often goes like this. First, because of historical poverty, Tanzanians have never had surplus resources and so have never had to set priorities. They needed, and still need, everything—food, clean water, education, electricity, paved roads, better health services. So, whenever a US partner suggests a project, the answer is "Yes." Because they need everything. Whenever they are asked to describe their needs, they provide a detailed list. Yet, when asked to set priorities, they are unable to do so. Everything is top priority and they have difficulty prioritizing one project over another.

Second, because everything is top priority, when funds from America finally arrive, it often happens that Tanzanians decide that the funds would be better used for another project rather than what was originally agreed upon. When the Americans learn about this, they are upset and Tanzanians are puzzled by this reaction.

Third, if contracting for a service is necessary, someone's brother-in-law is inevitably chosen. They have no concept of nepotism except to regard it as a good idea. These cozy relationships inevitably lead to overcharging or poor quality work—or both. We learned later that many wells dug with US money failed because they were not constructed properly.

Fourth, different cultural beliefs combined with lack of basic knowledge regarding money also means that Tanzanians have problems understanding cultures that require reporting and accountability. And the process of even getting money to the Tanzanians is a problem. The extreme poverty means there are almost no banks in rural areas and most churches, villages, and individuals don't have bank accounts or even cash. Nor do they have a real understanding of how banks work.

Americans help open a bank account for a project. After funds are deposited, they are completely withdrawn and the bank closed the account. When it is time to fund another project, there is no existing account to receive the funds.

Here is a prime example of one project that explains the common pitfalls. One US church congregation sent funds to their partner congregation to buy a milling machine to process harvested corn. After the funds arrived, the money was spent on replacing the roof of the church. The US congregation was not informed about this and there was no reporting of how the money was spent until a subsequent visitor learned that the funds had been diverted. This created mistrust on the part of the Americans and damaged the relationship. For the Tanzanians, diverting the money to something that at that time was deemed more important made complete sense. But for the American church, there was disappointment because the money was not spent as it was intended.

When the US congregation tried to send additional funds for a separate project, they discovered that the bank account had been closed because all the previous funds had been withdrawn.

These frustrating cultural differences highlight the essential need to establish good relationships between the donor country and the Tanzanians. This is vital for any project to succeed. Many communities have one-shot visits from Americans who drop off a project developed without any local input and then leave. Without a trusting relationship, projects fail.

THE FUTURE AHEAD

It is clear that there are many needs to be met in Tanzania and oftentimes first-time visitors are overwhelmed by this and the obstacles that must be overcome. But we have proven that we can overcome obstacles even with our limited resources. Some of our successes have been already described in this book. There are many others, as well as projects we continue to develop or have interest in developing.

Improving the cooking environment is one area. Women do all the cooking in Tanzania. Even in well-educated households with both people working, women still do the cooking.

In the rural areas, there are virtually no kitchens—at least not the way we know kitchens, but they cook there anyway. Although things are changing, many homes do not have electricity. Therefore, there is no refrigeration and shopping and cooking must be done every day. Virtually all cooking is done with wood. Woman gather the firewood, which is increasingly difficult to find due to the deforestation that is occurring in Tanzania.

Usually three stones are placed into a triangular shape and a wood fire is started between them. Most cooking happens indoors and explains why women and small children have asthma and other respiratory diseases caused by the polluted air from these cooking fires. Sometimes, cooking is done with charcoal which contributes to the deforestation by requiring a large tree to make a small amount of charcoal. Driving across the country, several smoky fires can be seen—sites where charcoal is being made. This is illegal, but rarely enforced. Bags of charcoal line the highway, available for sale. In some ways, cooking indoors with charcoal is worse than using wood. As with wood the particles given off during combustion cause respiratory diseases. Charcoal makes hotter fires than wood and children falling into these fires are more seriously burned.

There are several low technology substitutes for cooking over wood or charcoal, including varieties of solar ovens. But Tanzanian women are conservative about changing to these new ways and conversions to this method have been slow.

For those who have domesticated animals, we are slowly introducing a new way of cooking, Manure is shoveled into a tank which releases enzymes that break down the manure, releasing methane gas which can be stored or used in a cooktop, eliminating the need for firewood. It also produces a residual powdery substance which makes excellent fertilizer.

The tank is high technology developed in Europe. The program offering this technology to farers is subsidized so that it is affordable to a farmer with at least two cows that produce enough manure for the system to operate. Each farmer must buy cement to construct the chamber for the tank and supply the labor to operate the system. This successful program will expand as we identify sources of funding to replace the current subsidy.

For these women, this is literally a lifesaver. Cooking over wood indoors releases a great deal of carbon monoxide and other poisonous gases. Until natural gas or electricity is available, these bio-gas installations will save many lives by providing cleaner air and water and reducing the amount expelled for cooking meals.

Other stories we have been successful that were not covered in the book but information is available on are the Mramba Vulnerable Children's Club which has been replicated in the village of Msindo. Our integrated farming efforts with chickens and goats (using the Heiffer International model) has provided people with no other resources to become successful business people and elevate themselves out of poverty. Improving rainwater catchment and adding solar lighting have been instrumental in providing lifesaving food and services. And we are very optimistic about a new grain storage system and training which could protect against that 1/3 of grain that is lost to pests.

We encourage you to follow our projects at **www.empowerTZ.org** or on my blog at **www.philipflatessa.com** and reach out if you are interested in engaging in our efforts in improving the lives of our friends half a world away.

ACKNOWLEDGEMENTS

I want to thank all the volunteers from Iowa, Virginia, Arizona, California, and Arkansas whose expertise, energy and passion made the stories of this book possible. Without my brilliant editor, Glenda Stormes-Bice, this book would still be a disconnected bunch of Word files on my computer. My graphic designer, Mary Talbert, took a complex book and created a captivating cover and then inserted the photographs that help tell the stories. Andrea Klokow provided the skills that made the stories flow and who did much of the detailed proofreading. Rob Craig took the photographs for the back cover and provided many of the photographs illustrating the stories. Also providing photographs were Frank Trumpy, Judy Trumpy, and Dr. Jeff Carithers. Elaine Leggett and Christine Meraz did the thankless task of proofreading the entire book. Any remaining mistakes are my responsibility.

And, of course, I have to thank my loving--and very patient wife--Judy, who pushed me into writing all this down.

For my colleagues who think they recognize themselves in these stories and who remember them differently, my response is that this is my book and my memories. Go write your own book.

CLOSING

This book describes the work and escapades of a group of highly motivated and dedicated volunteers who selflessly endured hardships to give to others - volunteers who firmly believe that their efforts can, did, and will continue to improve the lives of the people they encountered in positive and lasting ways.

I volunteered with Phil in Russia and Tanzania on Gender Based Violence projects. His book reminds me again how difficult it is for many of the people we encountered during our volunteer work. How abject poverty abounds and items we, as Americans, take for granted simply do not exist in many regions of the world. Clean water, soap, food, medical care, electricity - the list seems endless.

Volunteering provided an opportunity to positively impact people's lives, and perhaps as significantly, all of the volunteers rapidly discovered that our own work changed each of us for the better. As Americans we are particularly ethnocentric. The work described in this book forced us to step into the world of others and experience the circumstances of the world of those we were serving. It challenged us to think and act differently, and to serve others for the sake of building a better world.

Phil, as you have read, has the rare and unique ability to assemble a group of people that possess the vision to see things not as they are, but as they could be. Not to see problems as insurmountable, but to see them as opportunities for change. Phil's courage, wisdom and conviction to ask the right questions was critical to the success of so many of these projects.

I want to thank Phil and his cadre of volunteers for allowing me be included in this unique and special family that believes we can and do change the world one person at a time.

Allan M. Hoffman
Cave Creek, Arizona
President and Professor Emeritus
Santa Barbra Graduate Institute